Extinction and the Human

ALEMBICS: PENN STUDIES IN LITERATURE AND SCIENCE

Series editors
Mary Thomas Crane
Henry S. Turner

Extinction and the Human

Four American Encounters

Timothy Sweet

PENN

UNIVERSITY OF PENNSYLVANIA PRESS

PHILADELPHIA

Published by
University of Pennsylvania Press
Philadelphia, Pennsylvania 19104-4112
www.upenn.edu/pennpress

Printed in the United States of America on acid-free paper
10 9 8 7 6 5 4 3 2 1

Library of Congress Cataloging-in-Publication Data
Names: Sweet, Timothy, author.
Title: Extinction and the human : four American encounters / Timothy Sweet.
Other titles: Alembics.
Description: 1st edition. | Philadelphia : University of Pennsylvania
Press, [2021] | Series: Alembics : Penn studies in literature and
science | Includes bibliographical references and index.
Identifiers: LCCN 2021003632 | ISBN 9780812253429 (hardcover)
Subjects: LCSH: American literature—History and criticism. | Human-animal
relationships—America—History. | Human-animal relationships in
literature. | Human ecology in literature. | Animals in literature. |
Mammals—Effect of human beings on—America. | Whales—Effect of human
beings on—America. | American bison—Effect of human beings
on—America. | Extinction (Biology)
Classification: LCC PS169.A54 S94 2021 | DDC 810.9/362—dc23
LC record available at https://lccn.loc.gov/2021003632

CONTENTS

From the Pleistocene to the Anthropocene

In 2017, a team of Harvard University scientists announced that they were close to creating a hybrid elephant-mammoth embryo.[1] Whether this creation could eventually lead to the successful de-extinction of the mammoth depends on the criteria by which we measure success. The closest hybrid that is hypothetically possible according to current science is an animal that is "capable of living where a mammoth once lived and acting, within that environment, like a mammoth would have acted" but that remains genetically "more elephant-like than mammoth-like."[2] We may be interested in cloning the mammoth for various reasons. For some, "it would be cool!"[3] For others, it would advance our understanding of reproductive biology; it might enable the restoration of the Arctic tundra ecosystem; it might bring back a species that we humans likely had a strong hand in exterminating. The Harvard team members are interested in ecosystem restoration and may be motivated by these other factors as well, but their immediate goal is to help preserve, albeit in altered form, the endangered Asian elephant by adapting it to a different environment. Their project is thus an attempt to use an extinct creature to intervene in our current crisis, often termed the Sixth Extinction event.[4] In this context, the Harvard team's work mixes responsibility, atonement, and assumptions about agency in one particular form of engagement with non-human beings. They hope to repair the results of human excess by caring for a species and, by extension, an ecosystem.

The mammoth may be the original charismatic megafauna.[5] Large, fascinating animal species onto which we can project humanlike qualities and with which we have a significant history of (often violent) interaction, megafauna invite us to reflect on human exceptionalism. The question of the human is more visible here than in cases of the endangerment or extinction of less charismatic animals, however important to human purposes (such as coral polyps), or plants, however beautiful or useful (such as the American

chestnut).[6] By human exceptionalism I mean any account of a distinction between humans and nonhumans that we use to deal with a troubling practice or to negotiate difficulties concerning our relation to nonhumans.[7] Human exceptionalism in this fairly broad sense is not necessarily unique to the modern West.[8] All humans who eat animals, for example, mark the distinction in one way.[9] Even so, a particular version of the human/animal distinction and its exceptionalist corollaries is specific to the modern Western separation of Nature from History.[10] The present study's focus on humankind's relations with certain large animals is one means to provoke reflection on this separation, its consequences, and its prospects. Rather than mount yet another theoretical critique of the human/animal distinction, however, *Extinction and the Human* brings some of this distinction's motivating concerns— morality, communicability, historical destiny, sovereignty—to case studies of human-animal relations in which animal species have become extinct or endangered.[11]

Extinction and the Human focuses on mammoths, whales, and the North American bison beginning with the moments that these species' extinction or endangerment began to generate significant print archives. These archives include transcriptions of traditional Indigenous oral narratives, historical narratives, scientific narratives, and literary narratives by Indigenous American and Euro-American authors.[12] If the Sixth Extinction is a hyperobject—an event so massively distributed in space and time that it cannot be experienced directly—these cases of particular megafauna have consistently commanded our focus and attention.[13] They form a starting point for a coherent, approachable history. Before Enlightenment naturalists identified the fossil bones of mammoths as differing from those of living elephants and established extinction as a geohistorical fact, those bones were often said to be the remains of extinct races of beastly giants, destroyed either by a deity or by a group of civilized humans.[14] Thus the book begins with a prehistory of the extinction concept, as manifest in early Spanish colonial historians' transcriptions of Nahua and Inca narratives and taken up in cross-cultural dialogs in eighteenth-century New York and New England. The mammoth became a national icon in the early U.S. republic because it connoted power and indigeneity, even as it was often characterized as a tyrant deserving of extinction.[15] The mammoth did not maintain this iconic status, as the fact of its extinction became firmly established, probably because its fate augured ill for the young republic's future. Later, the mammoth's fate was taken up as an object lesson for European settler-colonists. Whales and buffalo were threatened by extractive industries during the nineteenth century and became

objects of both instrumentalist concern and preservationist activism. For millennia prior to this modern trajectory, they had been subjects of human social engagement—and still are, especially in tribal traditions. Throughout these cases, various accounts of the distribution of agency and responsibility give rise to different accounts of the human role with respect to nonhumans. Analyzing these cases, I hope to inspire further reflection on this question of the human place and the related question of belonging.

Megafauna provide a focus because, as my opening example suggests, they have been perennial sources of fascination. Easy to anthropomorphize, they are limit cases for the human/animal distinction and thus can provide particular insight into the problem of exceptionalism. Animals can seem especially humanlike if they engage in ostensibly moral behavior, as for example the white whale does in Herman Melville's *Moby-Dick* or the mammoth does in Joseph Nicolar's *Life and Traditions of the Red Man*.[16] Accounts of animals' moral behavior and humans' moral judgments regarding that behavior, important components of many of the interactions examined in this study, are more frequent in stories of megafauna than in stories of, say, insects or plants. The focus on megafauna is not meant to discount whole ecologies, however, but rather to suggest larger networks of relations. In many instances, megafauna are key environmental shapers. Pleistocene-epoch megafaunal herbivores such as the mammoth, for example, were "constant gardeners," keeping forests in check and thereby producing a diversity of ecosystems including savannah and various kinds of woodland, depending on rainfall, temperature, soil, and other factors.[17] After their larger Pleistocene kin became extinct, the buffalo (*Bison bison*) "cultivated the prairie ... ecosystem" in the North American west.[18] On the other hand, the vast forests of precolonial eastern North America, in which the passenger pigeon flourished, may well have been an effect of the Late Pleistocene extinctions.

The project focuses on the Americas, primarily North America and its oceanic environs, because the Americas were the site of two distinct waves of human migration, during the Late Pleistocene epoch and the modern time of European settler-colonization, both associated with anthropogenic extinctions.[19] Of course, there is no doubt about the second wave's acceleration of extinctions and endangerments caused by market-driven hunting, the intensification of agriculture, and other kinds of habitat destruction. While this second wave has become part of the global Sixth Extinction with the carbon economy's alteration of the earth's geophysical processes, the present study focuses on cases whose histories began prior to the development of the carbon economy and, for whales and buffalo, continue into the present. While

the causes of the Late Pleistocene megafaunal extinctions remain an open question, recent reviews of evidence point, in the words of one study, to a "bigger kill than chill."[20] That is, strong correlations exist between extinction events and the arrival of anatomically modern humans in Australia (some 80,000 to 40,000 years ago), Europe (50,000), and the Americas (50,000? to 10,000). In contrast, only weak correlations exist between Late Pleistocene extinction events and climate changes.[21]

North America has an especially rich archive of implicit and sometimes explicit dialogs between Indigenous peoples' and Euro-American settler-colonists' stories of species extinction and endangerment. Such stories reach back to Late Pleistocene events, via associations with fossil remains, and forward to the present, when tribal buffalo projects enable the buffalo's persistence in an ethical manner (unless one brings a vegetarian perspective[22]) while the renewal of ancient tribal whaling traditions is criticized by many Euro-American environmentalists and by some Native Americans as well. Although South America and Australia saw these same two waves of colonization and extinction, here Indigenous stories of extinction and endangerment and their interactions with Euro-American stories have been less fully archived. While Chapter 1 explores archives from sixteenth-century Mexico and Peru, such sites invite further investigation.[23] In Europe, it is more difficult to parse extinctions neatly into separate Pleistocene and modern events, and the continuity of oral tradition seems difficult to trace.[24] Whether Indigenous American oral traditions preserve memories in unbroken continuity from the Late Pleistocene epoch remains an open question, which will be explored in Chapter 2. In any case, those traditions give accounts of Pleistocene megafaunal extinction that Euro-American settler-colonists engaged with from the sixteenth century on. In the colonial era and continuing into the present, encounters between Euro-American and Indigenous American stories have shaped memories of the mammoth and the fates of whales, buffalo, and other species.

This juxtaposition of Indigenous and Euro-American stories in the context of extinction will inevitably evoke two prominent images, the "vanishing Indian" and the "ecological Indian." Although productive interventions will be noted at relevant points, and Chapter 4 will necessarily engage with the "vanishing Indian" motif's linkage to the decimation of the buffalo on the Great Plains, this will not be my primary focus.[25] The counter-discourse of Native survivance, to use Gerald Vizenor's term, becomes pertinent here insofar as it focuses on human-animal relations.[26] We will see specific examples of survivance narratives in eighteenth- and nineteenth-century Indigenous accounts

of the mammoth, the revival of a tribal whaling tradition, traditional buffalo stories, and recent tribal buffalo projects. The "ecological Indian" is another matter. An updated version of the "noble savage" image, it is not generally conducive to survivance because it suspends Native Americans in a timeless past rather recognizing them as historical actors, and because it depends on Western concepts of conservation and environmentalism. That is, the "ecological Indian" is a fiction that Westerners hold up to other Westerners as a nostalgic example and to Indigenous peoples as an ideal against which they are measured and inevitably found lacking—although Indigenous peoples can use this image tactically in assertions of sovereignty against the Westerners who invented it.[27] As Shepard Krech has further argued, the image assumes an understanding of ecology in terms of balance and harmony rather than, as recent research indicates, in terms of dynamic systems prone to disequilibrium and sensitive to small actions.[28] Native Americans, like all humans, are dynamic forces whose environmental impact is uncertain in particular cases. The Late Pleistocene human migration to North America, for example, may very well have had a dramatic impact on indigenous fauna with significant consequences for North American ecosystems.

Whether humans caused the Late Pleistocene extinctions has no bearing, however, on present-day Indigenous nations' sovereignty or their right or capacity to manage natural resources: the latter follows from sovereignty and is a political right under the purview of treaties and other agreements such as the convention of the International Whaling Commission (IWC) and must be treated as such.[29] Moreover, other peoples ancient and modern have hunted animals to extinction in other places. The Maori's extirpation of the moa from New Zealand six hundred years before European colonization, for example, is the most familiar of some two thousand such extinctions caused by the Polynesian colonization of Pacific islands.[30] The Late Pleistocene extinctions do, however, have a bearing on later Indigenous and settler-colonial stories concerning the human/animal distinction and environmental relations. As such, along with stories of modern-day extinctions and endangerments, they bear investigation during the heightened awareness of the present crisis.

Belonging

The Sixth Extinction began to attract public notice in the mid-1990s, as evidenced by a handful of books bearing that title.[31] Humanities scholarship followed beginning in the late 2000s.[32] Of this work, only Mark Barrow's account

of the origins of species conservationism significantly addresses responses prior to the 1980s.[33] By contrast, *Extinction and the Human* investigates how assumptions about agency and responsibility—and thus judgments both factual and moral regarding human causality in extinction events—have varied historically.[34] Humans have been causing extinctions for about as long as we have been humans. We have not, however, always understood or admitted this, nor have we always felt it was wrong or sad. At the same time, there are limits to human agency—limits that Moderns, to use Bruno Latour's convenient terminology, now confront in the Anthropocene concept and that Nonmoderns, including Indigenous Americans and colonial-era Euro-Americans, have managed through attributions of superhuman or spirit-power agency.[35] The moral terms of responsibility and atonement persist in the Anthropocene, now in relation to superhuman agencies—geophysical forces—that seem fundamentally noncreative. Hence the Harvard project's response to one particular extinction event, an event in which humankind seems have borne a large measure of responsibility.

Extinction and the Human explores historically informed self-reflection at a time when, as conservation biologists realize, hard choices are inevitable and the possibility of "multispecies justice" remains in question.[36] One approach to the emerging field of extinction studies within the environmental humanities argues that there is no singular phenomenon of extinction. Each case is different and is experienced, measured, performed, and enunciated in different ways by all the forms of human and nonhuman life which are entangled in that case.[37] Each individual animal can be recognized uniquely as "a single knot in an emergent lineage, a vital point of connection between generations" that can provide insight into the precarity of a species.[38] Yet while each individual animal and each species or kind of life is undeniably unique, concerns over biodiversity and species extinction take shape, as Ursula Heise demonstrates, in one of several genres that make up the world's literary repertoire: elegy, tragedy, or apocalypse most obviously, but also other genres such as comedy, epic, or encyclopedia. Thus configured, they gain traction as stories that human communities can tell about themselves and their future. Such stories shape our assessment of "what we value."[39] From this perspective, biodiversity is a cultural question as much as a scientific question.

Incorporating the insights of both case-specific and genre-based approaches, *Extinction and the Human* investigates the ways in which several extinction and endangerment archives frame the question of human exceptionalism, in order to provoke moral reflection on questions of belonging and

the place of the human. I use *belonging* here in the sense that Aldo Leopold did in his now classic collection of environmental essays, *Sand County Almanac*, for its evaluative connotations.[40] If we reflect on human exceptionalism, such reflection cannot help but be evaluative. Leopold posited that we abuse our environment if "we regard it as a commodity belonging to us. When we see land as a community to which we belong, we may begin to use it with love and respect."[41] Assuming an expansive sense of "land" that includes a place's whole biota, Leopold famously formulated the Land Ethic, which directs us to "examine each question in terms of what is ethically and esthetically right, as well as what is economically expedient. A thing is right when it tends to preserve the integrity, stability, and beauty of the biotic community. It is wrong when it tends otherwise" (224–25). The Land Ethic is not based on the principles of deep ecology. For Leopold, humans are not harmful parasites on the body of Gaia but rather an integral part of the biotic community. The Land Ethic "changes the role of *Homo sapiens* from conqueror of the land-community to plain member and *citizen* of it. It implies respect for . . . fellow members, and also respect for the community as such" (204, latter italics added). While any number of environmental writers have used the idea of community, few have used the political language of "citizen." In this usage, readers of Latour might hear a resonance with the project of assembling a "parliament of things" to organize environmental relations.[42] Working out Leopold's criteria of "what is ethically and esthetically right," with or without Latour's help, would mean constant reflection on the assumption of human exceptionalism (although Leopold did not use this term). The Land Ethic looks like a rule, but really it provokes a set of questions, all centered on relations between humans and nonhumans. One feature of these relations is that only humans seem to be able to speak. Thus Latour has suggested that we expand our understanding of what counts as language, observing that nonhumans can participate in the "parliament of things" by means of the sciences, which provide "speech prostheses" through which nonhumans can speak (*parler*) their positions and interests.[43]

An alternate account of the program signified by "multispecies justice" or the Land Ethic is the Indigenous American practice of treaties with animals. As the Chickasaw novelist Linda Hogan puts it, "That we held, and still hold, treaties with animal and plant species is a known part of tribal culture. The relationship between human people and animals is still alive and resonant in the world, the ancient tellings carried on by a constellation of stories, songs, and ceremonies. . . . These stories and ceremonies keep open the bridge

between one kind of intelligence and another, one species and another."[44] To take just one example, for thousands of years the Mississauga Nishnaabeg met with the fish nations twice a year at a particular narrows between two lakes "to tend their treaty relationships and to renew life just as Gize-mnido (creator) had instructed them."[45] Such treaties are now difficult to maintain, Hogan asserts, since "the Western mind has resulted in a way of living in the world that has broken the trust between human and animal."[46]

The practice of treaties with animals bears further examination for several reasons. Like Latour's suggestion regarding scientific speech prostheses, treaties require a common language (or translation) in order to reach a legitimate agreement which would then be ceremonially renewable. Like Leopold's use of the term "citizen" and Latour's proposal for a parliament, the treaty form organizes environmental relations as political relations. As distinct from "biophilia," the cross-species love that conservation biologists such as Edward O. Wilson and Michael Soulé hope will promote species preservation, treaty relations are grounded not in love but in mutual respect.[47] Moreover, the treaty form suggests a historical dimension to the problem of human exceptionalism: the idea of a broken treaty holds out the possibility of repair, rather than the narrative of decline and mourning that shapes so much modern environmental discourse. It should be noted, however, as the subsequent discussion of Amerindian perspectivism will indicate, that treaties are not the only Indigenous American means of organizing human-animal relations.

Beyond the analogies to Leopold's and Latour's programs for multispecies justice, the treaty form foregrounds humankind's potential for violent, destructive relations with nonhumans. One formulation of human exceptionalism is the presumption of environmental sovereignty, naming humans as the sovereign exception in the biosphere, the "point of indifference between right and violence," as Giorgio Agamben puts it, in ecological relations.[48] Treaties with animals, by contrast, figure reciprocal recognitions of sovereignty. Treaties among humans presume the reciprocal recognition of sovereignty in order to resolve a history of (or potential for) violent relations. This history of violence may be formally encoded in treaty negotiations, as exemplified by the condolence ceremony that opened the Haudenosaunee's several treaty negotiations with the British during the eighteenth century, or it may remain implicit.[49] In treaties with animals, the resolution of a history of unorganized violence takes shape as a cycle of debt in which animals sacrifice themselves to humans, who reciprocally incur obligations to undertake certain practices, rituals, and ceremonies respecting the animals.

Responsibility and Agency

Leopold argued over a half-century ago that Darwin repositioned humans as "only fellow-voyagers with other creatures in the odyssey of evolution. This new knowledge should have given us, by this time, a sense of kinship with fellow creatures, a wish to live and let live, a sense of wonder over the magnitude and duration of the biotic enterprise" (109). Yet living and letting live have always encompassed countless individual acts of violence. The scale of these acts of violence has increased as the human economy occupies more and more of the biosphere through population growth and technological intensification.[50] Humankind itself now seems endangered, even as the anthropogenic nature of the Sixth Extinction event is being recorded in the indelible geological signature of the human, as denominated by the term "Anthropocene."[51] This term indicates the supposition of human responsibility for having shaped our environment, even as the resulting forces exceed the capacities of human agency to alter them.[52] Yet humankind has always been a shaper of environments, even before the Neolithic revolution and the development of agriculture.[53] Species extinctions have been a frequent consequence of that shaping. Since even preservationism, protectionism, and other such "wilderness" orientations involve the active shaping of the environment, our future depends on greater awareness of our capacities and reflection on the accompanying responsibilities.[54]

Each of the cases examined in this book poses the question of the human and related questions of responsibility and agency in different ways. Sixteenth-century Indigenous American narratives about the extinction of beastly giants were based on remains we now identify as those of Late Pleistocene–epoch megafauna, species that were very likely extinguished by humans. These narratives, whether or not they carried the historical memory of the Late Pleistocene extinctions, investigated the nature of society and social organization. Early Euro-American accounts of these Indigenous narratives, not fully able to take up the concept of extinction, further extended their investigation to the nature and history of organic life itself. Some narratives named human causal agents and appealed to human social norms in the moral assessment of extinction events; others named superhuman causal agents and appealed to transcendent norms. Eighteenth-century Indigenous American accounts of the extinction of mammoths named superhuman causal agents but appealed to an anthropocentric moral assessment of environmental management. Euro-American accounts during the same era shared this moral assessment but were divided on the question of causal agency, human versus superhuman.

Nineteenth-century concerns over the impending extinction of whales, as the whaling industry rapidly intensified its extractive processes, asked whether there is a natural limit on species' persistence and if so, what force might impose such a limit—and, in some cases, what such a limit might mean regarding humankind's ultimate fate. As recent controversy over Indigenous Americans' whale-hunting traditions indicates, such cases raise the question of sovereignty. Late nineteenth-century scientists' and preservationists' concerns over the impending extinction of the North American bison brought about by market hunting asked whether predation is a defining characteristic of humankind's species being and if so, whether there is a natural or a social check on this characteristic. While some preservationists blamed Indigenous peoples as well as white Americans for overhunting, Indigenous narratives from the same period resisted definitions of humans as heedless predators needing external checks. Rather, Indigenous narratives focused on ethics of access and distribution—thus anticipating considerations of the buffalo in terms of a communicative, social relation with humans that guide present-day tribal buffalo projects. The through-line of all these historical cases is reflection on the capacities of humankind as environment shapers. This line of reflection is critical in responding to our current crisis. We cannot help but intervene. The question is how and to what effect.

As forms of response and measures of responsibility have varied historically, so have accounts of agency and the occasions through which agency is produced or exercised. We might begin the analysis of these accounts in terms of Latour's refusal of the Moderns' de-animation of nonhuman nature and their concomitant reservation of agency only for humankind. [55] A refusal to de-animate nature is also modeled, as I have indicated, by Indigenous American accounts of human-animal relations. In narrating extinction, humans may come to occupy the positions of agent, observer, and/or object (the latter especially in the case of dark-ecological narratives) with respect to other agents, observers, and/or objects, any of which are given by the narrative various powers and capacities. These powers and capacities can be parsed in various ways depending on one's ontological frame.[56] Nonmoderns (to continue with Latour's terminology) have ways of maintaining the world's animation and thus of distributing agency among nonhuman as well as human actors. These ways became visible to the Moderns as superstitious appeals to supernatural agents such as spirit powers or idealist forces such as vitalism. Enlightenment thinkers such as Thomas Jefferson discounted Indigenous Americans' appeals to supernatural agents, even as these thinkers also imagined the world as being generated and held together by another kind of supernatural agent. Still later in

the nineteenth century, a teleological misreading of Darwin—perhaps encouraged by Darwin's own reluctant revision of the last paragraph of *On the Origin of Species* to insert "the Creator" as primary agent—provided another quasi-animate driver for extinction as well as evolution.[57] One kind of response to the Sixth Extinction returns to a theocentric account of agency, as manifest in humankind's evolved capacity for belief and a sense of the sacred, as the greatest hope for survival.[58] An agnostic version of this position is voiced by Timothy Morton, who asserts that since "nonhuman beings are responsible for the next moment of human history and thinking," we ought to respond with Zen-like techniques of "mindfulness, awareness, simple letting-be."[59] We have always needed to locate agency. The crisis of the Anthropocene has shown that Nonmodern accounts of agencies outside ourselves in powerful gods or other nonhuman forces are not misguided, for these accounts reflect on important universal questions for human being while rendering comprehensible certain powerful agents that shape our environment.

While a Latourian frame enables us to negotiate difficult matters of ontology—allowing, for example, Enlightenment and traditional Indigenous narratives to speak to each other, as we will see in Chapter 2 particularly—it does not necessarily help with the evaluative dimension that historically has been integral to extinction discourse. Moral evaluation has been important to critical analysis at least since Aristotle parsed the objects of literary imitation into "agents" that are either "admirable," "inferior," or somewhere in the middle, and organized the literary modes accordingly.[60] Northrop Frye added an environmental dimension to this modal analysis when he observed that Aristotle's evaluative terms "*spoudaios* and *phaulos* have a figurative sense of weighty and light." Frye's move from Aristotle's moral classification to the ontological question of "the hero's power of action" with respect to other persons and "his environment" as a literary mode's constitutive feature silently bore with it Aristotle's evaluative frame.[61] Of course, I am not making a case for Frye as a proto-ecocritic. But construing the question of "power of action" in a reanimated world that includes humans and nonhumans (and gods if they exist) returns us to ecocriticism's traditional function of linking moral evaluation with accounts of human environmental entanglement.

Moral evaluation has always been a crucial part of human responses to extinction. Those responses have varied historically. Investigating their variation will, I hope, provide us with perspective and a repertoire to draw on in our response to the present crisis, as we reflect on the question of belonging in relation to the possibilities and limits of humankind's environment-shaping capacities.

Species Being?

Typically, blame for the Sixth Extinction rests with either humankind's species being or capitalism: either we as a species are inherently destructive or capitalist accumulation is uniquely destructive. I will assume that this is a false binary.[62] Capitalism was a significant cause of the near extinction of North American bison, some whale species, and many others. As a driver of global warming, habitat destruction, and direct consumption of biota, capitalism is responsible for a great deal of devastation, while socialisms focused on extraction and industrial production regardless of environmental costs have contributed as well.[63] Whether we want to consider capitalism as the only cause depends on our frame of reference, for capitalism did not extinguish the moa, nor the mammoth and other Late Pleistocene megafauna. The extinction of the moa was a result of Neolithic colonization. The Late Pleistocene extinctions happened prior to the Neolithic revolution, to say nothing of the market revolution.[64] There is strong evidence, as I have indicated, that human colonization has been causing extinctions for fifty or more millennia.

Thus broader views—such as Ronald Wright's *A Short History of Progress*, Roy Scranton's *Learning to Die in the Anthropocene*, or Amitav Ghosh's *The Great Derangement*—locate capitalism in a larger trajectory of environmentally destructive behavior through the course of human existence.[65] Ghosh, for example, puts imperialism chronologically and materially prior to capitalism as the primary driver of environmental catastrophe. And even in responding to the present crisis, as Dipesh Chakrabarty argues in a frequently cited essay on the Anthropocene concept, "a critique of capital is not sufficient for addressing questions relating to human history," since human activity has altered the earth's basic geological processes. Reckoning with this crisis, according to Chakrabarty, requires an investigation of "the species history of humans," a process that will "prob[e] the limits of historical understanding."[66] One such broad investigation of species history is Kirkpatrick Sale's *After Eden*.[67] Sale speculates that the human will to domination is an evolved response to a climate crisis some seventy thousand years ago, when a massive volcanic eruption produced rapid and extensive global cooling. Although humans had become anatomically modern some ninety thousand years earlier, they responded to this drastic environmental change by developing a cultural complex based on the innovation of big game hunting and fishing supported by wearing animal skins and using fire for environmental management. Symbolic communication, the production of material abstract symbolic forms, also developed at this time according to archaeological evidence. It is possible that genetic

mutation enabled these cultural responses (and if so, could have enabled other species of the genus *Homo*, such as *neanderthalensis*).[68] This cultural evolution seems to mark *Homo sapiens* as distinctly different from other hominins—as exceptional—although evidence for the "humanness" of *Homo neanderthalensis* continues to mount.[69] Like Sale, Wright also recognizes the development of hunting as a key marker of human species being. He argues that the perfection of hunting was the first of many "progress traps," technological innovations whose success in turn threatens human persistence.[70] The perfection of hunting, on this model, inevitably led to local extinctions of game animals and thus to many local Neolithic revolutions.[71] The distinguishing feature of these Neolithic revolutions, agriculture, may in itself become a progress trap if global warming destabilizes the climate sufficiently. While Scranton tells a more conventional history of the development of agriculture and civilization focused only on the Middle Eastern Fertile Crescent, he emphasizes a feature that others overlook: the centrality of violence to human social organization. While he says little about humankind's stance toward other species, the consequences are readily extrapolated. Such histories of human world-shaping counter existentialist claims that humanity has no predetermined essence.[72]

The questions of whether or when humans became extinction-causing agents could not properly be asked prior to the establishment of species extinction as geohistorical fact in the early nineteenth century. Prior to that, however, local extirpations were familiar, as for example the deliberate extermination of wolves in Ireland during the seventeenth century. Examining fossil remains of the Irish elk (now known to have become extinct about eight thousand years ago), the physician and naturalist Thomas Molyneux speculated in 1697 that as Ireland "became peopled, and thickly inhabited," the elk "were soon destroy'd, and kill'd like other Venison, as well for the sake of Food as Mastery and Diversion." Accordingly, he urged his countrymen to take "some care . . . to preserve" the red deer, which "is much more rare with us in *Ireland*, than it has been formerly."[73] Not quite a century later, Jefferson commented on the effects of the fur trade, which caused "the general destruction of the wild game by the Indians, which commences in the first instant of their connection with us, for the purpose of purchasing matchcoats, hatchets, and firelocks with their skins."[74] Speaking in the same moment in James Fenimore Cooper's historical novel *The Pioneers*, the white hunter Natty Bumppo complains that he will have to travel far to the west to obtain the beaver pelts necessary to pay a court fine; in the sequel, *The Prairie*, Natty finds abundant game on the Platte River.

Whether humans were capable of extinguishing an entire species, beyond local extirpations, was another question. As we will see in Chapter 2, Jefferson

and many of his Enlightenment colleagues were slow to accept the idea of species extinction. Similarly, the Native Americans with whom they exchanged stories did not refer to the mammoth as extinct—in their languages, extinction and death could only be differentiated by context—but rather as escaped, hidden away, absent.[75] (Genetic engineering projects such as the Harvard lab's work on the mammoth may yet confirm this sense of temporary absence.) Georges Cuvier, whose work in comparative anatomy at the turn of the nineteenth century established species extinction as geohistorical fact, did not believe that humans were powerful enough to have caused the extinctions that were evident in the fossil record. Rather, he argued, evidence pointed to "a great and sudden revolution" of the globe, or perhaps several such revolutions over eons, that had buried many creatures alive, shifted the locations of oceans, and caused drastic climate change.[76]

By the early nineteenth century, however, naturalists began to generalize from local anthropogenic extirpations to the concept of anthropogenic extinctions.[77] Charles Lyell, whose uniformist geological theory would influence Charles Darwin, regarded extinction not as a result of geophysical catastrophe, as Cuvier had done, but rather as a result of ongoing regular natural processes. He argued that "no one of the fixed and constant laws of the animate or inanimate world [can be] subverted by human agency."[78] Yet humans had clearly caused extinctions and continued to do so. Lyell cataloged numerous animals that had been wholly extirpated from the British Isles—including "the ancient breed of indigenous horses, the wild boar, and the wild oxen," beaver, wolf, bear, and Scottish wood grouse—and predicted that the colonization of Australia would eliminate the kangaroo and emu.[79] Such anthropogenic extinctions must have proceeded from one of the "fixed and constant laws" that Lyell's uniformist theory championed. In elaborating these natural laws, Lyell refused the emerging modern elegiac narrative of extinction as loss: "If we wield the sword of extermination as we advance, we have no reason to repine at the havoc committed."[80] The extirpation of other species is part of the ordinary course of nature, Lyell asserted, and this is evidently a feature of humankind's own species being, as it is of every other species' being in different ways. Figuring competitive extermination in terms of "encroachments," he went on to erase the Indigenous human presence in colonial territories, arguing that extinctions will increase as "highly-civilized nations spread themselves over unoccupied lands."[81]

Lyell cast his account of anthropogenic extinction as an ontological rather than a moral claim, a claim of *is* rather than *ought*. Even so, the fact

that he paused to address the moral question suggests that he worked against a powerful impulse to "repine." Such exceptionalist logic worked to produce the human/animal difference, along with a colonialist corollary, that Lyell's disavowal refused yet reprised.[82] In this way, his claim about species being encoded the "sacrificial structure" according to which the animal is separated from the human through its designation as the potential object of "a noncriminal putting to death," while also claiming difference within the human species.[83]

Questions of human nature in this context—formulated perhaps as a question of whether humankind is inherently rapacious, or is inherently an invasive species, as environmental biologists might put it[84]—are related to the question of whether human culture results from a suppression of animal nature. In a suggestive critique of this question of human and animal natures, Marshall Sahlins argues that modern Western culture (since Hobbes, although with roots in Augustine) is unique in propounding the repressive hypothesis.[85] Many non-Western cultures by contrast treat the human essence not as an overcoming of animality but as a coming into sociality. This is consistent with the ontology that anthropologists such as Eduardo Viveiros de Castro describe as Amerindian perspectivism, according to which humanity is the world's originating substrate and all the various species differentiated themselves while retaining their humanness-for-themselves in the primordial time when the world came to order.[86] A perspectivist account of human being contrasts with the Western sense of human being in which a distinctively human quality, such as the soul or cognition, is layered onto a preexisting organic substrate, thus forming the topmost link in the Great Chain of Being. In a perspectivist ontology, every species is human for itself but not-human for other species. Perspectivism thus recognizes that human action inevitably leaves an impact on nonhumans—the difference from the Western conception of such interaction being the reciprocal recognition that nonhumans are equally alive and also have souls. In cross-species confrontations, such as getting food, "it is inevitable that one [species] will finish by imposing its humanity on the other, that is, that it will finish by making the other 'forget' its own humanity."[87] This is why, for example, the Runa of upper Amazonia advise you to sleep face up in the forest: if "a jaguar sees you as a being capable of looking back—a self like himself, like *you*—he'll leave you alone. But if he should come to see you as prey—an *it*—you may well become dead meat."[88] Perspectivism thus distributes the human exception to all species, even as it posits an animal's imposition of its own will, its humanness.

Responding to the Sixth Extinction

Responses to the Sixth Extinction are predominantly of two kinds, elegiac and optimistic.[89] The emergence of elegy as a modern response suggests a shift in attitude concerning the justness of extinction. That is, to the extent that mourning responds to death as an injustice, the elegiac response to extinction casts a species' death as unjust.[90] A prominent variation on the mode—we might call it future elegy—worries that the Sixth Extinction will include humankind, the ultimate injustice (or will it be justice after all?), because it will eventually extinguish so many species as to destroy the biotic networks necessary to support human life.[91] Thomas Jefferson, as we will see, had already arrived at such a position, speaking in the Enlightenment language of systems. Cross-species mourning is another matter, however. Historically, as this study will show, responses to the extinctions or endangerments of charismatic megafauna have not necessarily been elegiac—certainly not in the case of early modern accounts of the extinction of giants and many Enlightenment and Indigenous American accounts of the extinction of the mammoth, all of which view certain extinctions as instances of justice.[92]

Elegy also traditionally performs continuance, be it in the assertion of eternal spiritual life or the consolation of earthly community.[93] Again, cross-species mourning introduces a complication. One means of enacting the consoling function of elegy for species extinction would be to build allegiances for the future among persisting beings—making kin, as Donna Haraway would say.[94] A communal orientation is suggested in a different way by Indigenous American forms such as the Haudenosaunee condolence ceremony or the Tlingit potlatch, which restore vitality in human communities.[95] Although the capacity for public response is built into Maya Lin's web-based memorial to extinctions, *What Is Missing?*, its project of collecting accounts of loss does not produce communal relations.[96] Communal revitalization is performed, however—as Chapters 3 and 4 will suggest—by tribal buffalo projects and by the Makah nation's renewed ritual celebrating the hunting of a once-endangered species, the gray whale. In both cases, deaths of individual animals mark the recoveries of key species, cross-species relations, and human community.

As grief can be transacted through debilitating melancholia or restorative mourning, so too can optimistic responses take escapist or restorative forms. According to the escapist line of thinking, an intensification of the same feature of humankind's species being that caused the crisis—our world-shaping capacity—can also fix the problem. This takes the form of either

geoengineering solutions to end carbon pollution or other forms of toxic-ity or interplanetary colonization schemes to abandon the earth where, as Kim Stanley Robinson puts it in his novel *Green Mars*, "long-range carrying capacity . . . [is] massively overshot."[97] Fantasies of interplanetary colonization put any remorse for the extinction crisis forever behind us. From the van-tage point of colonies on Mars, where no indigenous biota exist (none larger than microbes, in any case) for humankind to extirpate, the Sixth Extinction might seem like a youthful indiscretion. Such present-day techno-optimistic responses resonate, as the following chapters will suggest, with anthropo-centric progress narratives that grounded Indigenous Inca and Nahua origin stories (Chapter 1), structured Enlightenment accounts of the mammoth's extinction (Chapter 2), and framed Euro-American preservationist writing on the buffalo (Chapter 4).

Other forms of optimism are evident in resurrection ecology and res-toration ecology.[98] Resurrection ecology focuses on preserving the DNA of endangered species against future extinctions or recovering the DNA of extinct species in order to revive the species through cloning.[99] Restoration ecology attempts to emulate an extinct ecosystem state by repopulating a space with the nearest living kindred species.[100] A combination of both is at work in the Harvard team's effort to clone the mammoth using the Asian elephant to produce a creature that belongs in a tundra environment. Such projects manage the guilt of the Sixth Extinction not by putting the crisis behind us but through atonement, a response that was anticipated in some nineteenth-century preservationist writing on the buffalo and is evident in recent pro-posals for "rewilding."[101] While technologies developed for de-extinction may be useful in preserving endangered species—for example, by introducing genetic diversity into small populations—nevertheless de-extinction projects may take up "intellectual bandwidth and financial resources" that could be used to address the extinction crisis in other ways.[102] Resurrection ecology thus potentially diffuses public concern over the extinction crisis, species conservation, and habitat preservation. A different kind of restoration is per-formed, however, by bringing an existing endangered species back from the brink of extinction through protectionist measures. Such projects have been variously motivated. The International Whaling Commission, for example, was formed in 1946 to promote "the conservation of whale stocks and thus make possible the orderly development of the whaling industry" and its 1982 moratorium on commercial hunting (which is not universally observed) fol-lowed from that.[103] On the other hand, tribal buffalo projects, as Chapter 4 will demonstrate, subordinate market principles to the goals of community

revitalization and the reestablishment of social relations between humans and buffalo.

In assuming normative measures of climate and biodiversity, however, both elegiac and optimistic modes of response evade the moral question of whether any species, including humankind, ought to persist at all.[104] This is the most radical form of the question of belonging, in which humanism's *ought* confronts Darwin's *is*. Ceding human exceptionalism—for example, through a posthuman account of the world as a set of interconnecting systems with no point of existential or epistemological privilege—would mean ceding any such moral judgment.[105] Of all species that ever lived, 99.9 percent are extinct and humans are fated for eventual extinction as well, as a Darwinian inevitability.[106] Deep ecologists have been insisting for decades that Gaia could get along just fine in our absence.[107] Yet this point has in turn been rehumanized by Alan Weisman's bestselling book *The World Without Us*, which reassuringly imagines a familiar, rational subject who surveys the ecological results of human extinction and the gradual recovery of nature.[108] Here, the imagination of the world without us becomes a Robinsonade: the imagination of a world without other humans. In the paleoecologist Jan Zalasiewicz's *The Earth After Us*, the role of rational observing subject is played by extraterrestrial scientists investigating earth's fossil record one hundred million years in the future.[109] More radically, Henry David Thoreau imagined the persistence of human thinking embodied in durable fabricated objects such as stone arrowheads, which will exist after the human species' extinction.[110] Freud's observation in the aftermath of the unprecedented carnage of World War I seems apt here: "We cannot, indeed, imagine our own death; whenever we try to do so we find that we survive ourselves as spectators."[111] Reflecting today on the extinction or endangerment of species, especially the human-like species on which this study focuses, we both register our fate and imagine our persistence.

A Prehistory of Extinction

Prior to the work of Georges Cuvier, who finally settled the question of extinction and established the existence of a previously unknown Pleistocene-epoch fauna, evidence indicating the disappearance of a kind of life invited two intertwined lines of inquiry.[1] One line concerned empirical accuracy within the field of natural history: the proper identification and classification of fossils, which included any rock or mineral substance dug from the earth (from the Latin *fodere*, to excavate). Another line concerned the question of cause: the powers and capacities of human and nonhuman agents responsible for the disappearance of a kind of life. The question of cause bore an implicit or sometimes explicit dimension of moral assessment.

Both the material and moral dimensions of causal inquiry became especially visible in American encounters between Indigenous storytellers and European historians. Notable encounters happened in two phases and locales: sixteenth-century New Spain and early eighteenth-century New England. In the intervening period, European naturalists investigated the provenance of fossils and this led to the investigation of the origin of a particular kind of life as the key to its extinction. While the Europeans' stance regarding the material dimension of Indigenous extinction narratives gradually shifted from Renaissance-era openness to Enlightenment skepticism, their stance regarding the moral dimension remained constant.[2] Both Europeans and Indigenous Americans agreed in assessing the disappearance of a kind of life positively or negatively according to whether this disappearance promoted human flourishing.

Nahua and Inca Ecology

As far as we know, the first colonial American fossil encounter took place between Hernán Cortés and a group of Tlaxcalans, a Nahua-speaking people

whom Cortés would soon enlist as allies in his conquest of Mexico.[3] In this encounter, the Tlaxcalans, who had never been conquered by the Aztec Triple Alliance, presented themselves to the Spanish as descendants of virtuous and powerful warriors. Parts of the Tlaxcalans' ancestral account of "how . . . they came to inhabit [their] land" were recorded by one of Cortés's warriors, Bernal Díaz del Castillo.[4] Díaz's purpose as memoirist of the Spanish conquest motivated him to present two episodes from the longer historical narrative he heard from the Tlaxcalans: first, their ancestors' conquest of the giants who originally occupied their land, which lay east of the mountains that separated them from the Aztec-controlled valley of Mexico; and second, the prophecy shared by all Nahua peoples of the return of the god Quetzalcoatl (although Díaz does not name him as such), whose emissaries the Tlaxcalans evidently believed the Spanish to be. Central to both episodes is the theme of conquest. The second episode had immediate consequences for the present context of encounter, for if the Spanish were indeed the men prophesied by the Tlaxcalans' ancestors, men who "would come from distant lands in the direction of the rising sun to subjugate them and govern them," then they would "defend [the Tlaxcalans] against the Mexicans," that is, against the Aztecs to the west (230).

The first episode recounted by Díaz presents an earlier instance of conquest. The Tlaxcalans' "ancestors had told them, that in times past there had lived among them men and women of giant size with huge bones, and because they were very bad people of evil manners . . . they had fought with them and killed them, and those of them who remained died off" (229).[5] Díaz credits this story because he had seen a fossil thigh bone "which was very thick and the height of a man of ordinary stature. . . . I measured myself against it and it was as tall as I am although I am of fair size" (229). By way of this historical narrative, the Tlaxcalans establish their presence in their current environment through moral right, and they project the continuation of that presence against their current enemies, the Aztecs, through alliance with the Spanish.

A question that puzzled Cortés—why the Aztec Triple Alliance had not conquered Tlaxcala when apparently they could have done so rather easily—bears on the environmental dimension of the Tlaxcalans' narrative of migration, extermination, and occupation.[6] This environmental dimension would be elaborated more fully in the versions given by the missionary historians Diego Durán, in *Historia de las Indias de Nueva España* (1581), and José de Acosta, in *Historia natural y moral de las Indias* (1590), both of whom drew on preconquest documents and Indigenous informants.[7] Like Díaz del Castillo, Acosta and Durán authenticate this narrative of extinction and civilization through

personal witness. Acosta reports that the excavation of the bones of a giant when he was in Mexico in 1586 yielded "a tooth, which, without exaggeration, was fully as large as a man's fist, and the rest of the bones were in proportion. I saw the tooth and was amazed by its extraordinary size."[8] Such finds were not uncommon in sixteenth-century Mexico, for as Durán reports, "In certain places of that region enormous bones of the Giants have been found, which I myself have seen dug up at the foot of cliffs many times."[9] Having seen the bones, none of the three Spaniards cast any doubt on the veracity of the accompanying Nahua story. They may have been prepared to credit these Indigenous American stories because they were familiar with Old World stories of giants that were sometimes based on the evidence of fossil teeth and bones of Pleistocene megafauna—notably St. Augustine's account of antediluvian giants in *The City of God* but also classical myths and vernacular legends.[10]

Acosta, a more philosophical and systematic historian than Durán, locates the Tlaxcalan narrative of extermination and settlement within a three-part, global proto-ethnographic ranking of cultures based on technological, economic, and governmental criteria. Lowest in the three-part scale are nomadic hunter-savages, Chichimecas, who have no government and practice no agriculture. The Aboriginal inhabitants of the valley of Mexico, including the race of giants exterminated by the Tlaxcalans, were said to be of this kind.[11] Analogously in Peru live the Uros, who "are so brutish that they do not even think of themselves as men" (83). At the midpoint of Acosta's evaluative scale are peoples who practice agriculture but live in independent towns and band together under the leadership of some larger chief only as necessary in times of war. The highest on the scale are kingdom-builders such as the Aztecs or Tlaxcalans, who have developed distinct social classes devoted to agriculture, trade, war, and religious offices. The Tlaxcalan settlement narrative as elaborated by Durán and Acosta demonstrates their progress from the middle to the highest form of culture.

Versions of the Tlaxcalan extermination narrative given by Durán and Acosta develop the moral evaluation of the war of conquest recorded in Díaz del Castillo's memoir, with its characterization of the giants as "evil," giving it an environmental dimension. The environmental dimension of the original Nahua sources is drawn out by Durán's and Acosta's interest in accounting for the peopling of the Americas within the frame of biblical history and especially by Acosta's more ambitious project of characterizing the climate of the New World, particularly that of the Torrid Zone, as habitable and even beneficent.[12] In this context, the Tlaxcalan extermination narrative becomes an account of putting the land to its best use to support a flourishing

civilization—a civilization that, according to Acosta, was inferior to European Christendom only in lacking alphabetic writing and true religion.[13]

According to the story transcribed by both Durán and Acosta, the Nahua lineages who settled Mexico emerged from seven caves and undertook separate migrations to different locations in Mexico, where they settled because they found good land. According to Acosta's sources, most of the Nahua lineages encountered Aboriginal populations of Chichimecas, "savage, forest-dwelling men who lived solely from hunting" and ate "even loathsome things like serpents, lizards, mice, locusts, and worms" (380–81). Or as Durán puts it, "Their whole life was reduced to a quest for food. In order to kill a snake they spent an entire day crouching behind a bush, watching the snake at its lair as a cat will wait for a mouse" (11–12). In most cases, with the coming of the superior Nahua, these people fled. They "showed no displeasure, nor did they make any resistance; they only departed and, seemingly astonished, concealed themselves in the most hidden part" of the mountains (Acosta, 384). However, the Aboriginal inhabitants of the land the Tlaxcalans wanted to settle were a race of savage giants who "refused to allow what the other Chichimecas had countenanced; rather, they began to defend the land, and as they were giants, they tried to expel the intruders by force" (384). The Tlaxcalans overcame the giants' superior strength by stratagem. Whereas Durán calls it "treason and deceit" (12), Acosta calls it "craft":

> Feigning peace with [the Chichimecas, the Tlaxcalans] invited them to a great banquet; and they had folk lying in ambush, and when all of them lay in a drunken stupor the Tlaxcallans secretly stole their arms, which consisted of great clubs and wooden shields and swords and other kinds of weapons. Having done this, they suddenly fell upon them; and in trying to defend themselves, and not finding their weapons the Chichimecas rushed to some nearby trees and, seizing the branches, stripped them off as if they had been so many leaves of lettuce. But at last, as the Tlaxcallans had come armed and in good order, they routed the giants and caused such ravages among them that not one was left alive. (384)

Both Durán and Acosta report that following the extermination of the giants, the other (ordinary-sized) Chichimec barbarians in the region "began to acquire some civilized traits, and to cover their flesh and to feel shame about things that had not caused them shame before" (Acosta, 385), emulating the Nahua.

Durán's and Acosta's accounts of the extinction of the Chichimecan giants, then, narrate the Nahua's successful competition for resources over more powerful humanlike agents. As in the account recorded by Díaz del Castillo, there is no invocation of superhuman or divine agency, no aid from spirit powers. The giants' evil nature evidently consisted in their hunter-savage culture, which they refused to give up, in contrast to those ordinary-sized Chichimecas who learned to emulate certain aspects of Nahua culture, although remaining separate. Acosta, ever more systematic than Durán, generalizes this narrative progression. "I am convinced," he writes, "that most of the provinces and nations of the Indies have developed in this same way," being occupied first by "savages," next by "others, seeking new and better lands," who "settled the better parts and instituted order and polity and a sort of commonwealth," and "later still, either from these or from other nations," men of "more energy and craft than the rest began to subdue and oppress the less powerful, until they formed great kingdoms and empires" (385).

These great kingdoms were, at the time of Cortés's arrival, engaged in perpetual war with each other. This kind of war was different from the war of extermination that the Tlaxcalans' ancestors had waged against the Chichimecan giants. The ongoing warfare between the Tlaxcalans and the Aztec Triple Alliance was characterized by highly formalized, seasonal battles in which the primary aim was to capture rather than kill the enemy. Whether or not Moctezuma II regarded such battles as strategic encounters in a long-term war of attrition against Tlaxcala, they evidently served two purposes.[14] As the king explained to Cortés, they provided training for his warriors and Tlaxcalan captives for ritual sacrifice.[15] The Tlaxcalans also took captives for sacrifice.

Human sacrifice was the key technology by which the Nahua managed their relation to their gods and thereby their environment, a relation that they regarded as precarious, not only at the fifty-two-year intervals when they prepared ritually for the end of the world, but continually. That is, to some degree the Nahua saw themselves as threatened by extinction and ritually organized their culture to persist. Mesoamerican human sacrifice and cannibalism have been famously explained by Marvin Harris as the distribution of animal protein as a reward for the warrior class's allegiance to the state in a context of protein deprivation.[16] However inadequate Harris's functionalist reduction is for an understanding of the ritual complex surrounding the sacrifice, it remains suggestive insofar as it attempts to get at the ecological significance of the ritual complex.[17] This significance emerges from a sense of environmental precariousness in an area that was prone to drought, hail, and blight—conditions that were more acute during the Little Ice Age of the

fifteenth century.[18] In the early sixteenth century when the Spanish arrived, the Nahua must have retained a cultural memory of the three-year drought and famine beginning in the year One Rabbit (CE 1454) when, as Durán's informants reported, "the earth burned like fire. . . . The prickly pear cactus no longer gave fruit; its leaves wilted and became limp, baked by the heat. As soon as maize sprouted it turned yellow and withered like all the rest of the crops" (143–44).[19] Around the time of the famine, Moctezuma I formalized the so-called flower wars, Tenochtitlan's perpetual war against Tlaxcala and other unconquered cities, in order to ensure a steady supply of sacrificial victims.[20] The environmental association of these wars, as manifest in the poetic association of a warrior's life and death with the blooming and fading of a flower, was pervasive at the time of Cortés's arrival.[21]

This association of warriors with flowers is just one indication that, as Inga Clendinnen puts it, ritual human sacrifice to the earth gods manifested the Nahua's understanding that "the human body . . . was no more than one stage in a vegetable cycle of transformations, and human society a human arrangement to help sustain that essential cycle."[22] The Nahua conceptualized their place in the vegetable cycle as one of involuntary debt to the earth gods contracted through eating the fruits of the earth. The Nahua's sense of debt was symbolized, for example, in the festival eating of cakes made in the image of the god Huitzilopochtli from maize and amaranth flours, which Acosta describes as a diabolical aping of the Roman Catholic Church's central sacrament: "Beginning with the eldest, [the priests] distributed [the cakes] and gave them in a sort of communion to all the people, young and old, men and women. And they received it with so much reverence, awe, and tears that it was a remarkable thing to see, saying that they were eating God's flesh and bones and that they were unworthy to do so" (304). While the masses fed on gods in the form of maize and amaranth cakes, the elite fed on gods in the form of the bodies of enemy warriors, who were made to impersonate the gods and were then sacrificed and distributed to the warriors who had captured them. The debt thus symbolized could be fully repaid only in death, when the earth gods in turn fed on all human bodies.[23] This understanding of the body as part of the vegetable cycle persists today, though now dissociated from the technology of sacrifice—for example, in a contemporary Nahua song: "We eat of the earth / then the earth eats us."[24]

While the Tlaxcalans and Aztecs whom Cortés encountered waged flower wars as a means of socially sustaining their place in the vegetable cycle, the ancestral Tlaxcalans had fought a different kind of war against the evil giants, not a flower war but an "angry war" of extermination.[25] In this war to

extinguish another kind of life, the Tlaxcalans did not take captives for sacrifice. Thus they excluded that other kind from the social reproduction of what they understood to be a just human ecology. The Tlaxcalans thereby present themselves as having used a purely human agency, unaided by superhuman powers, in order to shape the natural environment for their own benefit and to exclude another, harmful kind of life from it.

Indigenous Peruvian accounts of the extermination of giants, also associated with the fossil remains of Pleistocene megafauna, are more explicit in their environmental dimension. These accounts characterize the giants as male, sexually rapacious, and ravenous. The giants' appetitive qualities thus add to the extinction narrative an important moral dimension concerning human ecology: not only consumption, as in the case of the Chichimecas, but also reproduction.[26] With this increased moral urgency comes a shift in the naming of the exterminating agency from human to divine. Versions of the Peruvian extermination story are given in Acosta's *Historia*, Agustín de Zárate's *Historia del descubrimiento y conquista de la provincia del Perú* (1555), and Pedro de Cieza de León's *La Crónica del Perú* (1553). Cieza de León's account, the most detailed, is quoted in full by the first mestizo Inca historian of Peru, Garcilaso de la Vega, in his *Comentarios Reales de los Incas* (1609).[27] While Zárate provides a more exacting report of the excavation of the bones that was undertaken by the deputy governor of Trujillo to verify the local peoples' ancestral story, Cieza promises the most truthful account, saying, "I will relate what I have been told, without paying attention to the various versions of the story current among the vulgar, who always exaggerate everything."[28] According to this unexaggerated version, then, a party of male giants, some "dressed in the skins of animals, others only in the dress which nature had given them," landed by boat near Trujillo (then called Puerto Viejo) (189). After building a crude village and digging deep into "the living rock" to secure a supply of water, the giants began to devastate the land and terrorize its people (189). They "consumed all the provisions they could lay their hands upon in the surrounding country; insomuch that one of them ate more meat than fifty of the natives of the country could. As all the food they could find was not sufficient to sustain them, they killed many fish in the sea with nets and other gear" (189–90).[29] If this were not bad enough, they also raped and killed the local women and killed some of the men as well, when they attempted to drive the giants away. "After a few years," because "the native women did not match their great size" or perhaps because "of the counsel or inducement of the devil," the giants began to practice sodomy among themselves.[30] For their sins they were punished by "God our Lord":

"While they were all together, engaged in their accursed [sodomy] a fearful and terrible fire came down from heaven with a great noise, out of the midst of which issued a shining angel with a glittering sword, with which, at one blow, they were all killed, and the fire consumed them. There only remained a few bones and skulls, which god allowed to remain without being consumed by the fire, as a memorial of this punishment" (190).[31] Acosta similarly says that the giants were "consumed in fire that came from Heaven" while Zárate more vividly affirms that "a younge man came downe from Heaven, shyning like the Sunne, & fought with those Giants, throwing flames of fier at them with such vehemency, that the tokens and signes therof remained in the hard stone," and then chased the remaining giants into a valley where "hee made a finall ende of them."[32] This motif of fire from the heavens was also common to some Indigenous North American accounts of the extermination of the mammoth, as we will see in Chapter 2.

Since these Mexican and Peruvian narratives of the extermination of giants are associated with fossil remains, it has been suggested that they preserve traces of ancestral memories dating from the Late Pleistocene epoch.[33] In Acosta's figurative description of the battle between the giants and the ancestral Tlaxcalans, the giants' behavior, "seizing the branches" of trees and "stripp[ing] them off as if they had been so many leaves of lettuce," may seem to resemble that of proboscideans such as mammoths or mastodons (384). The resemblance is also preserved, albeit less effectively, in Durán's figure, in which the giants "tore branches from the trees with the same ease as one cuts a turnip" (12). If this motif was transmitted intact from the Late Pleistocene epoch, in which Clovis people flourished by means of technologies that were adapted to hunting mammoths and other megafauna, then the extermination narrative as a whole could be understood as a chronologically compressed account of cultural evolution, according to which Paleolithic hunting culture is replaced by Neolithic agrarian culture after the extinction of the megafauna.[34]

Such an interpretation would not, however, change our understanding of the narrative's basic account of environmental agency, in which human beings exterminate a kind of life different from themselves (although not all that different) without any aid from the gods. Nor would it change the narrative's implicit moral judgment, which values the extermination positively. The Clovis people may have mourned the extinction of the mammoths, having lost so great a food source, even if they had caused the extinction.[35] Yet the Nahua settlement narrative does not preserve any trace of mourning. It seems less likely that the Incan extinction narrative preserves ancestral memory of

encounters with mammoths or other Pleistocene megafauna. These narratives do not depict any action that might be taken as proboscidean behavior, as in the Nahua account of the giants stripping off tree branches like so many leaves of lettuce. Nor, despite the motif of a killing fire, does there seem to be any reference to a volcanic eruption.[36]

Whether or not the Mexican and Peruvian narratives encode ancestral memories of the mammoth, both narratives use evidence of the disappearance of an apparently humanlike kind of life to engage with issues of human ecology. In the Peruvian narrative, the giants, while resourceful enough to build boats and dig wells, are environmentally unfit in two ways. They are hunters who cannot find enough meat to sustain themselves, and when they turn to fishing they threaten to exhaust the sea's resources. (Zárate actually characterizes them primarily as fishermen). The giants do not remain long enough to test whether fishing could sustain them, however, because they cannot reproduce themselves. So large that they are unable to have sexual intercourse with ordinary women, they turn to nonreproductive sexual behaviors and for this—in the causal logic of the Spanish chroniclers—they are finally exterminated by divine power. This linkage of divine agency with the policing of sexual behavior differentiates the Peruvian from the Mexican narrative, which rests entirely on human agency. Two factors seem relevant in the different attributions of agency: comparative power and claims to Aboriginal occupation. The Peruvian story narrates an invasion, in which a divine agent preserves a morally superior but physically much weaker Aboriginal culture. By contrast, the Mexican story narrates a conquest in which organized human effort exterminates a physically stronger but morally inferior Aboriginal culture. Whether or not the Tlaxcalans' privileged position as Cortés's allies colored Spanish transcriptions of their ancestral conquest narrative, the dimension of moral assessment is similar to that of the Peruvian narrative. In both cases, the extermination of an inferior kind of life preserves or establishes a flourishing, morally superior human culture.

To put these Mesoamerican fossil legends into a larger perspective: we are familiar with stories that characterize the Neolithic revolution as humankind's original alienation from nature—the Mesopotamian and Hebrew story about the fall of Eden, the classical Greek story about the decline from a Golden Age, and the Taoist story about the lapse from a state of Perfect Unity. One interpretation of such stories is that they encode a nostalgic cultural memory of a pre-agrarian state of greater biodiversity and human freedom.[37] Yet this narrative is reversed in the Mexican and Peruvian fossil legends regarding the extinction of marauding giants, which encode Paleolithic culture as a state

of voracious resource exploitation. One explanation for this narrative shape is provided by ecological economics: working from the assumption that the human species has potentially infinite wants and limited environmental and technological means of satisfying those wants, agrarians will tend to regard hunter-gatherers like the Mexican and Peruvian giants as rapacious exploiters of resources.[38] These are terms on which Spanish historians, themselves products of an agrarian culture, could agree with their Nahua and Inca informants. The resulting sense of extinction as progress through the eradication of a powerful threat to humankind's well-being would recur in eighteenth-century North American accounts of the extinction of the mammoth—a context in which imperial politics more than shared ecological-economic assumptions shaped European transcriptions of Indigenous stories.

The Provenance of Fossils

During the sixteenth century, it had seemed reasonable enough to both Indigenous Americans and Europeans that large, otherwise unidentified fossil bones and teeth were the remains of ancient giants. With the development of natural history as a field of inquiry, however, Europeans linked such remains to other curiosities such as fossilized marine shells and petrified wood. While wood and animal bones and teeth posed the question of the mechanism of preservation, the remains of marine shells in inland locations were especially puzzling because they also posed the problem of transport and deposition. Naturalists debated whether such fossils were *lusus naturae*, tricks of nature that mimicked the shapes of living beings, or whether they were in fact the remains of living beings.[39] Of these naturalists, Robert Hooke is of interest because he was among the first to posit the extinction of species. In this he contravened the widely held belief of universal preservation by divine agency, as stated, for example, by the Irish physician and naturalist Thomas Molyneux in 1697. For Molyneux, the "Principle of Providence taking Care in general of all its Animal Productions" meant that "no real Species of Living Creature is so utterly extinct, as to be lost entirely out of the World, since it was first Created."[40] Such a view was held by Thomas Jefferson, as we will see in Chapter 2.

In a series of papers read to the Royal Society beginning in the1660s and published posthumously as "A Discourse of Earthquakes," Hooke advanced the theory that fossils which looked like wood, shells, bones, and teeth derived somehow from the "Soul or Life-principle of some animal" or plant rather than being produced by some "Plastick faculty inherent in the Earth

itself."[41] The idea of a "Plastick faculty" of the earth was ancient, with roots in the concept of a world-spirit as elaborated, for example, in Plato's *Timaeus*, and was being revived in England during the mid-seventeenth century by the Cambridge Platonists.[42] Hooke's explanation for fossils used the analogy of buried coins dating from the Roman occupation of Britain. Arguing that it was no more likely that the forces of inorganic nature would produce imitations of Roman coins than of oyster shells, Hooke proposed rather that displaced shells and the like were evidence of the earth's dynamic history. Where Georges-Louis Leclerc, Comte de Buffon would come to characterize the reading of the earth's archive as a purely human hermeneutic process, however, Hooke emphasized divine agency in both production and interpretation:

> There is no Coin can so well inform an Antiquary that there has been such or such a place subject to such a Prince, as these [fossil shells] will certify a Natural Antiquary, that such and such places have been under the Water, that there have been such kind of Animals, that there have been such and such preceding Alterations and Changes of the superficial Parts of the Earth: And methinks Providence does seem to have design'd these permanent shapes, as Monuments and Records to instruct succeeding Ages of what past in preceding. And these written in a more legible Character than the Hieroglyphicks of the ancient *Egyptians*, and on more lasting monuments than those of their Pyramids and Obelisks.[43]

For Hooke, the hand of Providence was evident both in causing the extinctions and in making sure humankind became aware of the extinctions and their causal mechanisms. These mechanisms, according to Hooke, were a combination of earthquakes, which raised submarine surfaces and sunk elevated terrain, and shifts in the earth's axis and center of gravity, which caused flooding. As a consequence, Hooke hypothesized, in past ages "there may have been divers Species of things wholly destroyed and annihilated, and divers others changed and varied, for since we find that there are some kinds of Animals and Vegetables peculiar to certain places, and not to be found elsewhere; if such a place have been swallowed up, 'tis not improbable but that those Animal Beings may have been destroyed with them; and this may be true both of aerial and aquatick Animals."[44] Through such a process, Hooke reasoned, the remains of ancient giants might also be preserved: "We have Stories that there have been Giants in former Ages of the World, and 'tis not impossible but that such there may have been, and that they were all destroyed, both they and their

country by an Earthquake, and the poets seem to hint as much by their *Gigan-tomachia*."[45] Given that Hooke believed he had worked out the mechanics of floods as well as earthquakes, it is curious that he did not specifically name the giants in Genesis 6:4 ("There were giants on the earth in those days"). As we will see, Cotton Mather would comment extensively on this possibility.

Hooke's emphasis on locale in his discussion of fossils suggests that he was not much troubled by questions of deposition and transport. For Hooke, fossils were remains of creatures indigenous to the locales in which they were found, although, of course, environmental conditions in those locales may have varied significantly from the present day. Natural agency in the form of earthquakes or floods had caused the demise of these creatures and the preservation of their remains, apparently through a Providential design that Hooke does not theorize in any detail. Nor does it seem that Hooke was much troubled by the idea that Providence would allow "divers Species of things [to be] wholly destroyed or annihilated," although whether he was using "species" as a term for something more than a local variety of creature remains unclear. Thus it is unfortunate that, as the editor of his posthumous papers noted in 1705, Hooke left no commentary on a drawing he had made to accompany the "Discourse of Earthquakes," which the editor labels as "the petrified Grinder [i.e., molar] of some large Animal, possibly of a Whale or Elephant."[46] If the tooth belonged to a whale, the explanation for its location inland would have been the same as that for fossilized marine shells: ancient submersion and then elevation of the terrain by means of an earthquake. Yet, from the accompanying drawing, the tooth looks rather like it belonged to a mastodon. Seventeenth-century naturalists ignorant of mastodons might have concluded that it belonged to an elephant, though a careful and informed observer would have noted that an elephant's molars have fairly flat surfaces rather than the conical points of the specimen in question. However, fossil remains of woolly mammoths, whose molars are much the same size as mastodon molars but are flat like those of elephants, were also sometimes found in England and were generally grouped, along with mastodon fossils, as the remains of elephants. As in Hooke's analogy likening fossils to antique coins, the remains of elephants could have been correlated with the Roman occupation.[47] Remains of any gigantic, apparently nonindigenous animal other than an elephant would have posed a greater puzzle in terms of deposition and transport.

In the Americas, where discoveries of elephant-like remains could not be explained by Roman occupation, other narratives emerged along with reconsiderations of the theory of nature's "Plastick faculty" that Hooke had

disavowed. In the 1680s, John Banister—a minister, naturalist, and one of the founders of the College of William and Mary—noted that such fossil teeth mixed with "petrified oysters, scallops, bones, &c." occurred in the banks of the James River and its tributaries far above the reach of the tide. Questioning whether these "strange stones . . . were ever reall teeth," he considered two explanations: "Now either ye sea in former ages came further up into ye country, which to the eastward lies very low & level, or ye earth by some kind of salts of its own, that naturally shoot into such figures, must have produc'd these there; which I know is ye more modern, & (if not in this) in many other places where such things are found, ye most plausible opinion." After reproducing the debate between proponents and opponents of the theory of plastic power, and even allowing for the claim that nature might be "as constant in the production of form'd stones as she is of those vegetables & animals which have no seminall principles in themselves" such as fungi, Banister finally conjectured that the shells and teeth in question were "petrefaction[s]," that is, formerly living organisms preserved through the mineralization of their corpses.[48]

Banister shared his specimens with another naturalist and Fellow of the Royal Society, the Reverend John Clayton, during the latter's two-year residence in Virginia. Clayton incorporated these into his "Account of Virginia," which was published in the *Philosophical Transactions* in five installments from 1693 to 1701. Commenting on the banks of fossilized oyster shells, Clayton differed from Banister in accepting an explanation based on the theory of plastic power: "I do not apprehend, why it may not be as feasible to suppose them to have been Rocks, at first shot into those Figures, as to conceive the sea to have amass'd such a vast Number of Oyster-shells one upon another, and afterwards subsiding, should leave them cover'd with such Mountains of Earth, under which they should petrefie." However, he characterized the fossil teeth found among those deposits specifically as "petrefied" remains rather than as original productions of nature, supposing that "they must have been of Fishes." Similarly, he identified specimens that Banister showed him, taken from "a Hundred and fifty Miles up into the Country," as "the Joynt of a Whale's Back-bone, and several Teeth."[49] Clayton did not attempt to explain why the remains of marine animals should be found so far inland, though probably like Banister he assumed that at one time the sea level had been much higher than at present.

In their observation of fossils, both Banister and Clayton wanted to preserve the theory of nature's "Plastick faculty" while limiting its scope by identifying different causal agencies in different cases: the biblical flood could account for many fossils. Their differential application of the theory—for

Banister, fungi versus mollusks, fish, and whales; for Clayton, mollusks versus
fish and whales—may be attributable to their respective perceptions of these
organisms' ranks in the scale of nature. Plastic power might generate comparatively simple creatures, as Banister assumed of fungi, or it might mimic the
forms of comparatively simple creatures, as Clayton hypothesized of mollusks,
but it did not produce the more complex creatures generated by "seminall
principles" such as fish or whales. For these more complex creatures, remains
indicated an existence and disappearance that called for explanation.

Extinction and the Origin of Life

Other, more extensive North American deposits of mammoth and mastodon
bones and teeth, especially those not found in the vicinity of marine fossils,
could not so easily be reduced to the remains of fish or whales. Nor could they
be explained by Roman occupation. The idea that they might be the remains
of giants, as Hooke allowed, was readily available in both Euro-American and
Indigenous American traditions and seemed more likely.[50]

The first such account appeared in America's first continuously published
newspaper, the *Boston News Letter*, July 30, 1705. Edward Taylor—a minister
and physician in the frontier town of Westfield, Massachusetts, who would
not become known as an important poet until his papers were rediscovered
in the twentieth century—was intrigued enough by this account to copy the
passage in his diary, making some minor alterations and emphasizing the
dimensions of the remains:

> On the 23d of July "one of the Gentlemen of the Council at York
> carried thither a monstrous *Tooth* that weighed *four* pounds & *three*
> *quarters*, said to be one of the great Teeth of a man, whole & sound
> on the Top but much decayed in its fangs, one of which being hollow
> contained *half a pint* of Liquor. It was dug out of a Bank or Hill that
> rose some 30 or 40 foot above the place, about 26 Miles below Albany,
> at a place called *Claverack*. They found another Tooth, that seemed
> to be a fore tooth that was *four fingers* broad; and dug up Bones that
> when they came to the Air turned to Dust, but one Bone they took up,
> judged a Thigh Bone of a Man, *seventeen foot long*."[51]

Taylor was thus prepared when, the following summer, "a Dutchman, that
came from Albany" showed him a similar tooth as well as two pieces of bone,

the dimensions and appearance of which Taylor recorded in detail before reporting the Dutchman's conjecture, based on the disposition of other bones at the site, that they were the remains of a "Monster" some "60 or 70 foot high."[52] Similar remains would be shown to Governor Joseph Dudley of Massachusetts, who would in turn report the find to New England's most highly esteemed naturalist at the time, the minister Cotton Mather.[53] Dudley and Mather concluded that these were the remains of the giants mentioned in Genesis and extinguished by the great flood. While the biblical flood offered one possible explanation for the remains, Taylor preferred the postdiluvian provenance suggested by Indigenous stories, as conveyed by his Dutch visitor: "The Indians flocking to see the monstrous Bones upbraided the Dutch with Unbelief in that they would not believe the Report of a monstrous person w^c. they had told them from their Fathers, viz. that about 240 years ago there was a monstrous person as high as the Tops of the Pine Trees, that would hunt Bears till they took to the Trees, & then would catch them with his Hands, and would go into the River 12 or 14 feet deep and catch 3 or 4 or 5 Sturgeons at a time & Broil them on the Fire for his food."[54]

Taylor would use this account from his diary as a prose preface to the 190-line poem he would write soon thereafter on the Claverack giant.[55] A memoir written by Taylor's grandson Ezra Stiles suggests that Taylor confirmed this account with local Native Americans, reporting from his uncle Eldad Taylor (Edward's youngest child) that "the Tradition among the Inds. was that the Giant 'was peaceable and would not hurt the little Indians', and that the little Inds. would give him meat to eat & he would receive it kindly; tho they said they always was afraid of him. They however [weren't] afraid of him when they approached him with a piece of meat or food, w^c he would take without hurting them. He would knock the Bears off the Trees with his fist or a Club. . . . When the Indians first saw Vessels passing in the Sound off against Paucatuck, they said at first it was *Weetucks* a coming again."[56] The additional detail and the specific reference to Paucatuck Sound (off the Connecticut coast east of New London) suggests that this version of the story—and perhaps the substance of the story that Taylor recorded in his 1706 diary entry as well—had not necessarily traveled with the tooth from Albany but rather was garnered by Taylor's further inquiry among Indigenous informants.

Taylor's inquiry into Indigenous narrative grounded one part of his twofold examination of environmental agency in his poem on the Claverack giant. Taylor refers specifically to the "Sopos indians" as a source.[57] The Sopos or Esopus were a Munsee people (one of the three branches of the Leni Lenape, often called Delaware by Euro-Americans) who had fought against

Dutch incursion in the mid-seventeenth century, but by 1705, when Taylor spoke with them, had been decimated by disease and war. As the Esopus' account of their mistaking a European ship for the giant Weetucks's canoe suggests, they told their story in the context of the hierarchical state of colonial relations around Albany and southward during the era of Queen Anne's War (1701–13). If, in this telling of a traditional Esopus legend, Weetucks stands in for the apparently peaceable yet implicitly threatening Europeans, the anecdote suggests that the Europeans could be placated with a bit of bear meat—metonymically, that is, by the animal pelts traded at Albany. Alternatively, given the date of "about 240 years ago," the story could function as a commemoration of the ancestors, Weetucks representing the Esopus people at the height of their strength just prior to the first European incursions on the New England coast. It is also possible that Taylor was familiar with southern Wampanoag stories about the giant Maushops, neither a world-creating culture hero in the mold of the Wabanaki Gluskap nor a terrifying monster such as the Stonish Giants of Haudenosaunee legend (both of which will be discussed in Chapter 2), but rather a morally neutral figure who lived apart, much like the Esopus' Weetucks. The local people sometimes placated Maushops with gifts of food and tobacco and Maushops sometimes reciprocally left the people food, especially cooked whale meat.[58]

In either case, the Claverack giant as Taylor describes him from Indigenous sources is a being whose powers and capacities seem well suited to his environment: stories imply that his favorite foods—such as bear, sturgeon, and whale—were abundant and his consumption of them was moderate and proportional to his size, evidently leaving plenty to support his ordinary-sized neighbors.[59] Since Taylor gives no account of the giant's death, he may have assumed that he died of old age. According to Indigenous stories, when foreigners arrived (in different versions, either other Indigenous Americans or Europeans) Maushops left New England (in some versions, with his wife) after transforming his numerous sons and daughters into killer whales.[60] Thus the narrative bears environmental content that Taylor seems to have missed. Unconcerned about carrying capacity and resource scarcity, Taylor may not have been prepared to understand the ways in which Esopus or Wampanoag accounts of the giant's powers and consumption patterns may have commented on these themes—especially during the early eighteenth century, when these peoples' cultural memories were fresh with the erosion of their traditional economic base by the Europeans' incursions.

Taylor's interest in a different kind of environmental agency is evident in his account of the giant's origin. He begins the poem with a prologue investigating

the origin of all creatures, from rocks and minerals through plants and animals to humankind, through the workings of nature's "Spirits." This survey prepares Taylor to examine the instance of gigantism evidenced by the Claverack remains, in which it seemed that "Nature exceeds itselfe."[61] Other naturalists examining fossils of giants posed a similar question of nature's agency and natural limits. Thomas Molyneux, for example, asserted that such remains "shew how far the power of Nature may reach, and does sometimes exert it self in the Productions of Humane Bodies beyond her usual bounds."[62] For Taylor, the giant's singularity posed a question regarding the assumption that the regularity of nature manifested divine wisdom. Taylor had reflected on this aspect of divine wisdom in a sermon composed in 1701:

> What wisdom must that needs be, that knew how to bring all things out of Nothing? . . . Cast an eye on the Elementary Bodies from the Stars to the Centre of the earth, the Various Sorts of Birds, fowls the various Sorts, and Kinds of Beasts, Serpents, Dragons, Scorpions, Worms, Insects, Fishes, etc. So the variety of Herbs, Flowers, Bushes, Shrubs, plants, Seeds, Fruits, trees: and all these made exactly according to the Draught of the Decree, in Nature, Matter, Form, Shape, Size, Properties, Qualities, Vertues, Spirits, Tempers, Springings, growing, Durations, Decayings, to keep their Natures, Seasons, etc., and so successively on to go by the hand of Providence to the end of the World. I say, the Wisdom that hath done all this, and chiefly that hath made Man, and put Wisdom into the inward parts, is Wonderfull. Here is Wisdom indeed.[63]

Whereas this sermonic passage emphasizes nature's regularity, Taylor had long been interested in finding evidence of the divine in the exotic as well. Thus, for example, in 1683 he had written to Increase Mather with observations on hailstorms, comets, and other unusual phenomena for the volume Mather was compiling, *An Essay for the Recording of Illustrious Providences* (1684). However, Taylor had not interpreted these phenomena as particular emblematic messages or other kinds of divine interventions into the usual course of nature, as other Puritans might have done. For Taylor, such phenomena posed a question similar to the one posed by gigantism: how to understand the unusual as usual, that is, as consistent with divine wisdom guiding the generative force of creation.

In the poem on the Claverack giant, Taylor thus found an occasion to explore the structure of nature's regularity and the manifestation of this

generative force. The prologue figures generation from "natures Kirnell" planted by God to become the "Tree of Nature to mentain / The glorious acts of Nature in the Same."[64] Notably this "Kirnell" generates what we would ordinarily think of as inanimate as well as animate things according to different manifestations of the same principle. As Taylor anatomizes the tree of nature,

> Her darksom root, bears melancholy Rocks,
> Breeds Stones, Lead, Churlish iron in their plots.
> Her brighter Spirits with good warmth refinde
> Through her rich Calendar breed richer kinde
> And so hatch Silver bright & Gold more fine
> And Sparkling Gems that mock the Sun & 'ts Shine.
> Her Spirits that ascen'd the florid Bough
> Of Vegetation ever do allow
> Our Eyes a paradise of speckld Spots,
> Of Orient flowers towerde on these twiggy tops.
> Whose bowells lodge Pomanders Sweet that rise
> In rich perfume, these kiss our nose, & eyes.
> Those Spirits that ascend to Sensitive,
> Sweet musicke for our Eares produce alive,
> By all her Bagpipes, Virginalls, & Harps
> The Wing'd musicians of the Woods imparts,
> Yea, & harsh notes from the rugged Organs roar,
> Displaying to us also natures Store.
>   Let me, my Lord, pick up of these a few,
> To set mine Eyes on, thy bright selfe to view
> As in a Looking Glass.[65]

From base rocks and finer gems through plants and flowers to birds and animals to the cognizant human observer of this continuum, the creatures are infused by the sap of the Tree of Nature, the "Spirits" that are all parts of one whole, different manifestations of "the Same" creating force. There is a division in this scheme between inanimate and animate creatures, root and branch, but they are all parts of one tree imbued with one sap. Thus the instances of gigantism that Taylor goes on to remark about are all of the same kind, albeit "Strange Steps" that nature takes "unawares" which appear to us as "Castles in the Aire," from giant oyster shells to mushrooms mimicking human heads to the human giants named in the Bible, classical literature, and medieval English legend. The key pun in Taylor's summary account of

the latter, "monstrous Bulks of Human kind / Kinde nature raised up," asserts a sameness between humankind and the basest rocks and fungi: even as all are different kinds, all nature is kin.[66] Human giants, like the animals, vegetables, and minerals anatomized in the prologue's opening lines, are all potentially "Looking Glass[es]" in which the enlightened viewing subject sees one thing, the "bright selfe" of the creating God—which must at the same time, according to the figure of the mirror, be the enlightened human subject who perceives in himself so much of God as is evident in the generative force of nature. Arranged in an ascending scale—nature's "Spirits" are "with good warmth refinde" to "breed richer kinde" as the sap, warmed by the sun, ascends the Tree—these manifestations all gesture upward toward God.

The generative force that Taylor figures as creating "Spirits" in the prologue to the Claverack poem appear—along with a similar tropology of refinement derived from Taylor's knowledge of alchemy—in a meditative poem on grace as the flowing life force that Taylor composed in 1702.[67] Meditation 2.47 on John 5:26, "the Son hath life in himself," figures salvation—and with it enlightened perception of what embodied nature both is (though temporally obscured) and will become at the resurrection—as a process of distillation that reveals and releases the life force. In the key stanza that unblocks the channel between the "golden Sea / Of Godhead Fulness" and the "Silver Ocean" of "All Created Fulness" (the latter including Christ's human nature), an alembic distills and channels this life force to every creature:

> Besides thy proper Lifes tall fulness-Wealth,
> There's Life in thee, like golden Spirits, stills,
> To ery member of thy Mystick Selfe,
> Through secret Chases into th'vitall tills
> Or like the Light embodi'd in the Sun
> That to each living thing with life doth run.[68]

The "Spirits" that appear in the Claverack poem as the sap of the "Tree of Nature" are homologous with these distilled "golden Spirits" that provide life to each creature. Taylor elaborates the idea in a sermon specifically associated with Meditation 2.47: "Nature . . . Communicates in its Prolifick Operation, vitall influences or a Principall of vitality, that goeth along, as absolutely essentiall to its propogation, with the propogating Matter it giveth forth. So that hence Naturall Life runs along the Chanell of nature naturally, and that according to the sort of Life that is thus propagated."[69] In the Claverack poem, sap of the "Tree of Nature"—that which flows "along the Chanell of

Nature"—specifically infuses inanimate things as well, which have their own form of "life." All manifest the generative principle that is especially visible in the case of gigantism, when "Nature exceeds itselfe."[70] Since this excess is produced through nature's own agency, nature cannot really be said to exceed itself except insofar as Taylor's poetics of contradiction sharpens his investigation of Nature's generative agency.

Nature's generative agency as thus characterized by Taylor was not the "Plastick faculty" that Hooke disavowed, though sometimes expressed in similar language, for here there was no question of the mere mimicry of natural forms. Rather, it was the orderly production of created beings, including mineral as well as plant and animal beings. We may be tempted anachronistically to characterize Taylor's belief in this sense of generative agency as vitalism but for Jane Bennett's reminder that the term names a "reaction formation to mechanistic materialism," the latter being a conceptualization of matter that would coalesce only through the elaboration of Enlightenment skepticism.[71] "Vitalism" is not a term used even by the Cambridge Platonists who were Taylor's contemporaries, although they may have spoken like Taylor of "vitall influences or a Principall of vitality."[72] Prior to the consolidation of mechanistic materialism, Taylor did not need to disagree with Indigenous historians regarding generative powers. This marks Taylor as a Nonmodern, in Bruno Latour's sense of the term, that is, one who does not undertake the modernist de-animation of nature.[73]

Despite what we might assume regarding the Puritans' fondness for seeing divine intervention into the regular course of nature, Taylor is thus able to give a full account of the giant's being, origin, powers, and capacities by means of nature without invoking the intervening hand of God. In contrast, Cotton Mather had more trouble avoiding reference to immediate divine intervention. And as we will see in the case of narratives deriving from mammoth fossils found at Big Bone Lick (Chapter 2), Enlightenment skepticism framed nonmechanistic accounts of extinction given by Native Americans as bearing ineligible appeals to supernatural intervention, even as some such as Jefferson, like Molyneux, appealed to God's preserving agency.

Like Taylor, Mather found in the Claverack fossils an occasion to reflect on two senses of environmental agency: first, the relations between a creature and its environment, and second, the forces of generation. While Mather agreed with Taylor, against mounting skepticism among European naturalists, that the remains were those of a humanlike giant, he disagreed with Taylor and local Indigenous peoples regarding the remains' historical provenance.[74] Mather identified the remains as those of antediluvian giants,

thereby enlisting them in the project of bringing America into the order of biblical history, which he had begun in his history of the New England church, the *Magnalia Christi Americana*, and extended in his voluminous work of biblical commentary, the *Biblia Americana*. These remains of giants are a key exhibit in the *Biblia Americana*, for they provided material evidence, "an Illustrious Confirmation of the *Mosaic History*," regarding passages such as Genesis 6:4 ("There were giants on the earth in those days").[75] Addressing skepticism regarding reports of the remains of giants from Pliny the Elder through St. Augustine and into the sixteenth century—"I find, the Credit of *Pliny*'s Relations, runs pretty low among the Learned in our Dayes"—Mather asserts that by virtue of these remains, "*America* too will come in to shelter the Reputation of these Historians."[76] In a slightly revised version of the *Biblia Americana* commentary that Mather sent to John Woodward, a geologist, physician, and provincial secretary of the Royal Society, with the hope of publication in the Society's *Philosophical Transactions*, Mather actually puts himself in the place of St. Augustine. In the *City of God* (book 15, chapter 9), Augustine cites his personal examination of the fossil tooth of a giant at Utica to support his claim that antediluvian men were of larger stature than postdiluvian men. Thus Mather, having examined a tooth from the Claverack site sent to him by Governor Dudley of Massachusetts, writes that "afterwards I was able to use the Language of *Austin*; *Vidi ipse non solus, sed aliquot mecum*" (I myself saw, not alone, but others with me).[77] Despite this attempt to appropriate Augustine's authority (an irrelevant appeal to ethos in addressing the Royal Society),[78] Mather twists the latter's argument. Whereas Augustine took the remains to represent all antediluvian humans, whom he claimed were larger and longer lived than Noah's descendants, Mather uses the remains to assert the antediluvian giants' difference from ordinary humans, who have always been the same size.

According to Mather, the giants functioned as God's agents "for the Punishment of a wicked World" but proved to be "such a Plague unto the World, that if a *Flood* had not exterminated *Them*, they might in a while have exterminated all the rest, without a *Flood*."[79] They wielded exterminating power, but they were exterminated. The giants' power resonates with a characterization Mather had quoted earlier in his commentary, from the apocryphal book of Baruch: "*Ingenti corporis magnitudine praediti, reique bellicae scientissimi*" (by nature enormously large in body, predatory, and highly skilled in matters of war).[80] The characterization of these predatory giants may have inspired Mather's interpretation of the local Indigenous account, which is more malign than Taylor's: "Upon the Discovery of this horrible *Giant*, all the

Indians, within an hundred Miles of the Place, agreed in a *Tradition*, which they said, they had among them, from Father to Son, for some hundreds of Years, concerning him; and that he lived upon the fish of [the Hudson] River, (usually swallowing Four Sturgeons in a Morning for a Breakfast) and that his name was, *Maughkompos*. But there is very little in any *Tradition* of our Salvages, to be rely'd upon."[81] As a colonial addressing a prospective European audience, Mather may have been especially motivated to dismiss Indigenous American tradition.[82] The only detail he retains from this tradition depicts the giant as a great devourer. Even the name Maughkompos, an unusual variant of Maushops, may be Mather's invention. As the *Biblia Americana*'s modern editor Reiner Smolinski suggests, this name may be a pun on maw-compos, "endowed with an able jaw or stomach."[83] If so, Mather may have been toying with the idea that the "Plague" visited on ordinary humankind by the giants included not only a war of extermination, but overconsumption of resources as well—an environmental theme that resonates with Inca stories recorded by Zárate and Cieza de León and inverts the Nahua stories recorded by Díaz del Castillo, Durán, and Acosta.[84]

Like Díaz, Durán, and Acosta, Governor Dudley reported a story of the extermination of giants by ordinary humankind. Dudley's account came not from Indigenous American sources, however, but from "a tradition of the Jewish rabbins" that interpreted the second clause of Genesis 6:4 ("and also after that, when the sons of God came unto the daughters of men") as denoting sexual intercourse between fallen angels and human women resulting in offspring who "were such as whose heads reached the clouds, who are therefore called Nephelim, and their issue were Geborim, who shrunk away to the Raphaim, who were then not found to be invincible, but fell before less men, the sons of the east in several places besides Canaan"—thus indicating a line of generation that somehow must have survived the flood, though Dudley does not pursue the matter. He also offered an alternative image of the particular giant whose teeth he was sending to Mather as a pathetic Last Man, "for whom the flood only could prepare a funeral; and without doubt he waded as long as he could to keep his head above the clouds, but must at length be confounded with all other creatures, and the new sediment after the flood gave him the depth we now find."[85] Both of Dudley's stories characterize the giants as vulnerable, either to human conquest or to natural forces; neither casts them in Mather's role as God's punishing agents who got out of control and had to be exterminated in order to preserve humankind. Yet the central environmental theme expounded by Mather, the extinction of one kind as the preservation of another kind, was common as well to both Dudley's

account of the degeneration of the Nephelim and the Tlaxcalan conquest narrative. Whereas the Tlaxcalans' ancestors were supposed to have managed this issue themselves by exterminating their competitors, Mather posits that supernatural power closely manipulates humankind's relationship to natural resources, calling forth and then suppressing monstrous quasihuman agents to transact these ends.

Notwithstanding Mather's assertion that "there was an Omnipotent, Immediate, Miraculous Hand of God in the whole Affayr" of the exterminating flood, he remained intensely interested in the natural means by which the flood could have occurred, as evidenced by the more than forty manuscript pages of commentary he devoted in the *Biblia Americana* to chapters 7 and 8 of Genesis.[86] He was especially interested in refuting the theory set forth in Thomas Burnet's controversial but ultimately quite influential *Telluris Theoria Sacra* (1681; translated as *The Theory of the Earth*, 1684). According to Burnet, the surface of the antediluvian earth was completely smooth; crustal collapse released subterranean waters and caused the earth to tilt on its axis, after which the waters receded; the receding waters left the modern continents and oceans.[87] Among other points, Mather objected to Burnet's idea that the earth's smoothness was a postlapsarian remnant of Edenic perfection that the flood finally destroyed. Mather agreed with Burnet however in ruling out some of the more extraordinary explanations that various commentators had proposed—for example, that God had created and then destroyed all the flood waters, or had transformed air into water and then back again into air. Presenting various hypotheses with varying degrees of credulity, Mather is concerned to discover an explanation that preserved both God's omnipotence and nature's regularity. Among the most plausible, he cites a hypothesis proposed by John Ray, according to which "the Divine Power might . . . employ the Instrumentality of some Natural Agent, which is to us at present unknown, to *depress the Surface of the Ocean*, so as to force the [subterranean] *Waters* of the *Abyss*, thro' the forementioned Channels, and make the whole Surface of the *Earth* feel the Effects thereof." Especially when combined with an unusual amount of rain, the results would have been "Tragical and Marvellous."[88]

Mather's interest in identifying a "Natural Agent" mediating between "Divine Power" and matter is evident in a different way in his speculations on the origin of the giants, which he thought might provide the key to their disappearance. Here, like Taylor, he would ultimately turn to the question of nature's "Plastick Power." Mather first refutes the interpretive tradition cited by Dudley according to which the giants were the offspring of fallen angels

and earthly women by invoking Matthew 22:30 on "how Disagreeable *Matrimonial Affairs* are, to the *Angelical Nature*."[89] Wanting to find an explanation acceptable in terms of natural philosophy, an explanation that preserved God's ultimate agency while not making God immediately responsible for the disposition of every particle of matter, Mather first turns to stamina theory. Disseminated during the mid-seventeenth century by the Cambridge Platonists and bolstered by new microscopic observations—as published, for example, in Hooke's *Micrographia* (1665)—stamina theory purported to explain God's agency "in creating the *Seminal Part* of the World":

> Among the *Vegetables*, the . . . True *Seed* lies in so *little Room*, that it is not visible to the Naked Eye. . . . But in that *little Room*, there lies the *whole Plant*, in all the *True Parts* of it: which is afterwards evolved, and extended, and filled up, with its *Adventitious Nutriment*, until it be carried as far as the original *Stamina*, are capable: And *then*, the Growth stops. But perhaps, towards the *Period* of the Growth, so weak may be the *Stamina*, that according to the *Strength* of the Soyl that nourishes it, the *Growth* may be more or less, but a little varied.
>
> And why may not the *Seeds* of *Animals* have the like said of *Them*? Yea, the *Microscopical Inquisitions*, have made it more than probable; That the *True Seeds* of *Animals*, floating in their *Suitable Vehicle*, have, lying in a *Space* much less than the naked eye can discern, the whole *Bodies* of the *Animals*, even to all their *Nerves* and *Fibres*: which afterward *Grow* as aforesaid, until their original *Stamina* can be no further carried out.[90]

Among the first to observe the "seeds of animals" in their "suitable vehicle" was Anton van Leeuwenhoek, who was inspired by Hooke's *Micrographia*. Mather may have known of Leeuwenhoek's microscopic observations of vegetable seeds and animal spermatozoa from his letters to the Royal Society and responses by other naturalists such as Nehemiah Grew, extracts of which were published in the *Philosophical Transactions* from the late 1670s through the 1700s.[91]

Mather's discussion of this work focuses particularly on the size of creatures as predetermined by the stamina. In the case of giants, he speculates that "God, having at first created Numbers of Humane Bodies, in these true Seeds of them," may have created some "whose original *Stamina*, may be much larger than others, and capable of being drawn forth, to the most *Gigantic Extension*." Since Leeuwenhoek and others could not by microscopic

observation determine how stamina reproduced successive generations, Mather explores the two logical possibilities: (1) that stamina of each subsequent generation (in this case, of giants) might be taken from the environment into humans' bodies, "perhaps in their *Food*"; or (2) that stamina of all subsequent generations were present "all at first, in the Body of the First Man," Adam. Either way, giants could have been "brought forth, by Parents not exceeding the common Stature." Mather may have been troubled by the implications of the preexistence of stamina for all creatures, for if this were the case, how could we be certain that stamina of giants had been extinguished by the flood? Might not some remain, to be ingested or transmitted by the sons of Noah? That "we now suffer no more of this Plague" of giants, Mather asserts, is owing only to the "*Vigilant* and *Immediate* PROVIDENCE OF GOD"—not the most satisfactory conclusion for a Christian philosopher attempting to discover the agencies mediating between matter and divine will (Mather, 597). He leaves the question there, begging the reader's pardon for such a flight of speculation.

Yet Mather continued his investigation of the extinct giants. Sometime before 1712, when he wrote to Woodward, he added two items to the *Biblia* commentary on Genesis 6:4. One was a summary of Spanish American accounts. He reports the Peruvian story, which he knew from Zárate, of divine punishment in which "*Giants* . . . were fought by a Man descended from Heaven" but does not repeat the Mexican story of a human war of extermination against the giants despite having read Acosta's account (597). From Acosta, Mather reports on the size of the fossil teeth and bones found in Mexico. The second item is a critique of his earlier account of stamina theory—"oh! the palpable Darkness, under which we are languishing!" (599)—garnered from his reading in James Drake's 1707 *Anthropologia Nova; or, a New System of Anatomy*. Quoting from Drake, Mather concedes that the stamina theory "won't account fairly & fully, for *Mix'd Generation*," that is, hybridization as in the case of mules (598). Thus, also quoting from Drake, Mather professes uncertainty: "However old and exploded, the Opinion of a *Plastick Power* be, I must however embrace it even tho' I know not exactly wherein it lies: at least, till I meet with somewhat more sufficient to Resolve my Doubts, than hitherto I have done" (599).

Mather may not have been fully satisfied with the theory of "Plastick Power" because, at least in some versions, it allowed for randomness. In cases where the power operated on matter in less than optimal conditions, it might produce *lusus naturae*, as for example in producing marine shellfish underground where they could not live, or, potentially, in producing mineral

formations that merely mimicked these shellfish or the bones and teeth of animals or human giants. The theory of "Plastick Power" had thus served naturalists in providing a convenient explanation for the existence of monstrosities of various kinds, living and nonliving.[92] Yet there is some hint of randomness in Mather's account of the giants as a "Plague" that, although sent by God, nevertheless seemed capable of escaping its intended purpose and threatening to "exterminate all the rest" of humankind (597). If Mather wanted to salvage the moral component of his account of the mediation of divine agency in his characterization of the giants as a punishing force, he would have found it difficult to do so by means of the theory of plastic power, which seems to lack a moral component. Thus he needed to reformulate the account of nature's mediating agency. A passage from *The Christian Philosopher* indicates that by 1721 he had begun to do so, ruling out the possibility of *lusus naturae* in the case of fossil remains, as Hooke had done. In Essay 25, on minerals, Mather states that "*Fossils*, which are but the *Exuvia* of *Animals*, have been erroneously thought a sort of *peculiar Stones*," and on that basis "must be excluded" from the mineral kind.[93]

Mather returned to this problem of mediating agency in his last major work, an unpublished medical treatise entitled *The Angel of Bethesda*. Here, he attempted to elaborate the concept of "Nishmath-Chaijim," which was generally translated from the Hebrew as "breath of life," as for example in Genesis 2:7: "God formed man of the dust of the ground, and breathed into his nostrils the breath of life; and man became a living soul." Of a "*Middle Nature*" between body and soul, the Nishmath-Chaijim was the "*Medium of Communication*" between them, "by which they work upon One another," forming the "*Vital ty*" between them by "receiv[ing] *Impressions* from *Both*."[94] Mather specifically brings the Nishmath-Chaijim to bear on stamina theory, which he describes using much the same language as he had done in the *Biblia* commentary on giants, again noting that the theory is "Encumbered with Difficulties."[95] Mather thus attributes to the Nishmath-Chaijim the function of the seed "as it Leads to the Acts requisite in *Generation*, without any further *Instructor*, So it is the *Spirit*, whose *Way we know not, for shaping the Bones*, and other Parts" of the fetus in the womb.[96] Further, it is the origin of muscular motion, the regulator of digestion and other functions, and the memory-form that remains after death to preserve the shape of the body for the resurrection. Thus characterized as a medium of communication, an instructor, and a subtle substance comprised of "Particles . . . which may be finer than those of *Light* itself," the Nishmath-Chaijim would, if rightly understood, answer all questions regarding animate life that "cannot

be solved by the Rules of *Mechanism*."[97] In this way, Mather develops a critique of the Cartesian account of humankind's animal nature that in certain respects anticipated vitalism's attempt to suture the mind-body split. Whereas Descartes famously posited, as a consequence of the mind-body spilt, that animals are mere machines, Mather argues that the animal operations of survival and propagation, like so many human operations, while "not the Effects of any *Rational Projection*," can nevertheless be characterized as the operation of "Soul" or "Spirit." In order to argue that these so-called "*Meer Instinct[s] of Nature*" are more than mechanistic operations, Mather observes that whereas a broken machine requires "Some Hand from Abroad" to repair it, the body is often self-repairing. This organizing capacity gives living creatures their natures: "The *Nidification* of *Bird*s, the *Mellification* of *Bees*," and thus perhaps, although Mather does not return to the Claverack fossils in *The Angel of Bethesda*, the magnification of giants. Such capacities, including the body's capacity for self-repair, Mather says proceed from the Nishmath-Chaijim "with such *Faculties* and such *Tendencies* from God imprinted on it."[98]

This notion of a self-organizing capacity, which Mather characterizes as an agent that transfers God's "imprint" to matter, has since been reconfigured in the life sciences, shorn of any dependence on a supernatural origin, as the concept of autopoiesis. Coined by Humberto Maturana and Francisco Varela in 1973, the term "autopoiesis" defines a living system as a system that is self-maintaining within a boundary, the primary example being the cell. Scaled up, the definition applies to multicelled organisms such as bees, birds, or human beings.[99] The self-maintained boundary specifies an organism's interaction with the world—some things such as nutrients and wastes cross the boundary while others such as certain toxins do not—and in this way an organism co-emerges with its environment, its particular configuration of the world. Mather, as we have seen, used the concept of Nishmath-Chaijim to account for these self-maintaining and co-emergent properties: the "*Mellification of Bees*" is a synecdoche for co-emergence based on a key interaction with nectar-producing flowers; similarly, the "*Nidification of Birds*" is a synecdoche from the habit of nest-building creatures.

Autopoiesis does not describe the actions of a mediating agency between (God's) mind and matter, as the theory of plastic power was meant to do, but rather describes the organizing agency of life as existing and operating within the living organism with no reference to an outside source. Even so, its claim for agency suggests an implicit idealism. Slavoj Žižek observes that the definition of autopoiesis "repeats almost verbatim the Hegelian notion of life as a teleological, self-organizing entity" thus bringing it back to the

conceptual domain of Plato's world-spirit.[100] As the preeminent Cambridge
Platonist Ralph Cudworth argued in a defense of the theory of plastic power,
"the mechanic philosophers, however pretending to solve all phenomena by
matter and motion, assign no cause at all. Mind and understanding is the
only cause of orderly regularity; and he that asserts a plastic nature, asserts
mental causality in the world."[101] Maturana and Varela, by contrast, locate
mental causality solely within the organism itself by defining cognition as the
organism's dynamic coupling with its environment as specified by its internal
processes. Cognition is the organism's recognition and use of those features
of the world that enable the organism to maintain itself (such as nutrients or
heat). In "exploding final causes," Maturana and Varela find themselves deferring, like the mechanists criticized by Cudworth, to an endless causal chain
that has no beginning. Thus they arrive, as Bruno Latour puts it in a similar
critique, at a "contradictory notion of an *action without agency*."[102] Maturana
and Varela conclude their study by observing that in view of their conceptualization of biological phenomena, "new problems arise, and old ones appear in
a different perspective: in particular, those which refer to the origin of living
systems on earth (eobiogenesis and neobiogenesis)," that is, the generation of
life from nonliving matter.[103]

   This is precisely the problem that Mather found in the remains of giants
and the problem he hoped to solve by means of theories of stamina and
plastic power which mediated between ultimate supernatural will and the
material manifestation of life and death on earth. Discussions of autopoiesis
and cognition tend to emphasize positive aspects of the system's coupling
with its environment. Mather's medically oriented accounts also emphasize
environmental threats to the bodily system. For example, the Boston small-
pox epidemic of 1721 and the attendant controversy over inoculation (which
Mather favored) invited further consideration of the proto-germ concept
which Mather had first entertained as a possible explanation for gigantism.[104] In his biblical commentary, Mather had hypothesized that before the
flood, God had raised giants from parents of ordinary stature, perhaps by
means of "stamina" of gigantism taken in from the environment that altered
the ordinary development of the human body. Similarly, in 1721 Boston,
it seemed to Mather that citizens were constantly threatened by external,
microscopic agents, "*unseen Armies* of Numberless Living Things, ready
to Seize and Prey upon us!"[105] Such were the "Invisible *Velites*" that God
might use to "Chastise, and Even destroy, the Rebellious Children of Men"
by operating on the Nishmath-Chaijim.[106] Human beings are always threatened by punishment for their transgressions. If giants had been destroyed by

the flood, then the active principle of gigantism, if it were indeed embodied in stamina, may still abide, ready to punish. The punishing giants are thus not so much extinct, by the implications of Mather's theorizing, as they are held in suspension as potential agents capable of being divinely activated. In this, as we will see in Chapter 2, the punishing giants function like the mammoths or "big buffalo" that, according to a Christian-inflected version of a Haudenosaunee extinction narrative, the Great Spirit held in reserve underneath a mountain, ready at any moment to be summoned forth to punish a transgressive people.

*   *   *

Mather, like the Nahua and Inca, argued that giants deserved to be extinguished because they did not belong to the earth; they inhibited human flourishing. Taylor and his Esopus informants believed that giants did belong; thus Taylor writes not of the extinction of a kind of life, but of the creation of an exceptional individual. These differing moral assessments of giants' lives and deaths do not line up neatly with differing accounts of environmental agency, however. Spaniards working with Indigenous Mexican sources foregrounded purely human agency in narratives of extermination through conquest for control of resources and the institution of Indigenous civilization; this narrative ironically echoed the Spanish conquest of Mexico. In Peru, by contrast, Indigenous narratives of the extermination of immoral monstrous giants accomplished by the gods could be taken up without major adjustment by Spanish historians, who merely had to rename those gods. English and Euro-American investigators focused similarly on nonhuman agency, one category of which was the theory of nature's plastic power. For Hooke, the notion of a plastic faculty implied an unacceptable potential for randomness that confused organic and inorganic forms. The truth of extinction was evident, for him, in the fossil remains of organic forms. For Taylor, organic and inorganic forms alike were produced by the generative "Spirits" infusing the "Tree of Nature" and manifesting divinely ordained regularity. Apparently anomalous phenomena such as gigantism inspired the perceiving subject to meditate on this regularity while accepting Indigenous accounts of environmental fitness. For Mather, Indigenous accounts were irrelevant to the question of divinely ordained regularity. Stamina theory frontloaded divine agency in the initial act of creation whereas the "Plastick Power" of the Nishmath-Chaijim was a constantly acting, mediate agency that sorted organic forms into kinds through divine imprint. Stamina theory allowed for

the persistence of predatory giants into the present age and thereby required God's "*Vigilant* and *Immediate*" agency to protect humankind.[107]

If Mather had brought the mediating agency of the Nishmath-Chaijim to bear on the remains of antediluvian giants, he could have concluded that when the source of gigantism was wiped out by the flood, giants themselves became forever extinct, thereby preserving humankind from one kind of environmental threat. Whether he would have done so is another question, for it is doubtful whether Mather would have agreed with Hooke that the possibility of "divers Species of things wholly destroyed or annihilated" was consistent with a divinely ordered world.[108] Rather, for Mather, species extinction was possible only with world-ending apocalyptic fire—after which an exceptional group of humans, the saints, resurrected in body, would live on eternally with the world's creator. This desire for human persistence remains among the most important themes in extinction discourse.

CHAPTER 2

Mammoths, the "Oeconomy of Nature," and Human Ecology

As we saw in Chapter 1, fossil remains of Pleistocene megafauna became sites of exchange between Indigenous American and Euro-American narrative traditions. An especially rich site was Big Bone Lick, a salt lick on the Ohio River near present-day Cincinnati. In 1739 a military expedition—commanded by the Baron de Longueuil and made up of French, Haudenosaunee, and Algonquian warriors—camped near Big Bone Lick and found some of the fossil bones, teeth, and tusks of giant animals for which the site was named.[1] The identity of these animals was obvious to the Haudenosaunee and Algonquians, who had seen similar remains at eroded sites in the Hudson River valley. They knew from traditional stories that the remains belonged to *"le père-aux-boeufs,"* the "father-of-oxen" or "grandfather of the buffalo."[2]

Longueuil shipped some of the Big Bone Lick fossils back to Paris, where they were placed in Louis XV's cabinet of curiosities under the direction of Georges-Louis Leclerc, Comte de Buffon and later examined by Georges Cuvier.[3] To European naturalists, these remains suggested not so much an ox or buffalo as an elephant. This raised numerous questions: How could elephants have survived in a cold climate? Had the climate changed over time? Were the animals in fact elephants, or another species? Were such animals still living, and if so, where had they gone? Or if they had become extinct—a new and strange concept—how long ago and of what cause? If the creatures were indeed elephants, then the climate must have changed, as Buffon argued in support of his theory of gradual global cooling. Buffon's successor, Cuvier, however, reasoned that the creature did not necessarily have to be tropical. Through painstaking research in comparative anatomy, Cuvier differentiated extinct mammoths and mastodons from modern elephants, announcing preliminary results in a paper published in 1799. He went on to demonstrate, in

Recherches sur les ossemens fossils de quadrupèdes (1812), that a whole ancient fauna, unknown to modern humans, had become extinct. The *Discours préliminaire* to this work soon became available in English as *Essay on the Theory of the Earth*.[4] While the *fact* of the Late Pleistocene extinctions was thus settled for Enlightenment scientists, the *cause* of these extinctions remained an open question, one that potentially involved human responsibility.

Euro-American collectors and naturalists followed Longueuil's practice of eliciting stories from Indigenous informants. At least four similar stories concerning the Big Bone Lick site were transcribed during the eighteenth century, and other versions persisted in oral traditions through the nineteenth century, as is evident from the Penobscot historian Joseph Nicolar's *Life and Traditions of the Red Man* (discussed later in this chapter). In the multicultural, multilingual context of the Ohio River valley in the eighteenth century, such stories must have been widely shared among the Haudenosaunee, Lenape, Shawnee, and others. Variably inflected according to context, audience, purpose, and taste, the stories bear two core motifs: giant animals pose a threat to the people, directly or indirectly; and all or most of the giant animals are killed by lightning bolts. Some stories report the survival of one or a pair of these animals, in a place where they no longer threaten humankind. While European naturalists paid increasingly less attention to Indigenous Americans' accounts of the mammoth's extinction over the course of the nineteenth century, they kept these stories' primary moral concerns in focus: they too were interested in the nature of extinctive agency and in human flourishing. The Indigenous Big Bone Lick extinction narrative returned to print in Nicolar's 1893 history, but without the earlier stories' speculation on the mammoths' preservation. Now extinction is permanent.[5] As Nicolar tells it, extinction thus became a lesson for human ecology.

Questions of Agency

The most widely circulated of the Big Bone Lick stories appears in *Notes on the State of Virginia* (1785), where Thomas Jefferson claims the mammoth as a key piece of evidence in his refutation of Buffon's theory of the inferiority of the American environment.[6] Jefferson opens his argument by integrating Indigenous American narratives into the European discourse of natural history: "Our quadrupeds have mostly been described by Linnaeus and Mons. de Buffon. Of these, the Mammoth, or big buffalo, as called by the Indians, must certainly have been the largest. Their tradition is, that he was

carnivorous, and still exists in the northern parts of America." Jefferson then transcribes a Lenape story concerning "the animal whose bones were found at the Saltlicks, on the Ohio." Jefferson does not make much of the story's historical claims, presumably because it described a supernatural actor similar to Zeus, a "Great Man above" who killed all the mammoths but one by hurling lightning bolts. However, Jefferson renders from the mammoth bones a similar story. He argues that mammoths were likely living to this day somewhere northwest of the Great Lakes, where the "aboriginal state" of the environment still provided habitat. "To add to this, the traditionary testimony of the Indians," he concludes, "would be adding the light of a taper to that of the meridian sun."[7]

Jefferson's treatment of the Lenape story typifies eighteenth-century naturalists' ambivalence toward Native American interpretations of fossils. For example, in an essay promoting the first museum exhibition of a complete mammoth skeleton in 1803, Rembrandt Peale argued that the Indigenous tradition of the "great Buffalo" from Big Bone Lick was "clouded with fable," but "not improbable" at its core.[8] Similarly, Benjamin Smith Barton, vice president of the American Philosophical Society, explained in a treatise on method, "I am far from insinuating, that such traditions should be received as *pure history*: but I am persuaded that, on some occasions, much interesting information might be educed from them. . . . To a discerning and virtuous naturalist, they are like mines, among the rubbish of which we dig, with success, for the most precious metals."[9]

Most naturalists—with the prominent exception of Jefferson—agreed with Native Americans that mammoths had threatened the security of humankind in ancient times and that the extinction of the mammoth had shaped the environment for the benefit of humankind. How to understand the cause of that effect was another matter, however, and varied with the narrators' political positions. During the mid- to late eighteenth century, Indigenous cultures in the Ohio River valley saw themselves as threatened, especially after the British defeat of the French in the Seven Years' War and the failure of Pontiac's Rebellion in 1763. Stories from these cultures minimized human agency with respect to the environment or relegated it to the past and emphasized supernatural agency—although the particular conception of spirit power, monotheistic or pantheistic, again varied with local context. Euro-American naturalists suggested that certain truths could be mined from these Indigenous stories through the disaggregation of fact from "fable," as Peale put it. This suggestion took shape within the larger Enlightenment context of the disavowal of supernatural intervention in the natural world, as wonders

were conceptually reduced to a regular order of nature.[10] Eighteenth-century naturalists thus anticipated the modern cognitive theory of myth, which purports to refine truth from the "rubbish" of mental distortions.

Despite their assumption that the truth of Native American environmental narratives was occluded by fictions of supernatural actors, eighteenth-century naturalists also assumed that the world was created and maintained by supernatural power, positing an implicitly Christian or deist conception of the world.[11] However, some who were invested in westward colonial expansion proposed an alternative account of the Big Bone Lick extinctions, developing a speculative political fiction of collective human agency according to which ancient inhabitants of North America had banded together to remove the threat of the mammoth. Jefferson alone among the commentators wanted to hold on to the belief that the mammoth was still living, though he did imagine that human activity might have diminished its range. As he eventually came to accept the fact of extinction, he posited that a supernatural agent ordered particular extinctions but kept nature from degenerating into chaos. If Jefferson's narration of extinction as loss marks him as peculiarly modern, anticipating our own elegiac response, his recourse to supernatural agency invites us to interrogate the ontological grounding of modern extinction discourse, which must account for the interaction of human and nonhuman agents.

Whereas some other eastern North American Indigenous stories associate fossil remains of Late Pleistocene–epoch megafauna with water monsters or humanlike giants, the stories from Big Bone Lick identify the remains as belonging to a large, carnivorous mammal.[12] The tellings of the earlier Big Bone Lick stories bracket Pontiac's Rebellion of 1763. Two were recorded in 1762, each collected independently and transmitted to the Philadelphia Quaker naturalist John Bartram. One of these comes via Bartram's English patron Peter Collinson, who had heard from the trader and deputy superintendent for Indian affairs George Croghan about the discovery of the giant skeletons at Big Bone Lick.[13] Croghan, who was based at Fort Pitt after it was rebuilt in 1759, visited Big Bone Lick several times while traveling the Ohio River on diplomatic and trading voyages; he heard a story about the giant animals from his escorts, who were probably Lenape, Shawnee, or Sandusky Wyandot. Croghan evidently sent Collinson a story along with a description of bones and teeth, which Collinson then passed on to Bartram: "The Indian tradition [is] that the Monstrous Buffalos so called by the Indians was all struck dead with Lightning at this licking place." Collinson doubted that the story fully explained the creatures' disappearance, asking Bartram, "but is it likely to think all the Race was here Collected & was Extinguished at one

Stroke[?]"[14] Evidently, Croghan or Collinson had isolated one of the story's core motifs, the lightning strike. While the adjective "Monstrous" character-izes the animals as a threat to humankind, the narrative is attenuated, leaving the agent of the lightning strike implicit.

After hearing from both Collinson and the commander at Fort Pitt, Col-onel Henry Bouquet, about the bones at Big Bone Lick, Bartram evidently wrote to James Wright, a fellow Quaker with an interest in natural history, to request more information. Working with an interpreter, Wright interviewed "two Sincible Shawanese Indians" who gave a detailed description of the site, including the positions of five skeletons of the giant animal in question, and a story about their extinction, which Wright transmitted to Bartram in 1762.[15] The Shawnees reported that although such bones were "Scattered here & there" across the Ohio River valley, nowhere else was there a large group such as this, all apparently killed at one stroke. At the time that these animals lived, according to the Shawnees, there also lived "men of a size proportionable to them, who used to kill them and tye them in their noppusses and throw them on their Backs As an Indian now does a deer." When this race of giant men disappeared, "God killed these mighty creatures, that they should not hurt the present race of Indians." The Big Bone Lick animals specifically were "supposed . . . to have been Kild by lightning."[16]

Another version was told at the site of Big Bone Lick in the summer of 1766, although it was not published until 1795. In the new and tenuous accommodation between the British and various Native American polities following the failure of Pontiac's Rebellion, Croghan organized an expedi-tion down the Ohio River to distribute presents to cement alliances as the French had formerly done. George Morgan, a Philadelphia merchant, acted as supercargo. At Big Bone Lick, the British party met a raiding party of Haudenosaunee and Wyandots headed south against the Chickasaws. The eighty-four-year-old head of the party, most likely Haudenosaunee, told Morgan that he had traveled this road against the Catawbas many times in his youth, and had often heard his grandfather's story about the bones.[17] This version begins with an account, which emerged in the context of Ohio River valley revitalization movements, of the Great Spirit's separate creations of the white, black, and red races, each on their separate continents. The "Red Man" was happy for a time but "the foolish young people, at length forgetting his rules, became exceedingly ill-tempered and wicked." Unique to this version of the separate creations story told to Morgan is an episode in which the Great Spirit punishes the red race by creating "the great buffalo," who "made war upon the human species and destroyed all but a few." When these remaining

few "repented," the Great Spirit killed the buffalos by means of lightning bolts, all but a male and female pair whom he "shut up in yonder mountain, ready to let loose again, should occasion require."[18] This motif of the great buffalo as an intermediary agent sent by a god to punish an errant people reminds us—although any direct connection is unlikely—of Cotton Mather's account of biblical giants sent as agents "for the Punishment of a wicked World."[19] In the latter account, however, the punishing agents threaten to escape the purpose of the god who sent them and Mather is at pains to explain how they were controlled. In the Haudenosaunee story, there is no such problem with the ordering of the world for human flourishing.

Jefferson attributes the story he published in 1785 in *Notes on the State of Virginia* to the "chief speaker" of a Lenape delegation who had visited him in his capacity as governor of Virginia, probably during 1781 in Charlottesville. After "matters of business" pertaining to the war "had been discussed and settled in council, the governor asked the delegation some questions relative to their country, including what they knew or had heard of the animal whose bones were found at the Saltlicks, on the Ohio." The chief replied that according to "a tradition handed down from their fathers, . . . in antient times, a herd of these tremendous animals came to the Big-bone licks, and began an universal destruction of the bear, deer, elks, buffalos, and other animals, which had been created for the use of the Indians." The "Great Man above" was "enraged" by this behavior and killed all the giant animals but the largest bull, who was wounded but escaped and "bounded over the Ohio, over the Wabash, the Illinois, and over the great lakes, where he is living at this day."[20] This story includes neither the 1762 Shawnee version's account of a prior hunting culture technologically adapted to killing the giant animals nor the 1766 Haudenosaunee version's moral narrative of separate creations followed by sin, repentance, and salvation. If Jefferson was gratified to hear from an Indigenous informant that the mammoth was living in the present day, he was skeptical of the means by which that information was transmitted, via what he would have regarded as an allegory in which one mammoth, retreating from an angry god, stands in for a population that actually migrated for some material reason to the northwest. Yet, while Jefferson expanded on the critique of Indigenous narrative suggested by Collinson, he agreed with his Lenape informant that the mammoth "may as well exist there [in the unexplored northwest] now, as he did formerly where we find his bones. If he be a carnivorous animal, as some Anatomists affirm, his early retirement may be accounted for from the general destruction of the wild game by the Indians, which commences in the first instant of their

connection with us, for the purpose of purchasing matchcoats, hatchets, and firelocks, with their skins."[21]

Thus attempting to disaggregate fact from fable by correlating narrative detail with observable material truth (market hunting was generally known to cause a game population to decline), Jefferson anticipated the modern cognitivist theory of myth. Working backward from assumptions about narrative distortions imposed by mental structures, the cognitivist approach attempts to discern the material truth of the geohistorical or astronomical event that the story seems to witness. For example, following this method, a Klamath story recorded in 1865, shorn of its fabulous aspects and correlated with geological evidence, seems to record eyewitness memory of the formation of Crater Lake some 7,700 years ago from the eruption of a volcano.[22] The cognitivist approach assumes the possibility of the unbroken continuity of oral tradition over millennia. On this point, some ethnohistorians, Native American scholars, and activists agree. The Sioux activist Vine Deloria Jr. claims absolutely that traditional stories bear witness to events such as the creation of Crater Lake.[23] The Pawnee historian Roger Echo-Hawk more cautiously writes that "verbal literature arguably preserves glimpses and echoes of the long-vanished Pleistocene world of our ancestors."[24]

A cognitivist approach to the Big Bone Lick stories would begin with the analysis of one core motif, the killing of giant animals by means of lightning bolts, because archaeological evidence could be sketchy at best for the other core motif, the claim that the animals posed a threat to humankind. Cognitivists would shear away any consideration of divine agency as a mental distortion (the belief that if something happens, some agent must have willed it to happen) in order to read the lightning bolt motif as evidence of a natural phenomenon. Thus the story might be interpreted as a garbled explanation of the onset of the Younger Dryas climate phase, a thousand-year period of cold and drought from about 11,000 to 10,000 years ago. The hypothesis is that a comet crashing to earth some 11,000 years ago caused widespread fires, the ash from which induced global cooling by partly blocking solar radiation.[25] In North America, the timing of the Younger Dryas climate phase correlates with the extinction of the mammoth, as verified by radiocarbon dating, and with the demise of the Clovis culture whose technology was specifically adapted to hunting the mammoth and other Late Pleistocene megafauna.[26] The 1762 Shawnee story maps most closely onto the Younger Dryas scenario, identifying a premodern culture that correlates with archaeological evidence of Clovis culture. Yet the story seems to refute the hypothesis that this culture hunted the mammoth to extinction, because here the humanlike giants

(the Clovis people) disappear *before* the mammoths do, to be replaced by the present-day Shawnees who hunt smaller animals such as deer, although no reason is suggested for the disappearance of the giants.[27] In this evaluative context, the Shawnee version would seem to point to climate change as the cause of the Late Pleistocene extinctions—the compression of time between the lightning strike/comet event and the eventual disappearance of the mammoths being a cognitive adaptation of long-scale environmental observation to conventional narrative chronology.

Yet none of the other Big Bone Lick stories preserves the Shawnee version's motif of the replacement of one culture by another. Without this motif, the story loses its window onto the Late Pleistocene epoch. Reduced to the core motif of an extinction-causing fiery event, the Indigenous Big Bone Lick narrative stands only to lose authority as further geological and paleontological findings confirm or disconfirm the impact of a comet and any resulting climate change and ecological consequences. The cognitivist approach thus allows the primitive subject to witness, but not to understand. In this way it reproduces the eighteenth-century naturalists' critique of Native American environmental narratives as so much raw ore, valuable only insofar as it might be "mine[d]" for the "precious metals" of original witness.[28]

The ground of dispute concerns the naming of causation, especially causation effected by nonhuman agents. The modern cognitivist interpreters of myth merely defer the question of agency to the physical sciences, where it becomes a matter of specifying geophysical, astrophysical, or biological forces. Since these forces have their causes, in turn, back to some unknown origin in the beginning of the universe, such a deferral instantiates, as Bruno Latour puts it, a "contradictory notion of an *action without agency.*"[29] However, the eighteenth-century Euro-American naturalists did not discount the question of agency, but rather named it in three forms, sometimes intermixed in a single narrative. Some, such as Jefferson, substituted a European conception of superhuman agency, vaguely equivocating "God" and "Nature," for the more localized conceptions of superhuman agency deployed by the Native American stories. Some naturalists appealed to geophysical forces such as a great deluge, thus deferring causation to an unspecified origin (implicitly, the Christian God). Others, however, developed a fiction of cooperative human agency that was no more verifiable (especially given the absence of any such motif in Native American stories) than the apparently more magical accounts of agency given by Native Americans.

In the first Euro-American account of the Big Bone Lick extinctions, a paper published in 1768 in the Royal Society's *Philosophical Transactions,*

the English physician and anatomist William Hunter argued that the fossil remains, like similar remains found in Siberia, were not those of elephants, but rather represented a distinct species. Hunter's speculation regarding the extinction of this species, which he thought "in former times has been a very general inhabitant of the globe," shares with the Native American stories a project of moral evaluation. Hunter asserts that "if this animal was carnivorous, which I believe cannot be doubted, though we may as philosophers regret it, as men we cannot but thank Heaven that its whole generation is probably extinct."[30] Even as he invokes a supernatural agent by "thank[ing] Heaven," Hunter does not speculate on the mechanism of extinction, a question that Native Americans had answered by reference to lightning strikes. Eighteenth-century naturalists were divided over the question of mechanism. Buffon posited a gradual climate change, regarding the Big Bone Lick and Siberian fossils as remains of a tropical elephant species that had either died out or migrated as the earth cooled. Many others, such as Cuvier, assumed a catastrophic climate event such as a flood, rather than a gradual cooling. With the weight of Christian tradition behind it, the story of the flood had remained the default narrative, first invoked in this context by the German naturalist Johann Breyne in 1737 to explain the location of elephant-like remains in Siberia.[31] The sublimity of the biblical deluge seems to have matched the scale of the creature. Rembrandt Peale similarly found the "sudden and powerful cause" of a great "deluge" the likeliest cause for the extinction of such "tremendous animals . . . which at all times must have filled the human mind with surprise and wonder."[32]

However, some Euro-Americans argued that humankind, rather than a supernatural agent or a nonhuman natural agent, was the beneficent shaper who had removed a threatening excess from the environment. These Euro-Americans developed a speculative political fiction centered on human agency. In a short book published in 1784 to promote the settlement of Kentucky, the land speculator John Filson reviewed the territory's "Curiosities" of natural history, including the extant literature on the remains at Big Bone Lick. Dismissing the stories told about Siberian remains by "ignorant and superstitious Tartars" but apparently unaware of Indigenous American accounts, Filson takes a moral stance similar to that of Hunter and the Indigenous Big Bone Lick stories, but shifts the attribution of agency:

Can then so great a link have perished from the chain of nature? Happy we that it has. How formidable an enemy to the human species, an animal as large as the elephant, the tyrant of the forests, perhaps

the devourer of man! Nations, such as the Indians, must have been in perpetual alarm. The animosities among the various tribes must have been suspended till the common enemy, who threatened the very existence of all, should be extirpated. To this circumstance we are probably indebted for a fact, which is perhaps singular in its kind, the extinction of a whole race of animals from the system of nature.[33]

In this scenario, the normal politics of warfare and diplomacy are suspended in favor of international cooperation to remove a threat to humankind. Imagining human rather than supernatural agency as causal, Filson develops a politics rather than a theology of extinction.

This political narrative was reiterated by George Turner, a federal judge who was interested in western lands and had personally traveled to Big Bone Lick.[34] In a scientific paper arguing that the mammoth was carnivorous, Turner concludes, "With the agility and ferocity of a tiger; with a body of unequalled magnitude and strength, it is possible that the Mammoth may have been at once the terror of the forest and of man!—And may not the human race have made the extirpation of this terrific disturber a common cause?"[35] Filson's and Turner's narrative of cooperative human action fit the late eighteenth-century context that is the occasion for Filson's promotional tract, the shaping of American nature for European culture—a project that would require the removal of Native Americans. (Filson's text includes the first biography of the Indian fighter Daniel Boone.) Like the Indigenous narratives, this narrative takes an anthropocentric stance toward the shaping of the environment. However, the imperial prospect elicits an emphasis on the potency of human agency where the Indigenous narratives relegated shaping power to superhuman actors.

Differences among the Big Bone Lick stories thus show how the naming of environmental agency is contingent and context-specific. Even as we translate between Indigenous American and European practices for naming agency, we can observe that all these stories are fundamentally concerned with a primary distinction between the human and the nonhuman. That is, the stories as a group become a site for the examination of the powers and capacities of humans and other agents with respect to a given world. With this modal approach, we can reread the Big Bone Lick stories more closely as shaped by environmental concerns in the present of the telling.[36]

All the Native American stories make three claims: (1) giant animals are associated with past environmental conditions that are less hospitable to humankind than present conditions are; (2) human beings do not possess the

capacity to manage this kind of environmental threat; and (3) some superhuman power does possess that capacity. The nature of that superhuman power remains in question, however, indicating a conflict between monotheistic and pantheistic cosmologies. Monotheism was a central component of the Pan-Indian revitalization movements that emerged beginning in the mid-eighteenth century in the Susquehanna and Ohio River valleys, so it is not surprising to find it here in the Great Man who hurls lightning bolts.[37] Another motif bears on the question of power, however, as evidenced by Longueuil's warriors' 1739 identification of the bones as those of *le père-aux-boeufs*. This motif is a "master of the game," an embodied tutelary spirit who organizes the behavior of a species of game animal and mediates human interaction with it, as for example the Great Beaver was said to do in northeastern Algonquin territory.[38] Similarly, from Euro-American hunters and traders working west of the Mississippi in the early 1760s came Indigenous accounts of "the Rhinosses or Elephant Master," which became associated with the bones at Big Bone Lick.[39] The master-of-the-game motif, traditional in the pertinent Indigenous cosmologies, is absent from the 1762 Shawnee version, which is told at the moment of monotheistic revitalization's greatest promise, just prior to Pontiac's Rebellion. However, the master-of-the-game motif returns in altered or attenuated form in the versions told after the failure of Pontiac's Rebellion, suggesting a reintegration of a traditional pantheistic cosmology. The 1766 Haudenosaunee story imports the master-of-the-game motif into the revitalizationist master narrative of sin, repentance, and salvation: the Great Spirit creates the great buffalo as an agent of punishment and preserves that agent should humankind need to be punished for future transgressions.[40] In the 1781 Lenape story, the big bull is evidently more powerful than the others of his kind, able to fend off the lightning bolts with his forehead until he is wounded, and even then he is able to escape to safety.

In the Lenape story, the struggle between the big bull and the Great Spirit suggests a tension between a traditional pantheistic cosmology, in which environmental agency is dispersed and accessible to humankind through ritual interaction with natural-supernatural agents such as masters-of-the-game, and an emergent monotheistic cosmology, in which environmental agency is consolidated in a single supernatural force which is comparatively remote from human access. Read as a political allegory (to counter Jefferson's allegorical reading) in the context of the Lenapes' concerns with the colonial militia's occupation of several Ohio River settlements, with the Great Man standing in for colonial power and the big bull for the Lenape people, the 1781 Lenape story projects a geographic limit on Euro-American expansion.[41]

Read ecologically, with the people as beneficiary of the Great Man's goodwill, the story projects a benevolent supernatural agent with strong but limited power to shape the environment. Unforeseen changes, such as the disruptive mammoths, may yet appear at any time. The Lenape version draws out the anthropocentrism of the earlier versions, stating specifically that the game animals "had been created for the use of the Indians."[42] The Great Spirit decides who has a greater right to eat the game animals—the mammoths or the Indians. The decision is not based so much on moral evaluation, as in the 1766 Haudenosaunee version, but rather on assumptions about the centrality of human culture to ecosystem dynamics. Anthropocentrism thus receives both theological and ecological warrants. At the same time, the debilitating effects of European colonization on Native American polities seem to have precluded any narration of a political account of environmental management in the manner of Filson and Turner—even though such an account could conceivably have drawn on the transmitted memory of Clovis-culture mammoth hunting as a collective enterprise.

In general, the Big Bone Lick stories, Euro-American as well as Indigenous American, characterize the mammoth as an environmental excess, not merely a superfluous presence but an invasive agent that threatens the well-being of humankind (albeit with a jeremiadic twist in the 1766 Haudenosaunee version). By contrast, Jefferson's story, as distinct from the Lenape story he transcribes, anticipates the modern narration of extinction as loss. Arguing against mounting claims by European naturalists that the mammoth was likely extinct, Jefferson asserts that "such is the oeconomy of nature, that no instance can be produced of her having permitted any one race of her animals to become extinct; of her having formed any link in her great work so weak as to be broken."[43] Jefferson's story shares with the Indigenous stories an assumption that a larger-than-human force shapes the environment. Here, a powerful agent, "nature," acts on the world, figured as both structure (chain) and system ("oeconomy," that is, household management). Reprising these figures in a scientific paper on the fossil remains of another giant animal he named the megalonyx (great claw), Jefferson again argues against extinction: "The movements of nature are in a never-ending circle. The animal species which has once been put into a train of motion, is still probably moving in that train. For if one link in nature's chain might be lost, another and another might be lost, till this whole system of things should evanish by piecemeal; a conclusion not warranted by the local disappearance of one or two species of animals."[44] In the fear that "this whole system of things should evanish," Jefferson confronts the possibility of the extinction of humankind. Thus he pushes

the personified, superhuman shaping agent into the background, imagining its work both as an initial act of propulsion whose momentum continues perpetually and as an initial act of creation whose structure endures indefinitely.

After Cuvier made an overwhelmingly persuasive case, in his *Recherches sur les ossemens fossils* (1812), that the mammoth, mastodon, and megalonyx were in fact extinct, Jefferson revised his view of this environment-shaping agent, imagining a more active role. He wrote to John Adams,

> It is impossible, I say, for the human mind not to believe, that there is . . . design, cause and effect, up to an ultimate cause, a Fabricator of all things from matter and motion, their Preserver and Regulator while permitted to exist in their present forms, and their regeneration into new and other forms. We see, too, evident proofs of the necessity of a superintending power, to maintain the universe in its course and order. Stars, well known, have disappeared, new ones have come into view; comets, in their incalculable courses, may run foul of suns and planets, and require renovation under other laws; certain races of animals are become extinct; and were there no restoring power, all existences might extinguish successively, one by one, until all should be reduced to a shapeless chaos.[45]

While the context here, a debate with Adams over Calvinism, required theological speculation, it is clear that Jefferson had come to believe that the careers of species are governed by a supernatural agent that is fabricator, preserver, regulator, and regenerator. This agent, external to the material universe, quite actively exercises its power to "restore" order in the face of matter's inherent tendency to disorder. So while Jefferson reversed his position on extinction, he retained his notion of a divine, ordering force. The apparent modernity of Jefferson's response—his narration of extinction as loss—remains bound up with a Nonmodern appeal to supernatural agency.

Jefferson's use of the phrase "the oeconomy of nature" registered the beginning of a shift in Euro-American discussions of extinction: functions that had been assigned to a Christian or deist god were reassigned to the quasipersonified or nonpersonified category of nature.[46] A clear transition point is marked by the last sentence of Darwin's *On The Origin of Species*, which metaphorically assigns evolution a cause that is traceable back to an original action, but withholds its agent's name: "There is grandeur in this view of life, with its several powers, *having been originally breathed* into a few forms or into one; and that whilst this planet has gone cycling on according to the

fixed law of gravity, from so simple a beginning endless forms most beautiful and most wonderful *have been, and are being, evolved*."[47] The two agentless passive constructions, "having been ... breathed" and "have been, and are being, evolved," moreover divide evolutionary causality—and by extension, extinctive causality—between an agency external to the species (that which does the breathing into) and agencies internal to the species (those which have been or are being evolved). Positing senescence or vulnerability within the species itself was one means of locating extinctive agency, as we will see in Chapter 4. Thus Richard Owen, a paleontologist most famous for coining the word "dinosaur," speculated that while climate change may have caused the extinction of the Pleistocene megafauna in Europe, in many cases in Australia and the Americas, where "sufficient signs of extrinsic extirpating cause or convulsion" were absent, it was "possib[le] that species like individuals may have had their death inherent in their original constitution"; the "period of exhaustion of the prolific life force, may have been ordained from the commencement of each species."[48]

The unnamed, external agent of creation, transformation, and extinction, which Darwin figured with breath and which Owen registered with a similarly agentless passive construction, remained the source of some uneasiness. For the 1860 edition of *On The Origin*, Darwin reluctantly revised his concluding sentence to name an agent that his contemporaries could easily understand as the Christian or deist God: "There is grandeur in this view of life, with its several powers, having been originally breathed *by the Creator* into a few forms or into one."[49] The gist of this revision persists in claims for intelligent design.[50]

Darwin's 1860 revision implied a moral evaluation of the processes of evolution and extinction. Darwin himself never explicitly voiced such an evaluation, but his competitor in the development of evolutionary theory, Alfred Russel Wallace, did. "We live in a zoologically impoverished world, from which all the hugest, and fiercest, and strangest forms have recently disappeared," wrote Wallace in 1876, "and it is, no doubt, a much better world for us now they are gone."[51] Wallace thus extended a line of natural theology that had emerged during the Enlightenment to reconcile the phenomenon of extinction with God's omnipotence to answer the likes of Jefferson who thought extinction violated nature's coherence. For example, in 1811 the physician and paleontologist James Parkinson responded to Cuvier's apparent refusal to address theological matters in his account of extinction, arguing that "the total extinction of some species, and the late creation of others ... afford a direct proof of the Creator of the universe continuing a

superintending providence over the works of his hands."[52] Such reasoning fit well with earlier Euro-American accounts of the Big Bone Lick extinctions by the likes of William Hunter, who "thank[ed] Heaven" that the mammoth had been exterminated, and with the Indigenous accounts of a protective super-human agent who shaped the environment for human benefit.[53] The idea that the Pleistocene megafauna posed a threat to human flourishing persisted into the twentieth century. H. G. Wells's account of "primitive man," for example, posited that "the mammoth used to chase him."[54]

During the nineteenth century, as science depersonalized and detheologized nature, climate change initially became the predominant narrative concerning nonhuman extinctive agency. Cuvier, who first definitively established that the remains of mammoths belonged to a distinct species and traced their extinction to nature's agency, scoffed at the "fabulous account" given by Indigenous Big Bone Lick stories of the mammoth's destruction by "the Great Spirit, to prevent them from extirpating the human race." Rather, he argued, scientific evidence pointed to "a great and sudden revolution" of the globe, or perhaps several such revolutions over eons, that had buried many creatures alive, shifted the locations of oceans, and caused drastic climate change—without, however, venturing any causal explanation for these revolutions.[55] Lacking a theory of the generation of new species through evolution or transformation, Cuvier's catastrophism indicated a vision of ever-decreasing biodiversity. Louis Agassiz, who consolidated the history of the geological era known as the Ice Age, also posited rapid climate change as a cause, but he did so by reembodying nature. Rather than Cuvier's catastrophic global revolutions, Agassiz posited climate pulses analogous to the death and resuscitation of a human body. The climate cooled at the end of an era, causing a mass extinction event; new life appeared with each warming pulse, although within a trajectory of overall gradual global cooling consistent with theories posed by Buffon and others.[56] Agassiz vividly presented his theory of the Ice Age in a series of sketches first published in the *Atlantic Monthly*. Here, he pictured the onset of the cooling pulse that exterminated the Pleistocene megafauna:

> The long summer was over. For ages a tropical climate had prevailed over a great part of the earth, and animals whose home is now beneath the Equator roamed over the world from the far South to the borders of the Arctics. The gigantic quadrupeds, the Mastodons, Elephants, Tigers, Lions, Hyenas, Bears, whose remains are found in Europe ... and in America from the Southern States to Greenland

and the Melville Islands, may indeed be said to have possessed the earth in those days. But their reign was over. A sudden intense winter, that was also to last for ages, fell upon our globe; it spread over the very countries where these tropical animals had their homes, and so suddenly did it come upon them that they were embalmed beneath masses of snow and ice, without the time even for the decay which follows death.[57]

Of the cause of this sudden climate change, Agassiz conceded, "we have as yet no clew."[58] Any moral evaluation—"their reign was over"—thus remains attenuated. Wallace similarly felt no need to speculate on causes, stating that "there must have been some physical cause" for the extinction of the Pleistocene megafauna and "it must have been a cause capable of acting almost simultaneously over large portions of the earth's surface, and one which . . . was of an exceptional character. Such a cause exists in the great and recent physical change known as 'the Glacial epoch.'"[59] Darwin remained uncommitted, however, writing to Wallace in 1876, "I cannot feel quite easy about the Glacial period, and the extinction of large animals, but I must hope that you are right."[60] Some of Darwin's unease about the Glacial period was due to the fact that as paleontologists fleshed out the fossil record, they discovered remains of apparently warm-adapted and cold-adapted species in the same locale. Eventually, a more sophisticated account of the era emerged, according to which cold glacial periods oscillated with warm interglacials, although with less extreme fluctuation than posited by Agassiz.[61]

Perhaps another reason why Darwin hoped that Wallace was right about the Glacial period was because the only plausible alternative, within the terms of Enlightenment science's disenchantment of the world, was human agency. In the eighteenth century, the anthropogenic explanation of the Late Pleistocene extinctions had been a minority position held by a few Euro-Americans with imaginative or financial investments in westward expansion. During the nineteenth century, the anthropogenic explanation gained adherents for various reasons. Cornelius Mathews, a founder of the Young America movement, shared the investment in U.S. westward expansion that had underwritten the positions of John Filson and George Turner.[62] Mathews's strange quasihistorical novel about the extirpation of the mammoth, *Behemoth*, adapted the widely held fiction that present-day American Indians had been preceded in North America by a civilized race that had built the mounds at Cahokia and numerous other places from southeastern to midwestern North America, works that are now attributed to the flourishing of Mississippian culture

(c. 800–1600 CE). The Mound Builders, according to this fiction, had either mysteriously vanished or had been exterminated by the ancestors of present-day American Indians.[63] By means of this fiction, white Americans could claim a European pre-Columbian past for North America, setting ideological precedent for the colonization of the West.[64]

Mathews sets the stage by following the general form of the Lenape Big Bone Lick narrative, which he probably knew from Jefferson's *Notes*: "in an age long past and dimly remembered, [mammoths] had wasted the fields of their fathers and made desolate their ancient dwellings," as in the Lenape narrative when the mammoths had threatened human existence by destroying all the game animals, and were all exterminated but one animal.[65] One legend retold by Mathews's Mound Builders held that the mammoths "had been swept from the earth by some fearful catastrophe," albeit evidently not catastrophic enough to have obliterated the Mound Builders as well. Yet one great mammoth "still lived and might, from a remote and obscure lair, once more come forth, to shake the hills with his trampling, and with the shadow of his coming darken the household of nations" (4). Another, "more thoughtful" legend held that "in that distant age" when the mammoths had reigned, "a new and majestic race of heroes, moulded of Nature's noblest clay, had sprung into life to battle with and finally vanquish these brute oppressors of their country" (4–5). So Mathews shows a new generation of "heroes" responding to the return of the mammoth, which "seemed, in these terrible incursions, to be fired with a mighty revenge for some unforgiven injury inflicted on his dead and extinct tribe by the human family" (22). The mammoth's depredations prompt a revitalization of Mound Builder culture: their "forges, whose fires had smouldered in long disuse, were again rekindled" and they craft steel weapons and build forts and wheeled battle-engines (32). Thus *Behemoth* becomes a narrative of the killing of a great beast through cooperative human effort, a narrative whose general shape is most familiar to us in Herman Melville's *Moby-Dick*.[66] (As Melville's Ishmael calls the whale a "salt-sea mastodon," one of Mathews's Mound Builders calls the mastodon a "land leviathan."[67]) The beast does not succumb easily, even though the Mound Builders marshal an army of "one hundred thousand strong" (32). They pursue the mammoth from the Mississippi River, where he began terrorizing the Mound Builders, across the Great Plains, through the Rocky Mountains, and to the Pacific Ocean—as if tracing the path of the Lewis and Clark expedition, which Jefferson had hoped would find living mammoths in the West. As Behemoth finds a place of retreat, the Mound Builders develop a new plan to undermine this retreat and bury him alive, but he hears their digging and escapes. This attempt to bury the mammoth mirrors and

Figure 1. Charles Willson Peale, *Exhumation of the Mastodon* (c. 1806–8).
Baltimore City Life Museum.

inverts the narrative of Charles Willson Peale's painting, *Exhumation of the
Mastodon* (c. 1806–8), which depicts the unearthing of skeletal remains from
a site in Orange County, New York, in 1801.[68]

Peale's painting, like Mathews's narrative, illustrates the mastery of megafauna through technological prowess and cooperative human effort. The
Mound Builders finally succeed in luring Behemoth into a box canyon, where
they charm him with music while they pen him in by building a wall made of
twelve-foot blocks of quarried stone set in place with an elaborate crane. Thus
penned in, the mammoth eats all the canyon's vegetation, drinks its stream
dry, and starves to death after forty days, leaving "his huge bones extended on
the plain like the wreck of some mighty ship stranded there by a Deluge, to
moulder century after century, to be scattered through a continent by a later
convulsion, and, finally, to become the wonder of the Present Time" (127).
Mathews gives no account of the Mound Builders after this episode, leaving
their fate to the reader's speculation.[69] Yet the Mound Builders' cooperative
technological mastery of their environment, to an extent far beyond what

Mathews knew of American Indians' practices, seems to present an allegorical claim made on the western territories by Young America.

Anticolonial Ecologies and Human Flourishing

Like Filson, Turner, the Peales, and Mathews, the Tuscarora historian David Cusick marshaled a narrative of coordinated human agency. He did so, however, to counter the expansionist territorial claims that were implicit in those Euro-Americans' narratives of megafaunal encounter. Cusick's 1827 *Sketches of the Ancient History of the Six Nations* narrates the eradication of several large, harmful beings that pose a threat to the Haudenosaunee people from the creation era forward, including barbarian giants, mammoths, and creatures unknown to Linnaean taxonomy such as "monsters called Ko-nea-rau-neh-neh, i.e. Flying Heads."[70] While spirit power sometimes plays a role, coordinated human agency is often more important. These stories of the peoples' efforts in removing threats are part of Cusick's overall project of asserting the sovereignty of the Haudenosaunee confederacy in New York and his subsidiary project of locating the Tuscarora, his own late-coming nation, solidly within that confederacy. Whereas the Mound Builder fiction on which Mathews drew represented a preemptive claim on North America by casting present-day American Indians as uncivilized interlopers, Cusick's history grounds the Haudenosaunee in their homeland precisely in order to argue against Euro-American preemption—that is, against the claim, used so often to warrant Indigenous peoples' removal, that because they did not use the land in a European manner, white settler-colonists had a superior claim. As Cusick wrote, the Haudenosaunee were embroiled in a struggle against preemption that dated back to the late eighteenth century and had recently intensified. In the early 1820s, speculators enlisted the U.S. government in their efforts to extinguish Haudenosaunee titles to lands around Buffalo and in 1826 used a new treaty to force a large land sale. Cusick published his *Sketches* the following year.[71]

Extinction narratives formed part of Cusick's effort to establish Haudenosaunee land tenure by demonstrating a continuous history of occupation and nation-formation on their own cultural terms. Among the threats that the five original families extinguish prior to their formal confederation is "the Big Quisquiss (perhaps the Mammouth)" (14). Here, Cusick strategically aligns Haudenosaunee history with Euro-American paleontology. Undoubtedly familiar with the interest of white Americans such as Peale in mammoth

remains from Upstate New York, Cusick translates the Haudenosaunee name for the creature to ground his narrative for such readers. When the Big Quisquiss "invaded the settlements south of Ontario lake," pushing down houses and otherwise wreaking havoc, "a certain chief warrior collected men from several towns—a severe engagement took place, the monster retired, but the people could not remain long without being disturbed: the Big Elk invaded the towns" (14). Again, "men were collected—. . . the monster was killed" (14). In addition to megafauna such as Big Quisquiss and Big Elk, the families were also harassed by "giants called Ronnongwetowanca, who came from the north" (10). After suffering several depredations, the people assembled "a few hundred warriors . . . to subdue them; after decisive contests, the warriors gained the victory, and it was supposed that the Ronnongwetowanca tribe has ever ceased to exist" (13). The next monsters to threaten the people were the Flying Heads, which in Cusick's illustration looks something like a two-legged, trunkless woolly mammoth (19). The Flying Heads see a woman parching acorns over a fire and eating them. They are "amazed" because they think she is eating the coals. Fleeing in fear, the Flying Heads "disappeared and were supposed concealed in the earth" where, as Cusick knew, the fossil remains of giant creatures were buried (19). In a different way from Peale's *Exhumation of the Mastodon*, the story of the Flying Heads represents human technology as mastering a monstrous creature.

The next threat to the five families is the Stonish Giants, who arrive from the west. According to Shawnee tradition, Cusick notes, these were descended from an isolated family: among them, "the rules of humanity were forgotten," much like the Chichimecas encountered by the Nahua or the barbarian giants who threatened the Incas, and they "eat raw flesh of animals" (20).[72] To deal with this threat, the people need the help of "the Holder of the Heavens," who leads them in an attack, driving the Stonish Giants into a deep hollow. The Holder of the Heavens then ascends the mountain and starts an avalanche of rocks, killing them all, but "one escaped . . . and seeks an asylum in the regions of the north" (22). Thus the families who would soon formally confederate under Atotharo's leadership "were now preserved from extinction" (22). Perhaps the families needed the Holder's help because the Stonish Giants presented an especially dire threat. If so, the story ends by implying a need for continual vigilance, should the Stonish Giants descend again from the north. This motif, the escape of one dangerous being from mass extermination, reiterates a motif from the Haudenosaunee and Lenape stories of the extinction at Big Bone Lick. There, too, a threatening form of life is nearly but not entirely eradicated.

The anthropogenic extinction narrative advanced by Cusick gained credence among scientists as well. This was partly because the effects of modern
human depredation were becoming evident on species such as the dodo or, as
we will see in Chapters 3 and 4, whales and buffalo, and partly because other
explanations such as a catastrophic event, gradual climate change, or species senescence increasingly seemed inadequate in the face of new evidence.
This shift did not, however, change the overall positive moral assessment of
the Late Pleistocene extinctions. If anything, those assessments became more
positive. Although Charles Lyell saw modern humans "wield[ing] the sword
of extermination," early on he believed that the Late Pleistocene extinctions
predated the appearance of the human species.[73] By 1873, however, Lyell had
modified his position following the accumulation of archaeological evidence
that located humans contemporaneously with the Pleistocene megafauna.
Regarding "the disappearance of many large pachyderms and beasts of prey"
during the Glacial era, he agreed that "the intervention of Man" played a significant part along with climate change.[74] Owen similarly became dissatisfied
with his early view that the cause of extinction lay within the nature of each
species as a given term of existence and looked to other agencies including
human as a primary cause in his summary text on extinct mammals. He
regarded extinction as "a natural law, which has operated from the beginning of life."[75] "In times anterior to man," "external agencies" such as predators or competing species or climate change or other such "ordinary causes"
seemed the most likely cause, but noting modern instances of the extinction
or endangerment of species such as the Great Auk "due to the direct agency
of man," it made sense to extrapolate (398, 399). In the case of *Elephas primigenius* (later reclassified as *Mamuthus* spp.) and similar species, "a rude
primitive human race may have finished the work of extermination, begun
by antecedent and more general causes" (401). Immediately following this
point, Owen goes on to describe the archaeology of flint weaponry found
in strata containing mammoth fossils. Wallace, returning to the problem of
Late Pleistocene extinctions in biogeographical context, concluded that gla-
ciation was "not held to be a sufficient cause for so general a destruction of
the larger forms of life," especially because there was no evidence of glaci-
ation or significant cooling in tropical or subtropical places such as Brazil,
Argentina, or Australia.[76] Rather, he agreed with Lyell and Owen regarding
anthropogenic causation acting in combination with other factors, but put
the case more strongly: "The fact that man should everywhere have helped to
exterminate the various huge quadrupeds, whose flesh would be a highly val-
ued food, almost becomes a certainty" (265). Against the view that primitive

weaponry would not have been sufficient, Wallace asserted their power: "It is therefore certain, that, so soon as man possessed weapons and the use of fire, his power of intelligent combination would have rendered him full able to kill or capture any animal that has ever lived upon this earth; and as the flesh, bones, hair, horns, or skins would have been of use to him, he would certainly have done so even had he not the additional incentive that in many cases the animals were destructive to his crops or dangerous to his children or himself" (267). In this late-career statement, Wallace's view of agency shifted away from climate change to focus on humans working in "intelligent combination," but his moral evaluation remained consistent: the Late Pleistocene megafaunal extinctions were a good thing for humankind.

The Penobscot elder Joseph Nicolar's *Life and Traditions of the Red Man* (1893) takes another turn in this project of moral evaluation, using the mammoth's extinction as an object lesson. Nicolar retells the Indigenous Big Bone Lick stories so as to link the extinction of the mammoth with a prophecy of the extinction of Euro-Americans. We have seen that in Cusick's account, humans working in "intelligent combination" (as Wallace put it) also occasionally required supplementary effort by a spirit power. The eighteenth-century Haudenosaunee account discussed earlier attributed the mammoth's eradication—with the exception of a pair who were preserved and might be brought to life again in case they were needed to punish errant humans—entirely to spirit powers. Cusick's version, told in a context that invited strong affirmation of the Haudenosaunee history of confederation, occasionally invoked spirit powers while emphasizing human agency. Nicolar's account is a product of Wabanaki, not Haudenosaunee tradition.[77] While oral transmission over generations probably linked Nicolar with the Abenaki speakers who participated in the Baron de Longueuil's 1739 expedition, Nicolar's account of the mammoth forms a key part of his retelling of the traditional Penobscot origin story in the late nineteenth-century context of land loss and environmental degradation. He does not locate the cause of the mammoth's extinction in direct human agency, as both Cusick and westward-looking Euro-Americans had done (albeit for opposing political and cultural reasons). Nicolar locates the cause within the species itself, but not in the manner of Owen's early speculation on species senescence, nor yet in terms of species being as some preservationists writing on the buffalo would do, as we will see in Chapter 4. Rather, using the familiar lightning-strike motif of the Big Bone Lick stories, Nicolar crafts a narrative of the fall of pride and greed with significant implications for human ecology. Aimed at the late nineteenth-century context, the lesson remains pertinent today.

Since the colonial era, the Penobscots had seen the effects of habitat destruction and overhunting on animal populations. In 1823 they had petitioned the governor of Maine, stating that "in consequence of the white people killing [moose and deer] off merely for the sake of their skins, they have now become nearly extinct." They asked that hunting by whites be regulated and stated that they themselves "have come to a conclusion to kill no more of the aforesaid game, Moose and Deer, at present."[78] The Penobscots lost most of their traditional land base during the nineteenth century and suffered a decrease in population from disease and outmigration. At the low point of Penobscot population around 1890, Nicolar undertook to write their history as a revitalization project. In this "full account of all the pure traditions which have been handed down from the beginning of the red man's world to the present time," Nicolar referred to "no historical works of the white man."[79]

The narrative begins with the work of the first man, Klose-kur-beh, a culture-bearer who receives instruction from the Great Being and learns the prophecies, which include the coming of the white people and their eventual extinction.[80] His first mission is "to clean the earth of all obstacles" and "to subdue the animals and beasts, so that man will not have much trouble in conquering them afterwards" (116, 117–18). "In those days," Nicolar informs us, beasts "sought after man's life, not only devouring him when they met, but also roving through the forest seeking after him." Thus Klose-kur-beh called all the animals to him one by one and "asked if they were willing to become small" (118). All but one agreed, in effect ratifying a treaty concerning their place in the world. Some needed to be persuaded, such as Miqu-go-a (squirrel), who leapt into a tree in resistance. Klose-kur-beh told him he could stay there but he would need to become small so he could travel from branch to branch without breaking them. Miqu-go-a agreed and received his name and present form. One animal refused, however—an animal that was "much larger than those near him, and the form of his body was not like the others—his back was the shape of the half moon with a very small head for the body, with large but thin ears hanging down each side of the head; eyes and mouth small and the upper lip so long he could reach out with it seven paces and up among the branches of the trees; and there were two long horns on each side of his long lip" (118). The animal is later named as "Par-sar-do-kep-piart—mammoth" but its identity is already clear from the description (119). Whether or not Indigenous tradition transmitted the memory of American proboscideans from the Pleistocene era forward (as discussed earlier), by 1893 these animals were widely known.[81]

According to Nicolar, the mammoth refused to join the emerging world order as shaped by Klose-kur-beh. The mammoth explains his refusal in a much longer speech than any other animal in Nicolar's entire narrative:

> No, I will not go forth to man and humble myself to obey his bidding; I will never obey the bidding of my enemy as long as he can not show the power and strength that I can. Even the trees bend when I touch them; I can break branches with my long lip and tear up the earth when I choose; and when I meet your children, ... I will dash them against my teeth so that my teeth will go through them. Seven of your children I can hang on my two teeth and go my way to meet more. Their weapons I do not fear, because my skin is so thick and hard even hair will not grow out of it; and my flesh is so deep that it covers my life, there can nothing reach that life which can be brought against it by your children; therefore I will repeat and say no. (118–19)

Klose-kur-beh "paused with sorrow" at the mammoth's expression of "vanity," sorrow that it refused an ordering of the world that would accommodate the flourishing of all creatures. "Woe unto you," says Klose-kur-beh, "your pride will fall with your body." The mammoth's destruction "will show my children that there is a power somewhere which is far greater than your power that can protect them from any violence you can press against them. . . . When the power does its work, it will be final, none of your kind will escape, but will all perish alike. My children shall stand around and gaze upon your bones; and the bones will last as long as the world stands, but your skin and flesh that gives you so much pride will never be seen again by any of my children" (119). A voice from above in a dark cloud warns Klose-kur-beh to depart, taking with him "the animals that obey," after which "the clouds began to roar very loud all over the heavens and the lightning shooting in every direction, and the howling of the animal was heard no more" (119, 120).

Nicolar thus retains key motifs from the Indigenous Big Bone Lick stories, such as the characterization of the mammoth as a threat to human flourishing and the causal agency of lightning strikes wielded by spirit power, but he adds other motifs as well. The narrative of the downsizing of the animals in early times has parallels in other Wabanaki stories and in other Indigenous traditions.[82] The Dakota memoirist Charles Eastman, writing at about the same time, tells a similar story of the primordial time when "all the animals were considered people" and all spoke the same language. The game animals "became conceited" and made war on the people. The "Great Mystery"

transformed them and gave the world its present order.[83] Eastman's story does not, however, contain an extinction component. Deloria's take on such stories is that it was not a matter of species extinction but rather of universal transformation through the downsizing of animals and humans during the primordial time: all are now smaller versions of their former selves.[84] This echoes the Shawnee Big Bone Lick story transcribed by James Wright, according to which both humans and animals were bigger in ancient days. Nicolar tells it differently, however. In contrast to the eighteenth-century Big Bone Lick stories to which his story is clearly related, here no individual escapes or is preserved for some future purpose. Thus Nicolar emphasizes two points that earlier Indigenous versions do not: the permanence of extinction and the consequences of pride in exercising power over vulnerable others, as the mammoth had done.

These motifs of pride and power connect the mammoth's extinction narrative to Nicolar's great prophecy of the extinction of the white race. Both are foreshadowed in the early days by a sign of the coming of the whites, "a very dense fog" that descended "over the whole country and remained seven moons" during which fishing and hunting became nearly impossible (164).[85] At this time, Mata-we-leh (loon) predicts the coming of the whites from across the ocean; they "have brought upon you this trouble and hunger, you cannot find animals because the days have been so dark, you cannot find fish because there is a covering over all the fish which the power of these people have placed there, it is the spiritual power that is in them, and if the power that is in you has not the force to overcome it, woe unto you" (165). Several men and women try without success to penetrate the covering over the fish, until the Mata-we-leh transforms herself into a great ball of fire and dives into the ocean, freeing the fish and dissipating the fog. It is yet some time before the whites will arrive. When they do, their power to prevent access to fish and game becomes manifest and there is a time of hardship continuing to the present day. Nicolar has already prepared his readers, however, with a saving prophecy given by the Great Spirit to Klose-kur-beh in the beginning, stating that the white man "wants all the world; he shall slay his brother because he wants all things; he shall know no one because he wants the power over all the earth" (112). This pride of power will be a curse, however, as it was with the mammoth: "The sweetness of the earth and love of power will destroy them. Before the day of destruction comes, this man shall have enjoyed all the power and possession he desires, and he shall have tasted the sweetness of the earth. . . . He need only reach forth his hand to grasp all things for his comfort; he will draw things for his convenience from the water, from the air, and

from deep down in the earth" (113). Yet the Great Spirit will show a superior power: "He shall shake the earth, because the substance of the water, air and earth have been drawn out, and used for comfort sake, and all these things have been left like the empty hornet's nest shall cave into these great pits, and the people shall fall into them, like the sand; And the powerful man shall be no more" (113). For those few who remain after this mass human extinction event, says the culture-bearer Klose-kur-beh, "then the Great Spirit shall call me forth . . . to teach you more" (113). Nicolar states in his conclusion, however, that the Penobscot remain at risk. He has told his story in order to enlighten them, for they "are now on the descending slide scale to a point not yet settled" (195).

Longueuil's Abenaki warriors, a likely source of transmission for the story of the mammoth that Nicolar adapts, probably also knew another, similar story of the Great Beaver, who behaves selfishly, like the mammoth, and is similarly punished. Although he does not retell it in *Life and Traditions of the Red Man*, Nicolar may have known this story as well. A recent version by the Abenaki writer Cheryl Savageau tells of the extirpation of the beaver during the fur trade and their twentieth-century survivance. In the old days before the fur trade, according to this story, the Great Beaver begins to act selfishly: he "patrols the edges [of his pond], chasing everyone away. This is all mine, he says. The people and animals grow thirsty." The Creator punishes the Beaver "for living out of balance," turning him to stone, much as the mammoth was punished in Nicolar's story. This in turn impacts human behavior as the Beaver's descendants are "killed by the millions" in the fur trade. The Beaver "dreams a hard dream: a world without beavers." But unlike the mammoth's extinction, here extinction is not permanent. There is new hope as the Great Beaver "dreams the rivers back, young mothers building, secure in their skins, and a pond full of the slapping tails of children."[86] Animals' and humans' agencies are entangled. "Balance" requires proper behavior of both.

*   *   *

While some of Jefferson's contemporaries recognized humans as extinctive agents—a position that would gain more support through the nineteenth century—Jefferson himself worried that recognizing the fact of extinction would mean admitting that the "whole system of things should evanish by piece-meal."[87] That is, the extinction of the mammoth or megalonyx portended the extinction of humankind. Narrating extinction as loss, Jefferson anticipated the emergence of the modern, elegiac response. In contrast, the

Indigenous American narratives from Jefferson's day, like Savageau's story of the Great Beaver, do not necessarily recognize extinction as an absolute. This position has gained new grounding with genetic engineering, for as we saw in the Introduction, efforts to clone the mammoth and other projects in resurrection ecology are ongoing. Yet Nicolar, like Jefferson, understood the extinction of the mammoth as an absolute and also connected the mammoth's extinction with human extinction, albeit in a different way. He went beyond Jefferson in identifying a political cause and providing a moral evaluation, both in terms of ecological fitness: the mammoth and the Euro-American colonists are doomed to extinction because neither wants to leave room for the mutual flourishing of all beings. Unlike the mammoth, for Nicolar the extinction of humans will not be absolute. Rather, as in the Indigenous Big Bone Lick stories, a remnant of the species is preserved for some reason. Under the Great Spirit's guidance, this reason is to promote the flourishing of all species.

Does the Whale Diminish?
Will He Perish?

In the whaling tradition of the Nuu-chah-nulth and the Makah, Wakashan-speaking peoples of Vancouver Island and the Olympic Peninsula, the whale comes willingly to the hunters. The whaling chief prepares by praying, "Whale, I want you to come near me. . . . Whale, if I spear you, I want my spear to strike your heart. . . . Whale, when I spear at you and miss you, I want you to take hold of my spear with your hands."[1] If the chief has successfully prepared, purified himself, and performed the necessary rituals, the whale will accept his prayer. After harpooning the whale, the chief recognizes this acceptance, praying, "Whale, I have given you what you are wishing to get—my good harpoon. And now you have it. Please hold it with your strong hands, and do not let go. Whale, turn toward the fine beach, . . . for when you come ashore there, young men will cover your great body with bluebill duck feathers and with the down of the great eagle, the chief of all birds; for this is what you are wishing, and this is what you are trying to find from one end of the world to the other, every day you are travelling and spouting."[2] As characterized in such prayers, the whale wants to be hunted. As a Nuu-chah-nulth elder explains, the whaling chief "identified the [whale] that he was intended to kill. That one was looking for him, too. They recognized each other. The whale gives himself to the hunter."[3]

By contrast, in the Euro-American whaling tradition that spread from New England's coastal waters in the eighteenth century to the Pacific Ocean in the nineteenth, the whale flees from the hunters or—as in the sinking of the whale ship *Essex* and the novel it inspired, *Moby-Dick*—the whale attacks to save itself or fellow whales.[4] Yet, as Herman Melville writes the story of one such attack, there is an element of recognition that while not parallel to the Nuu-chah-nulth elder's account, nevertheless draws Ahab to the white whale and perhaps the white whale to Ahab.

Both Ahab and Indigenous whale hunters recognize moral behavior in whales, albeit of different kinds: self- and species-preservation for the former versus cross-species cooperation and altruistic self-sacrifice for the latter. These different kinds of moral behavior are linked to different versions of community consolidation and, in turn, to different extinction narratives. Ahab's charismatic tyranny welds the *Pequod*'s crew into a killing unit whose obedience and efficiency are finally undone by an encounter with one superior whale. The sinking of the *Pequod*, as Melville tells it, becomes a symbolic moment in a larger narrative that predicts the whale kind's eternal persistence and humankind's ultimate extinction. Narratives of extinction and persistence have figured differently for the Makah and Nuu-chah-nulth. Traditionally, a successful hunt culminated in the ritual celebration of the whale, from the landing of the whale and the offering of prayers, duck feathers, and eagle down (often by women instead of or in addition to the young men) to the communal distribution of whale meat and oil through the whaling chief's potlatches, ceremonies that maintained social relations through an intricate system of reciprocity.[5] These whale potlatches were lost from community life in the early twentieth century, when commercial whaling had reduced the population of the key species, gray whales, to the brink of extinction. At that time, the Makah and Nuu-chah-nulth decided to stop hunting whales, intending to revive the hunt when the population recovered, meanwhile maintaining their cultural identification with whaling through names, stories, music, and art.[6] When the gray whale population recovered in the late twentieth century and the Makah revived their whaling tradition, the role of whales in community life became a point of contention that pitted claims of tribal sovereignty and survivance against claims for whales' exceptional moral status. The controversy did not split neatly along Indigenous versus Euro-American lines, however, but involved an array of parties, motives, and understandings of relations between humans and whales.

The Extinction of the Human and
the Persistence of the Whale

When Ishmael asks two questions central to the nineteenth-century whaling industry—"Does the Whale's Magnitude Diminish?—Will He Perish?"— he draws together lines of investigation into degeneration, extinction, and deep time that are threaded through *Moby-Dick*.[7] Jefferson had resolved the question of degeneration spatially in his refutation of Buffon by means of a

comparison of American and European species. Since the mammoth was a key exhibit, Jefferson hoped to resolve the question of extinction as well, by finding living mammoths somewhere in the great Northwest, as his Lenape informant's story of the Great Bull allegorically suggested. Melville, writing after Cuvier had established the fact of extinction through his anatomical reading of the fossil record, addresses the question of degeneration in terms of both deep time and human time, "all the generations of whales, and men, and mastodons, past, present, and to come" from the thirty-million-year-old fossil Zeuglodon onward (497).[8] He found that the whale had not diminished, but had become larger over geological time.

These chronological investigations led Melville to the more problematic question of species extinction. We have seen that even in the face of the confirmation of ancient extinctions by Cuvier and others, Jefferson held on to a belief in an active, supernatural "restoring power" that would prevent nature from being "reduced to a shapeless chaos."[9] Reflecting on extinction in *Notes on the State of Virginia* and other natural history writing, he did not figure human agency into his calculus of the "oeconomy of nature" in any significant way.[10] To admit human agency would be to set up a potential moral conflict between human and supernatural agencies in shaping the environment. In the case of the mammoth, Jefferson's contemporaries John Filson, George Turner, and the Lenape, Shawnee, and Haudenosaunee storytellers had avoided any such moral conflict by means of anthropocentric narratives that characterized the mammoth as a harmful environmental excess which was best extirpated to promote human flourishing.

In the nineteenth century, the moral calculus seemed more pressing as more species became visibly endangered, even as theories of evolution complicated the assessment of agency. In the late eighteenth century, for example, Filson wrote of the "amazing herds of buffaloes" that had recently populated the Blue Licks of Kentucky, "before the first settlers had wantonly sported away their lives."[11] By the early nineteenth century, naturalists began to generalize from numerous local anthropogenic extirpations to the question of global extinctions.[12] Charles Lyell, whose uniformist geological theory influenced Charles Darwin's understanding of species' evolution and extinction, regarded anthropogenic extinctions as consistent with "the fixed and constant laws of the animate [and] inanimate world" rather than as exceptional.[13] All species, he argued, have "marked [their] progress by the diminution, or the entire extirpation, of some other [species]."[14] Because anthropogenic extinctions were no exception to this general law of nature, Lyell argued, we

should not "repine at the havoc committed."[15] Nineteenth-century accounts often used Lyell's logic, appealing to the idea of species being in order to regulate the moral response that evidence of anthropogenic extinction demanded.

In this context, Melville surveyed the paleontological and contemporary evidence and asked of the whale kind generally, "Will He Perish?" (500). This question opens onto the more general questions of human and nonhuman agency that Melville explores in *Moby-Dick*. As far as Melville is concerned, the conditions for answering these questions are specified in the memorable quarter-deck scene in which Ahab first addresses the crew of the *Pequod*. Sometimes read as political allegory, the scene stages a nineteenth-century debate concerning species being.[16] Ahab, we recall, seeks vengeance on the great whale Moby Dick as either "agent" or "principal" of the "unknown but *still reasoning* thing" that has wounded him, psychically as much as physically (178, italics added). Ahab, Ishmael, and many of the *Pequod*'s crew come to understand the whale not as a mere commodity, not as a "dumb brute," much to the pragmatist Starbuck's dismay, but rather as a deliberative, intending being—thus a subject worthy of vengeance (178). This understanding, which is emphasized particularly during the novel's three-day chase sequence, blurs the human/animal distinction. Moreover, in construing the whale as either "agent" or "principal," Ahab leaves room for, although he does not insist on, the possibility of supernatural agency. As Ishmael reframes the difference between Ahab and Starbuck to draw out its moral significance, he imagines "admonitions and warnings" not only in Starbuck's sense of "foreboding" but even in the natural environment, as potentially signified by the "presaging vibrations of the winds in the cordage" (179). For Ishmael, these "vibrations" register our existential condition: they are "not so much predictions from without, as verifications of the foregoing things within. For with little external to constrain us, the innermost necessities in our being, these still drive us on" (179).

Over the course of his narrative, Ishmael comes to recognize what Ahab regards as the whale's intelligence and what Starbuck regards as the whale's animality is, rather, a configuration of species being unknowable either in terms of a cross-species understanding, which Ahab posits and resents, or in terms of mastery, which Starbuck assumes to legitimate the whale's commodification. Knowable neither in terms of mutuality nor possession, the whale's species being thus poses the question: Is humankind's historical relation to whales (or mammoths, dodos, bison, polar bears, etc.), which has been characterized as stemming from a differential of intelligence, merely a differential of behavior? And if so, are other terms of response possible than those

proposed by Lyell's amoral calculus, which regarded anthropogenic extinctions as consistent with the natural order?

In *Moby-Dick*, Melville does not deny the logic of competitive extermination that Lyell and others developed in the nineteenth century. Yet he, or his narrator Ishmael, argues that whales will not be exterminated through human agency, despite the concerns of some contemporary observers. Rather, in a narrative that begins as displaced suicide and remains preoccupied with human mortality—both individual and species—the whale offers hope for the infinite extension of life, with all its violence, beyond good and evil. Ishmael reserves supernatural narrative for human fate, leaving whales to persist according to their own natural agency. He marshals his cetological investigations in support of the proposition that "the unspeakable terrors of the whale, which, having been before all time, must needs exist after all humane ages are over" (498). The effect is twofold. First, Ishmael's argument, like Lyell's, grants agency to species, considering them as responsible for their own preservation or extinction. Second, the narrative in which Melville frames these arguments links Ahab rather than Moby Dick with extinction, thus displacing the predatory violence of the whaling industry away from whales and back onto humankind's fate, at a time when the Anglophone world was reminded anew of Christian millennialism's narrative of the end of the world. In imagining human extinction, Melville asserts the exceptional belonging of the whale, as contrasted with the evanescence of human presence. Whales (not the meek) will inherit the earth.

Although at one point early on Ishmael calls the whale "salt-sea mastodon" (70), he does so to evoke the attributes of ancientness and power that made the mastodon an aspirational symbol for the young and vulnerable U.S. nation in the early federal period.[17] Although the mammoth did not gain long-term traction as a national symbol, these attributes of ancientness and power remained compelling, and it is these on which Ishmael draws to argue against the possibility of the whale's extinction: "We account the whale immortal in his species, however perishable in his individuality. He swam the seas before the continents broke water; he once swam over the site of the Tuileries, and Windsor Castle, and the Kremlin. In Noah's flood he despised Noah's Ark; and if ever the world is to be flooded again, like the Netherlands, to kill off its rats, then the eternal whale will still survive, and rearing upon the topmost crest of the equatorial flood, spout his frothed defiance to the skies" (503–4). Ishmael takes this position against the concerns of certain "recondite Nantucketers" who worried that, as a result of overhunting, the whale "cannot now escape speedy extinction" (501, 502).

Those Nantucketers were not alone in discerning a pattern of population decline that augured extinction. The pattern is all too clear in retrospect in the history of whaling's expansion from New England's coastal waters outward to the Pacific. Each new whaling ground yielded the bulk of its harvest in the first few years. Increased exploitation led to the failure of the ground and the search for new grounds.[18] In the late eighteenth century, J. Hector St. John de Crèvecoeur reported, in his history of the Nantucket fishery, that "when the whales quitted their coasts . . . by degrees they went whaling to Newfoundland, to the Gulph of St. Laurence, . . . the coasts of Labrador. . . . In time they visited the western islands, the latitude of 34°, famous for that fish, the Brazils, the coast of Guinea. Would you believe that they have already gone to the Falklands, and that I have heard several of them talk of going to the South Sea!"[19] As Crèvecoeur indicates with his use of the verb "quitted," commentators understood this pattern in terms of the retreat of whales from areas of hunting pressure to areas where they were not hunted, rather than in terms of the extirpation of local populations. As we will see in the next chapter, early commentators held similar assumptions regarding the bison's extirpation from eastern North America.

Yet the end point of the narrative of retreat was extinction, as even some optimistic commentators recognized. In an 1834 review of four books on the whaling industry—including two of Melville's source texts, William Scoresby's *An Account of the Arctic Regions* and Scoresby's *Journal of a Voyage to the Northern Whale-Fishery*—the *North American Review* observed that with the global expansion of the industry, whales "have been driven to the deepest recesses of Baffin's Bay" or to "the very confines of the Pacific." As a result, "whether their mammoth bones in some distant century shall indicate to the untaught natives of the shores they now frequent that such an animal *was*, or whether, lurking in the inaccessible and undisturbed waters north of Asia and America, the race shall be preserved, is almost a problem." *Almost*, because according to this reviewer, the whale will not suffer the mammoth's fate at the hands of humankind: "Certain it is that subsistence can never fail, teeming as all waters do, with such profusion of life. That a squadron of 700 vessels scour every sea and bay, in the eager and unremitted pursuit, without exterminating or apparently diminishing the species, leaves us to wonder at the exhaustless resources of nature."[20] Others were less optimistic regarding nature's "exhaustless" potential, especially after the industry expanded into the Pacific. One such was M. E. Bowles, an officer on a New England whaling ship and frequent contributor to Hawaiian newspapers that catered to the shipping trade. Reviewing the past "ten or fifteen years" of the Pacific

whale fishery in 1845, Bowles concluded "that the poor whale is doomed to utter extermination, or at least, so near it as that too few will remain to tempt the cupidity of man, I have not a doubt."[21] He was similarly concerned for the fate of the sea elephant, as he reports after an 1844 hunt on a coastal California island: "The sea elephant are now very scarce, and if all who hunt them carry on the same war of extermination that we did, they will soon become extinct."[22]

Melville may or may not have been directly aware of these statements. One of his source texts, however, took up the topic as well. Borrowing silently from Bowles and the 1834 *North American Review* article, the Rev. Henry T. Cheever predicted the extinction of whales in his account of a Pacific whaling voyage, *The Whale and His Captors*:

> An experienced captain [evidently Bowles] thinks that . . . the poor whale, chased from sea to sea, and from haunt to haunt, is doomed to utter extermination, or so near to it, that too few will remain to tempt the cupidity of man.
>
> The history of the sperm whale fishery . . . confirms this calculation. Before the end of the present century, therefore, judging from the past, is it likely that the hunting of whales on the sea will be any more prosecuted as a business than the hunting of deer on the land? . . . "Whether their mammoth bones in some distant century shall indicate to the untaught natives of the shores they now frequent that such an animal *was*, or whether, lurking in the inaccessible and undisturbed waters north of Asia and America, the race shall be preserved, is almost a problem."
>
> > They roamed, they fed, they slept, they died, and left
> > Race after race to roam, feed, sleep, then die,
> > And leave their like through endless generations:
> > So HE ordained, whose way is in the sea,
> > His path amid great waters, and his steps
> > Unknown![23]

The concluding poetic quotation with which the Rev. Cheever assigned whales to their divinely ordained sentence of extinction is spliced together from an undersea vision in canto 2 of James Montgomery's "Pelican Island" (1828). After the line ending on "generations," Montgomery's original reads as follows:

—Incessant change of actors, none of scene,
Through all that boundless theatre of strife!
Shrinking into myself again, I cried,
In bitter disappointment,—"Is this all?"[24]

Cheever substitutes another passage after "generations" in order to emphasize divine ordination of death rather than human existential despair. Earlier
in the poem, Montgomery had observed that beneath the sea,

While ravening Death of slaughter ne'er grew weary
Life multiplied the immortal meal as fast.
War, reckless, universal war, prevail'd;
All were devourers, all in turn devour'd;
. . . .
So He ordained, whose way is in the sea,
His path amid great waters, and his steps
Unknown.[25]

Splicing these last three lines of Montgomery's vision of divinely ordained
"universal war" among the creatures of the deep—an image that Melville
echoes at several points in *Moby-Dick*—into his account of "endless generations," Cheever in effect maintains Bowles's description of human agency
in cutting off the generations, but he absolves humankind of responsibility.
Thus Cheever supplies a theological warrant for Lyell's refusal to mourn the
ostensibly natural act of one species exterminating another. Such predictions,
whether or not they appeal to a theological warrant, treat whales as mere
animal resources. Their primary concern is not so much for the preservation
of whales in themselves—the question that animated Melville's inquiry—but
rather for the continuance of an extractive industry.

A different sort of appeal, closer to Melville's investigations of the whale,
appeared in 1850 in the Pacific seaman's newspaper the *Friend*. Signed "Polar
Whale" and dated "Anadir Sea, North Pacific, The second Year of Trouble,"
"A Polar Whale's Appeal" presents the voice of an "Old Greenland" whale
pleading for mercy on his kind.[26] Using a disorienting alternative chronology
to plunge the reader into the whales' subjective being, Polar Whale refers to
a potentially apocalyptic event in whale history. In the human reckoning of
time, the "second Year of Trouble," the letter's date line, is CE 1850, the date
of its newspaper publication. From Polar Whale's point of view, the "Trouble"
began in the human year 1848, when a whaling ship first penetrated north

of the Bering Strait—where, to anticipate one of Melville's arguments against the likelihood of extinction, whales might have been assumed to find safe haven from the predation of the Pacific whaling fleet.[27] Having thus reoriented human chronology, the spokes-whale begins:

> MR. EDITOR,—In behalf of my species, allow an inhabitant of this sea, to make an appeal through your columns to the friends of the whale in general. A few of the knowing old inhabitants of this sea have recently held a meeting to consult respecting our safety, and in some way or other, if possible, to avert the doom that seems to await all of the whale *Genus* throughout the world, including the Sperm, Right, and Polar Whales. Although our situation, and that of our neighbors in the Arctic, is remote from our enemy's country, yet we have been knowing to the progress of affairs in the Japan and Ochotsk seas, the Atlantic and Indian oceans, and all the other "whaling grounds." We have imagined that we were safe in these cold regions; but no; within these last two years a furious attack has been made upon us, an attack more deadly and bloody, than any of our race ever experienced in any part of the world.

Measuring local suffering as more intense than distant suffering in a very human way, Polar Whale nevertheless links that suffering to a universal cause, reporting on a parliament of whales of all species who have somehow found voice—as Bruno Latour imagines nonhuman nature can do through scientific "speech prostheses"—and now claim representation.[28] The spokes-whale enlists human communicative media, "the power of the 'Press;' pray give these few lines a place in your columns, and let them go forth to the world."

Mixing pathos with grim humor that shows cross-species awareness of the human bodily perspective—"Multitudes of our species (the Polar) have been murdered in 'cold' blood"—Polar Whale elaborates a petition whose generic form is familiar from antebellum American reform rhetoric, as for example activism against slavery or Indian Removal, which counted on powerful friends to take up the cause of the powerless oppressed. The Cherokees had petitioned Congress in 1830 to "preserve us from ruin and extinction," stating that they merely "desire to remain in peace and quietude upon their ancient territory." They conceded that "the power of a State, may put our national existence under its feet," but contended that this "would be contrary to legal right." Thus they asked the United States to prohibit the state of Georgia from "tak[ing] possession of [their lands] forcibly."[29] Culturally prominent

whites such as Ralph Waldo Emerson took up the Cherokee cause, to no avail. The United States used force not to protect the Cherokees from the state of Georgia, but to remove them westward. While Polar Whale's rhetorical appeal is similar in its desire for peace and its diagnosis of positionality, the tone is heightened to emphasize the prospect of violence: "We polar whales are a quiet inoffensive race, desirous of life and peace, but, alas, we fear our doom is sealed.... Is there no redress? I write in behalf of my butchered and dying species. I appeal to the friends of the whole race of whales. Must we all be murdered in cold blood? Must our race become extinct? Will no friends and allies arise and revenge our wrongs? Will our foes be allowed to prey upon us another year?" We might wonder how many "friends and allies" Polar Whale might have hoped to find among the readership of a seaman's newspaper. One historian has imagined whalers reading it "doubled over with laughter."[30] It is possible that the text is an elaborate satire on the idea that whales deserve something like human rights or, in nineteenth-century parlance, the Rights of Man, as it was repeatedly argued that Africans and Native Americans did. Claims for such rights depend on drawing a distinction between those that do and do not deserve them, a point that depends on a deep structure of human/animal difference.[31] Melville's Ishmael, however, was one whaler who would not have read the text as satire (even as he would have appreciated its punning humor), for like "A Polar Whale's Appeal," he also realized that the context of extinction invited considerations of agency that could trouble the difference between humans and animals.[32]

As Polar Whale asserts the quasihumanity of whales, Ishmael argues that whales will escape extinction, despite the increasing pressure of human predation, through the apparently humanlike means of developing new behaviors. He draws an explicit comparison to the bison, saying that where the bison are doomed to extinction because of overhunting, whales are not. The difference lies in their natures, which is to say their mode of relation to their environment. This varies according to whale species' jaw shapes. Krill-straining baleen whales such as the Greenland and humpback whales possess little capacity for defensive attack. "Driven from promontory to cape" by whalers, they will retreat "at last resort to their Polar citadels, and diving under the ultimate glassy barriers and walls there, come up among icy fields and floes; and in a charmed circle of everlasting December, bid defiance to all pursuit from man" (502, 503). In the mid-nineteenth century, the assumption of the climate stability of polar ice was quite reasonable—although as Polar Whale's appeal indicates, whether or not polar ice would provide enough of a refuge after the whaling fleet's penetration north of the Bering Strait was

another question.[33] Sperm whales have developed other strategies. Possessing predatory jaws, they have become more aggressive and have taken to congregating for mutual protection in response to increasing attacks by whalers. "As of late," Ishmael reports, "the Sperm Whale Fishery had been marked by various and not infrequent instances of great ferocity, cunning, and malice in the monster attacked" (195). "In more than one instance, [a sperm whale] has been known, not only to chase the assailing boats back to their ships, but to pursue the ship itself" (228). Moreover, in response to "unwearied" pursuit by whale hunters, "Sperm Whales, instead of almost invariably sailing in small detached companies, as in former times, are now frequently met with in extensive herds, sometimes embracing so great a multitude, it would almost seem as if numerous nations of them had sworn solemn league and covenant for mutual assistance and protection" (417). Thus they sail in "widely separated, unfrequent armies" such as the "Grand Armada" the *Pequod* encounters in chapter 87 (502, 415). Moby Dick himself combines both of these behavioral developments—increased aggression and mutual assistance—when he frees a fellow whale by "snapping furiously at [the] fast-line" that secures a whale to a boat commanded by Captain Boomer of the *Samuel Enderby* (478).

One of Melville's sources on whale behavior was an account of a sperm whale's attack on the whale ship *Essex* in 1819, published by the ship's first mate Owen Chase.[34] Melville had, as Ishmael reports in chapter 45, spoken with Chase's son in the Pacific in 1841 and had annotated a copy of Chase's narrative in 1851 as he was completing the final draft of the novel.[35] Of the several first- and secondhand accounts of the event that have survived, Chase's is the most reflective. No doubt all accounts are colored by the three months of hunger and thirst the crew endured as they drifted in whaleboats hoping to reach the coast of Chile. Several died and the survivors resorted to cannibalism. If they had been rescued immediately, perhaps more of them would have recounted the whale's attack with more curiosity, for as another recollection puts it, the *Essex* was "attacked in a most deliberated manner."[36] Chase initially found the "design" of the attack "unaccountable" because the sperm whale species was "never before suspected of premeditated violence, and [was] proverbial for its insensibility and inoffensiveness." Even so, he reflected,

> Every fact seemed to warrant me in concluding that it was any thing but chance which directed [this whale's] operations; he made two several attacks upon the ship, at a short interval between them, both of which, according to their direction, were calculated to do the most injury, by being made ahead [i.e., into the bow of the ship as the ship was sailing

toward the whale], and thereby combining the speed of the two objects for the shock; to effect which, the exact manoeuvres which he made were necessary. His aspect was most horrible, and as such indicated resentment and fury. He came directly from the shoal which we had just before entered, and in which we had struck three of his companions, as if fired with revenge for their sufferings.... The whole circumstances taken together, all happening before my own eyes, and producing, at the time, impressions of decided, calculating mischief, on the part of the whale, (many of which impressions I cannot now recall), induce me to be satisfied that I am correct in my opinion.[37]

As with Captain Boomer of the *Enderby*, Chase concluded that this whale was deliberately motivated by a desire to protect and avenge his fellow whales, whom the *Essex* had attacked. In this attribution of humanlike qualities to the whale, such stories of whale hunting thus figured the human-animal relation differently than stories of hunting other giant beasts such as Cornelius Mathews's *Behemoth*.

This developmental account of whales' behavior contrasts with Ahab's fateful refusal to change his course, which renders the entire crew vulnerable. Ahab's refusal and the *Pequod*'s fate may have resonated, for nineteenth-century American readers, with predictions of the extinction of Native Americans who ostensibly refused to change their savage ways. Ahab, who "lived in the world, as the last of Grisly Bears lived in settled Missouri," is said to be a "wild Logan of the woods" (166). Figured as Logan, the Mingo warrior whom Thomas Jefferson positioned as the last of his line—although differently because he has not sated his thirst for vengeance, as Logan had done—Ahab becomes both an individual tending toward death and the avatar of a people tending toward extinction.[38] The Native American harpooner Tashtego goes down, as D. H. Lawrence observed nearly a century ago, with the "Red Indian bird" hammered to the *Pequod*'s main topmast.[39] The *Pequod* itself, "a noble craft but somehow a most melancholy" like Jefferson's Logan or any number of "vanishing Indian" figures, is said to be named after "a celebrated tribe of Massachusetts Indians, now extinct as the ancient Medes" (77). Melville adds an additional layer of determination, however. Ahab is figured deeper in time as a dinosaur—an animal that to the nineteenth-century popular imagination became extinct because it could not adapt—his peg leg leaving the *Pequod*'s deck "all over dented, like geological stones" (174).

Such allusions to extinction encourage the projection of individual mortality onto species mortality. Heightening this effect is the depiction of the

whaling industry itself as death-bound, especially in the "Try-Works" chapter. Earlier associated with Starbuck's prudent rationality, here the industrial ship, "laden with fire, and burning a corpse, and plunging into that blackness of darkness, seemed the material counterpart of her monomaniac commander's soul" (463). Affected by this underworldly experience, Ishmael feels that the *Pequod* "was not so much bound to any haven ahead as rushing from all havens astern. A stark, bewildering feeling of death came over me" (464). By the time he narrates the tale, Ishmael has recovered from these effects of "look[ing] too long in the face of the fire," recollecting that "to-morrow, in the natural sun, the skies will be bright; those who glared like devils in the forking flame, the morn will show in far other, at least gentler, relief" (464). Such was the naive American Captain Amasa Delano's response to the recollection of mortal danger onboard the *San Dominick* in a story that Melville would write four years later, "Benito Cereno." Delano prescribes a course of pastoral nature imagery to heal Don Benito's posttraumatic suffering. Don Benito rejects this prescription, for "the bright sun" and "the blue sky" "have no memory" because they "are not human." The mild trade winds, he says, "but waft me to my tomb."[40]

Following the "Try-Works" chapter, as the narrative approaches its conclusion, it addresses human mortality from another direction, engaging with reproductive futurity. This topic is interwoven with accounts of sightings of Moby Dick by the ships *Rachel* and *Delight*, who have lost men in encounters with Moby Dick. The captain of the *Rachel* begs Ahab to help him search for a lost whaleboat whose crew includes his twelve-year-old son. Ahab refuses, and the ship *Rachel* is left "weeping for her children, because they were not" (579).[41] The *Delight* is a floating hearse, fulfilling the first part of the harpooner Fedallah's prophecy regarding Ahab's death. Finally, the chapter just prior to the beginning of the *Pequod's* chase after Moby Dick opens on a revealing environmental meditation. While such meditations are characteristic of the novel's texture, this one particularly evokes possibilities of reproductive sexuality, pairing the "gentle thoughts of the feminine air" with the "murderous thinkings of the masculine sea" in a dialectic in which the apparent "contrast was only without"; within, "those two seemed one; it was only the sex, as it were, that distinguished them" (589). In this moment, in which "the stepmother world, so long cruel—forbidding—now threw affectionate arms round [Ahab's] stubborn neck," Ahab recalls his wife in Nantucket, whom he has hardly seen: "I widowed that poor girl when I married her" (590, 591). In this mood, Ahab begs Starbuck not to lower his boat in the hunt for Moby Dick: "I see my wife and child in thine eye" (591). Yet, as

Ahab articulates his sense of fate, in which he is compelled in the hunt "by some invisible power," reproductive futurity ceases to matter: "Toil we how we may, we all sleep at last on the field. . . . Aye, and rust amid greenness; as last year's scythes flung down, and left in the half-cut swaths" (592–93). Listening to Ahab's meditation on death, Starbuck "blanched to a corpse's hue with despair," recognizing his own removal from the reproductive narrative (593). He will go down with the rest of the *Pequod*'s crew, excepting Ishmael.

The sinking of the *Pequod* confirms the human vulnerability that is the source of Ahab's rage. Ishmael reports that "the great shroud of the sea rolled on as it rolled five thousand years ago" (624). The narrative ends on this apocalyptic image, the biblical flood, echoing the conclusion of Ishmael's reflections on extinction in chapter 105: "In Noah's flood [the whale] despised Noah's Ark; and if ever the world is to be again flooded, like the Netherlands, to kill off its rats, then the eternal whale will still survive, and rearing upon the topmost crest of the equatorial flood, spout his frothed defiance to the skies" (504). The whale spouts defiance where Ahab, finally, cannot. The whale displaces Ahab as the figure who rages against our human pain, our vulnerability, our mortality, and translates this rage into the fantasy of our eternal persistence.

This translation depends on Melville's oscillation between two chronological scales. Having used deep geological time in his natural history of the whale to index the whale's invulnerability—from the epoch of the Zeuglodon to the endless future beyond "all humane ages" (498)—Melville reverts in his concluding measure of "five thousand years" to the shallow, biblical time that had traditionally measured human history.[42] No rainbow appears to signal God's covenant as the *Pequod* sinks, but if one had appeared, it would have suggested to readers not a flood, but the millennial fire to come. Such a conflagration would destroy whales as well as humankind: "The elements shall melt with fervent heat, the earth also and the works that are therein shall be burned up" (2 Peter 3:10). Yet, as Polar Whale informs us, whales use their own chronology. Melville finds that the whale exceeds the scope of the biblical chronology which serves as a common reference point for human history. The undecidability of biblical versus geological chronologies in *Moby-Dick* thus differentiates humankind's fate from the whale kind's fate.

Melville undertook his investigations of the fate of the whale kind and humankind in an Anglophone world that explicitly entertained the possibility of human extinction even as it fantasized eternal persistence. The millennialist prophet William Miller's *Evidence from Scripture and History of the Second Coming of Christ, About the Year 1843* (1836) had attracted considerable attention in the United States and Great Britain, including commentary by Edgar

Allan Poe, Nathaniel Hawthorne, Ralph Waldo Emerson, James Fenimore Cooper, William Lloyd Garrison, John Greenleaf Whittier, Henry Wadsworth Longfellow, and Oliver Wendell Holmes.[43] The appearance of the brightest comet of the century in March 1843 seemed to lend credibility to Miller's prophecy. The image of a destroying comet had already been taken up by Poe in 1839 in "The Conversation of Eiros and Charmion," a speculative piece evidently written as a scientific reflection on Miller's *Evidence* that was later reprinted in *Tales of the Grotesque and Arabesque* (1840). Melville may have been especially intrigued, however, by the four Millerite tales in Hawthorne's *Mosses from an Old Manse* (1846), which he reviewed for the *Literary World* in 1850 while he was drafting *Moby-Dick*. Giving himself over to Hawthorne's "ravishments," Melville penned his famous descriptive phrase "the power of blackness" in response to one of these tales, "The Christmas Banquet."[44]

In his prophecy concerning the end of the world, Miller like other millennialists counted on human persistence in the form of the resurrected saints who would live with God in the "new heaven and new earth" as prophesied in Revelation 21:1.[45] Poe and Hawthorne use other narrative devices to imagine the extinction of human life as we know it but its persistence in consciousness nevertheless. Poe recounts "the final destruction of the earth . . . by the agency of fire" in a conversation between two souls in the space-time of the afterlife.[46] In Hawthorne's "The Hall of Fantasy," the narrator objects, on meeting Father Miller among the dreamers and speculators in the allegorical Hall, that "if the world should be burnt to-morrow morning, I am at a loss to know what purpose will have been accomplished." His companion attempts to reassure him that "man's disembodied spirit may recreate Time and the World for itself, . . . should there still be human yearnings amid life eternal and infinite."[47] In "The New Adam and Eve," Hawthorne asks us to imagine that "the Day of Doom has burst upon the globe, and swept away the whole race of men" but has left all human artifacts intact. Into this environment, which anticipates the scenario of Alan Weisman's bestselling *The World Without Us* (2007), "a new Adam and Eve have been created" and muse on the material remains of human culture.[48] In "Earth's Holocaust," Hawthorne imagines the destruction of all material culture but the persistence of "the human heart" with all its "shapes of wrong and misery."[49]

Melville was equally concerned to preserve human consciousness in the face of impending apocalypse. "And I only am escaped alone to tell thee" (Job 1:15) begins the epilogue (625). Within the novel's chase narrative, Ishmael serves this preserving function. Yet the outcome of the chase, as registered in chapter 42, "The Whiteness of the Whale," "stabs" him "with the thought

of annihilation." It "shadows forth the heartless voids and immensities of the universe" (212). That is, the encounter with the whale has inspired a powerful presentiment of extinction, which Melville counters by exploring the consciousness of the powerful annihilating agent. Melville thus imagines the extinction of humankind—not by fire but by flood, as if to anticipate global warming's rising sea levels—and the persistence of the whale kind. He displaces the violence emblemized by the whaling industry away from whales and onto humankind's fate while transcoding Ahab's defiance as the whale's defiance. Thus he projects humanlike consciousness into the deep, whale-kind chronology that, Ishmael says, will outlast humankind's fated time.

The Whale's Personhood

The voice of Polar Whale sounded anew in 1997, echoing issues of Native American sovereignty and survivance, when the Makah Nation petitioned the International Whaling Commission (IWC) to revive their ancient whaling tradition. Controversy regarding the Makah whale hunt engaged one of *Moby-Dick*'s primary topics, the question of whales' personhood. After the IWC granted a quota of five gray whales and the Makah announced their intention to plan a hunt, Earth Island Institute published an "Open Letter," signed by numerous NGOs and activists, opposing the hunt and giving this rationale: "The undersigned group respectfully appeal to the Makah Nation to refrain from the resumption of whaling. People from many cultures worldwide hold whales to be sacred and consider each species a *sovereign nation*, worthy of respect and protection."[50] The rhetoric of sovereignty took a slightly different inflection in the Chickasaw novelist Linda Hogan's arguments against the Makah whale hunt, which drew on interviews with some Makah women who opposed the hunt.[51] Hogan asserted that "in the traditional and historic past, we [Indigenous Americans] recognized the *sovereignty* of other species, animal and plant. We held *treaties* with the animals, treaties shaped by mutual respect and knowledge of the complex workings of the world."[52] (Such an agreement, as we will see in Chapter 4, provided terms for Great Plains peoples' relation to the buffalo.) Even so, Hogan argued, conditions had changed, bringing new considerations to bear on the Makah's ancient treaty with the gray whales, with consequences for their actions as specified in the 1855 Treaty of Neah Bay with the United States, which guarantees the Makah right to hunt whales. Hogan argued against the proposed hunt because the Makah no longer depended on whales for material subsistence:

"If the Makah are granted the right to whale by the International Whaling Commission, and they choose not to do it, it would truly make a statement about how strong a culture can be. It would be a statement that it will look to other means for the true and deep wellspring of a culture, of a people, one that holds to a reverence for life, a concern that the whale will continue into the future."[53] Hogan later took the hunt as material for her 2008 novel, *People of the Whale*, altering actual events and motivations in an effort to align the modern, Euro-American anti-whaling agenda with tribal tradition. The novel thus continues a theme that is present in Hogan's other novels, "conflicts between indigenous religious freedom and the Endangered Species Act."[54] In this case, for Hogan, the Endangered Species Act evidently took precedence. Yet, by the time the Makah proposed the hunt, the gray whale was no longer endangered.[55]

As the Makah tribal council and many others saw it, the question was not so much whale species' sovereignty—a term used in both Hogan's newspaper reportage and the Earth Island Institute's letter—as Indigenous nations' sovereignty. The Makah believed that they had taken whales' sovereignty into account by deciding to resume the ancient tradition, after a hiatus of seventy years, only when it became clear that a hunt would not endanger the conservation of the gray whale species. The decision and its effects, as documented by the Tseshaht Nuu-chah-nulth scholar Charlotte Coté, put the renewal of whaling at the center of cultural revitalization.[56] The difference between Coté's and Hogan's accounts of tradition turns on their assumptions regarding the endangerment of whales. For Hogan, a claim that the gray whale remains endangered provides a reason to eliminate whaling from Makah tradition. For Coté, a claim that gray whales can be hunted sustainably in small numbers, as indicated by their removal from the endangered species list, provides an opportunity for the renewal of the Makah's traditional relationship with whales and the revitalization of Makah culture.

The whaling history of the Makah, whose traditional home is the Olympic Peninsula, and the Nuu-chah-nulth, whose traditional home is on Vancouver Island's west coast, goes back millennia. The Treaty of Neah Bay guaranteed to the Makah "the right of taking fish and of whaling or sealing at usual and accustomed grounds and stations."[57] The state of Washington began to obstruct treaty rights soon after it attained statehood in 1889, in the case of salmon fishing targeting "accustomed grounds" that were outside the Makah Nation's geographical borders on land. United States law similarly refused to recognize individual villages' claims to particular offshore halibut banks, instead treating the ocean as a commons open to exploitation by all

(a position that will be examined further in Chapter 4) until a 1974 U.S. District Court case held that off-reservation marine resources were included in the 1855 treaty's guarantees.[58] The District Court decision continues to be a target of anti-treaty rights activism.

Whaling is more complicated than salmon or halibut fishing, partly because whales are more readily personified, as I will discuss below, and partly because whaling involves international agreements beyond the United States and Canada. These agreements posed additional challenges to the exercise of treaty rights. International regulation of whaling began with the establishment of the IWC in 1946 in response to the global decline of many species of whales from overhunting. The IWC's stated purpose was "to provide for the proper conservation of whale stocks and thus make possible the orderly development of the whaling industry."[59] The IWC membership voted to end commercial whaling entirely in 1982, allotting small quotas of whales to be taken only for scientific research and "aboriginal subsistence."[60] When the Makah themselves decided to end whaling in 1928, in view of the decline of gray whales resulting from non-Native commercial whaling, they intended to resume the tradition when the population permitted.[61] Meanwhile, they kept whaling traditions alive through place names, family names, stories, songs, dances, and plastic arts.[62] An important story tells of Thunderbird, the first whaler, who uses Lightning Serpent as a harpoon to kill whales and then carries them into the mountains to feast.[63] Another tells of how Thunderbird saved the people from starvation by bringing them a whale, thus instituting the practice of whaling.

When the Endangered Species Act was passed in 1973, the list of species included gray whales, which numbered 1,500 at that time. In 1994, when the gray whale population had rebounded to some 26,000, they were taken off the list and there was some speculation that the population had reached environmental carrying capacity. Since the Makah had intended to revive whaling all along, they were conceptually prepared. In 1995 they began to plan the hunt. The National Oceanic and Atmospheric Administration (NOAA) and the National Marine Fisheries Service (NMFS) found that the Makah plan to harvest a small number of whales would have no significant environmental impact.[64] The IWC moratorium was still in effect, however, and the Makah did not have a quota. Because the Makah had not taken a whale in seventy years, they apparently did not fit within the IWC's rules governing whaling, which excepted hunts by Aboriginal peoples only if they had a continuous tradition of whaling. In response to debate surrounding the U.S. proposal to grant the Makah a quota, however, the IWC amended its rules granting exceptions to Aboriginal peoples to read as follows: "The taking of

gray whales from the Eastern stock in the North Pacific is permitted, but only by aborigines or a Contracting Government on behalf of aborigines, and then only when the meat and products of such whales are to be used exclusively for local consumption by the aborigines whose traditional aboriginal subsistence *and cultural needs* have been recognised."[65] The IWC granted the Makah a quota of five gray whales after the Siberian Chukchi people traded with the Alaskan Inuits for part of their bowhead whale quota and ceded part of their quota of grays.[66] In 1999 the Makah killed one whale in a manner that updated whaling traditions: the crew prepared, fasted, and prayed in the traditional manner, but after the whale was harpooned, a specially modified rifle was used to ensure a humane kill and the whale was towed to shore with a motorized tug rather than by the whalers' cedar canoe. With requisite ceremony, the whale was divided among the people and some of it was saved for a potlatch to which they invited people from tribes across the United States and First Nations peoples from Canada.

Even before the 1999 hunt, a loose coalition of anti-treaty rights activists, animal rights activists, and the whale-watching tourist industry began to wage an ongoing legal campaign, first attacking the initial environmental assessment by the NMFS and NOAA and subsequently arguing that the 1972 Marine Mammal Protection Act's (MMPA) exemption of Alaska Natives did not extend to the Makah. The MMPA exempted Alaska Natives because they did not sign treaties with the United States; the act was thus a means of guaranteeing these people the right to take whales as they had always done.[67] The Makah, on the other hand, depended on rights guaranteed by the 1855 Treaty of Neah Bay, and particularly on the interpretation of the phrase "accustomed grounds," which they had always claimed included marine areas: halibut and salmon banks and whaling grounds. This argument regarding treaty grounds was not accepted by the Ninth Circuit Court of Appeals, which ruled in 2002 that the Makah could still apply for an exception to the MMPA, but only after an environmental impact statement was filed. In 2015 NOAA finally released the Draft Environmental Impact Statement (DEIS) prepared by the NMFS.[68] In the public comment meeting on the 2015 statement, anti-whaling activists adduced the usual arguments, including a claim that "since whales are no longer needed for Makah subsistence, allowing them to whale constitutes a 'cultural' exemption" from the MMPA, "setting a dangerous precedent that might be exploited by other groups."[69] The matter of the MMPA exemption remains in doubt.[70]

The cultural question is also the ground of ecofeminist objections to the Makah whale hunt, which are somewhat different from Hogan's objections. Both stand on the claim that the Makah whale hunt is no longer a

subsistence hunt, but some ecofeminists proscribe nonsubsistence hunting in general based on the position of "contextual moral vegetarianism."[71] Moreover, ecofeminists might observe—and here they would seem to agree with Hogan—that whaling was traditionally practiced not by all Makahs but only by elite men. As such, they might argue, support for the hunt advances support for traditional gender roles in Makah society at the expense of women and animals. As not all traditional cultural practices are worthy of preservation—for example, the Makah practice of slavery—analogously the tradition of whaling is not worthy of revival. Yet it might be argued that the latter critique ignores the distributive nature of the traditional Makah economy, in which whales are hunted by elite men and processed by women and the products distributed to all members of society—for example, through potlatches. Such a counterargument does not, however, fully address the question of "subsistence" versus "cultural" rationales for the revival of whaling.

The objection to a "cultural" as distinct from a "subsistence" exception to the MMPA (the kind of exception that, as we have seen, the IWC had granted in its 1998 revision to the rules governing international whaling) goes to the question of Indigenous sovereignty. As Vine Deloria Jr. puts it in a key essay, beyond political self-determination, "continuing cultural and communal integrity" is a key aspect of Indigenous sovereignty.[72] From the Makah perspective, "the intricate web of cultural practices, social relationships, and subsistence methods associated with their reserved right to whale are the guarantors of Makah cultural persistence."[73] The 2015 DEIS found that the resumption of whaling would have "beneficial impacts" in categories such as "Ceremonial and Subsistence Resources," "Traditional Knowledge and Activities," "Spiritual Connection to Whaling," and "Cultural Identity."[74] Coté thus concludes her account of the centrality of whaling to Makah revitalization by focusing on a little-recognized feature of cultural sovereignty, the capacity to maintain traditional foodways. She develops a critique of "culinary imperialism," that is, the Euro-American claim of power over what Indigenous peoples eat, as a key component of the project of Native American assimilation.[75] Implicitly, this critique might be directed toward the modern, Western position of contextual moral vegetarianism (although Coté does not explicitly address this point). Moreover, Coté argues, reintroducing whale products into the Makah diet is important for health, beyond the merely medical dimension. While several studies have shown the protective effects of marine mammal oil, rich in omega-3 fatty acids and other nutrients, in decreasing heart disease, diabetes, and arthritis symptoms, the revival of traditional foodways also has broad cultural, social, and spiritual significance.[76] Before the 1999

hunt, most living Makah had not tasted whale. After the hunt, they ate whale both at home and at a potlatch, a communal ceremony that persisted despite being outlawed in the nineteenth century by the Canadian government and strongly discouraged by Indian Affairs agents and missionaries in the United States. A Nuu-chah-nulth man invited to the potlatch noted its significance for his people's traditions as well: "I cannot thank the Makah people enough for allowing me to share in the 'Back to Tradition' feast. They have given me treasured memories and renewed pride in being a Nuu-chah-nulth person."[77]

Beyond the question of cultural endangerment versus survivance, other challenges to the Makah right to hunt whales would seem to proceed from different claims about the nature of whales. Even before the 1999 hunt was accomplished, the Makah faced opposition not only from anti-treaty rights activists (who use protest slogans such as "Save a whale, harpoon a Makah") but also from animal rights and save-the-whales activists who invest whales with special qualities not said to be at issue in activities such as salmon or halibut fishing.[78] Like Ahab, save-the-whales activists anthropomorphize whales, but their moral judgments differ from Ahab's—for example, they remark that gray whales "are well known for approaching humans in a curious and friendly manner."[79] Yet anthropomorphism per se is not the ground of disagreement, for Makah and Nuu-chah-nulth whaling culture also anthropomorphizes whales, as does Hogan in referring to sovereignty and treaties. As Coté explains, "The First Species Ceremonies of my people, for example, is a sacred event that affirms the 'personhood' of these animals and mammals and honors them for giving themselves to feed us."[80] Killing a whale thus evokes grief and remorse, even as it is a sacred act. As a crew member from the 1999 hunt put it, "You feel sad. . . . You have to. You've taken a pretty big life there." The crew also knew, however, that their ritual practice had been correct, rendering their spirits "so in tune" with the whales, that the whale's spirit agreed to come home with them.[81] Not to take the whale as he offered himself would have shown a lack of respect. The sense of the whale spirit's coming home, venerated in landing ceremonies, affirms the integration of whale belonging and human belonging in a tradition of ritually regulated practice.

The terms of the whale hunt in Hogan's novel *People of the Whale* are quite different from those observed of the actual hunt by Coté and other scholars. Whereas the latter describe the Makah as largely unified in their support for the whale hunt, Hogan describes their fictionalized counterpart, the A'atsika, as divided, with most women and a group of elders opposed and many men in favor, supported by the tribal council.[82] In Hogan's novel, the motivation for the whale hunt is not cultural revitalization but rather profit. The leader of

the whaling crew, a Vietnam veteran and small-time criminal named Dwight, has secretly arranged to sell the whale meat to Japanese businessmen. The fictional hunt takes place in 1988, before gray whales were removed from the endangered list. Hogan does not include any details regarding the MMPA, the IWC, or the permitting process, suggesting that this hunt is clearly illegal; even so, the federal government makes no effort to stop it, although plans have been widely publicized and have come to the attention of anti-whaling activists. Caught between tribal divisions are Thomas Just, another Vietnam veteran who decides to return home to the Dark River Reservation when he hears of the whale hunt, and his son Marco, who has been raised by his mother in his father's absence. Father and son are descended from a whaling lineage—Thomas's grandfather, Witka, was the last great A'atsika whaler—and Marco particularly shares his great grandfather's affinity for the sea. Marco leaves school to live with the elders, not so much in order to prepare specifically for whaling as to become a bearer of the traditional ways for the next generation. When he learns of the whale hunt, he agrees with the elders that "it was not the right time to hunt; the people were not prepared . . . but if the hunt was going to happen, his being there was the only thing he could do, no matter how knotted his heart."[83] Yet Marco "knew only a part of what led up to the decision to hunt, the politics, the dealings. . . . He couldn't stitch together the truths of divided worlds, double people, let alone the factions and jealousies within his own tribe" (79).

During the hunt, Marco is the only one of the crew who conducts himself traditionally—and for this he sacrifices his life. The rest of the crew do not purify themselves; they do not pray; they drink beer in the canoe. When they locate a whale, Marco tells them, "This is the wrong whale to kill," for it is too young and has merely approached the canoe in an inquisitive, "friendly" gesture (93). Dwight, angry at Marco's attempt to forestall the hunt, kills him and throws him overboard and the sea washes his body away, never to be found. In the confusion, Thomas does not see this and later assumes that Marco has been inadvertently injured and fallen overboard. With a semiautomatic military rifle in his hand (as contrasted with the specially modified hunting rifle the Makah used to ensure a humane kill), Thomas feels like he is back in Vietnam, and he fires many rounds, wounding the whale, even as he asks himself, "*Why?* Why am I doing this?" (93, italics in original). After the whale is towed ashore, the desecration of tradition continues: "The men cut it, laughing, talking about its sex organs, calling it names, all the love for the animal missing" (95). They even put a beer can in the blowhole. For Thomas, this is all too much. He perceives that the whalers "are like men at war" (95).

After the hunt, which takes place a third of the way into the narrative, he goes to live at his grandfather's shack, beginning a long healing process through which he will come to embrace traditional values as taught by the elders.

In the world of the novel, the hunt disrupts both cultural and natural orders. It exacerbates intratribal division and, as one of the elders predicts, "There's going to be a drought. A wrong thing was done. Maybe more than one wrong thing [i.e., the killing of Marco as well as the whale]. There will be a drought. . . . Get ready for it" (108). Fulfilling the prediction, the streams dry up and the ocean recedes from the American coast while a tsunami floods Asian coastal islands. The natural order is restored by a Rain Priest from the north, to whom Marco's mother must sacrifice her fishing boat. Division within the cultural order persists. Thomas decides to live with the elders, as Marco had done, to learn traditional ways, while Dwight and his crew plan another whale hunt.[84]

Hogan's account of the facts of the actual Makah whale hunt on which her novel was modeled differs from those given by others such as Coté, and this difference supports a differing stance toward tradition and renewal. In an interview, Hogan contended that "the men were whaling for a million dollars a whale for sushi in Japan," that the whalers used "submachine guns and automatic missiles," and that the Makah did not eat the harvested whale.[85] None of this was true of the Makah hunt.[86] Even so, Coté and Hogan share the same concern, the problem of maintaining tradition in the modern world, as focused particularly on human interaction with an anthropomorphized animal species. Hogan recognizes the intermingling of humans and whales in traditional Makah culture, as she paraphrases the song sung by the last great whale hunter, Thomas's grandfather Witka, and his wife, to entice migrating whales to come inshore and offer themselves to the hunt:

> Oh brother, sister whale . . . Grandmother whale, Grandfather whale. If you come here to land we have beautiful leaves and trees. We have warm places. We have babies to feed and we'll let your eyes gaze upon them. We will let your soul become a child again. We will pray it back into a body. It will enter our bodies. You will be part human. We'll be part whale. Within our bodies, you will dance in warm rooms, create light, make love. We will be strong in thought for you. We will welcome you. We will treat you well. Then one day I will join you. (22–23)

For Hogan, the time for this fleshly intermingling of whales with humans has passed. Tradition must change. For Coté, the persistence of tradition means

a respectful renewal of this fleshly intermingling, updated in certain modern ways such as a quicker, less painful method of killing the whale. Hogan similarly does not see tradition as being bound to the past, arguing that it is not a matter of language or dress but a matter of "how you behave within the world." The first step is "to decolonize your own mind and heart and soul, and then reeducate yourself into understanding what tradition is. Understanding and loving the earth." This means "living in a certain way where you do the least damage."[87]

Assuming that Coté shares this basic value of "do[ing] the least damage," she and Hogan are at odds as to how this value shapes practice. While Coté and Hogan would seem to have no disagreement regarding the harvest of salmon or halibut—both of which are anthropomorphized in traditional stories and possess the kind of sovereignty recognized by "treaties with the animals, treaties shaped by mutual respect and knowledge of the complex workings of the world"—they do disagree specifically regarding the harvest of whales.[88] If we do not attribute to Hogan the values motivating many modern, Western anti-whaling activists—that is, the belief that whales are more humanlike than salmon and thus more deserving of protection—the difference would turn on claims of endangerment. Perhaps oversimplifying, it seems that, for Hogan, whales are more endangered than traditional Makah culture is; whereas, for Coté, the reverse is true. Even so, while much of Hogan's *People of the Whale* supports the position of anti-whaling activists, it offers some faint possibility of reconciling pro- and anti-whaling positions—more possibility than Hogan would seem to offer in her nonfiction commentary. Thomas's decision to immerse himself in tradition, going to live with the elders after the debacle of the hunt, leads to a multisensory experience in which the ocean speaks to him. After fasting, purifying himself, and praying, Thomas enters the water as Witka did: "He hears the sounds of all the life in the water, the clicks and ticking, and for a while time changes. It seems he was there listening, hearing what almost amounted to words and now he no longer needs to breathe. He hears a low rumble . . . of a whale and it comes to him and looks at him with its wise old eye and he knows everything in that gaze. He knows how small a human is, not in size, but in other ways" (283). This visionary experience is meant to clarify for Thomas, and for us, the relationship between whales and humans going forward. Thomas sees himself now as the bearer of tradition and a vehicle of revitalization. He attempts to communicate that to the people: "[He] says, 'We are going to be better people. That is our job now. We are going to be good people. The ocean says we are not going to kill the whales *until some year when it may be right*. They are our mothers. They are our

grandmothers. It is our job to care for them.' Then he sings an old whale song he has never learned. He looks toward the ocean, and the song, it comes from him out of a hole opened in time. He sings it, a little embarrassed at first, then growing stronger in voice" (283–84, italics added). The ocean, as voiced by Hogan through Thomas, does not absolutely rule out hunting whales in the future. Meanwhile, however, it casts humans in a protective role, emphasizing the social nature of that role but now reversing the typical role of mothers and grandmothers as caretakers.

Thomas begins his revitalization project by training the whaling crew (the ones who sullied the first hunt) in the skill of paddling a cedar canoe. But on one of these practice voyages, Dwight kills Thomas as he had killed Marco. In the end, Dwight goes to prison. Thomas's ghost appears to his ex-wife and others before it is borne "to the old land where they hold to what is valuable" (289). Recounting Thomas's appearance, some say he was carried out to sea by the waves, some say by a whale, and "some just say the spirit world searches for us. It wants us to listen" (301). The relationship between humans and whales remains unresolved in the novel—as does the actual future of Makah whale hunting. For Hogan, the murder of Thomas is among the signs that any future "when it may be right" to hunt whales may never arrive. For Coté, who credits the science on endangered species as well as tribal tradition, that future is now.

*   *   *

For Lyell and many of his nineteenth-century colleagues, the extirpation of one species by another was a natural phenomenon separate from moral or religious questions.[89] That this stance did not satisfy Melville is evident not only in Ahab's and Ishmael's metaphysical inquiries but in the narrative's oscillation between biblical and geological time scales to measure and predict species' fates. Polar Whale's letter in the *Friend* presented the moral question as a matter of whales deserving rights ordinarily accorded to human beings, but helpless to protect those rights. That is, Polar Whale attempted to bring whales into the domain of politics as active participants, the *Friend*'s newspaper pages serving as his Latourian "speech prosthes[i]s."[90] Ishmael, exploring and blurring the human/animal boundary, in effect entertains Polar Whale's appeal. Even as he repeatedly characterizes the whale using humanlike qualities—such as volition, calculation, deliberation, retribution, and malice—Ishmael comes to believe that the inscrutable whale is another form of life. This other form of life cannot finally be rendered in terms of the human distinction between

the animal life of mere existence and (human) political life premised on communicability. Questions of the whale's malice, deliberation, mutual protection,
and other such qualities remain indeterminate, however much these qualities
invite human recognition. *Zoe* or mere animal life, as theorized by Giorgio
Agamben, "belonged to God as creaturely life" whereas *bios* or political life—a
key feature of Polar Whale's appeal for sovereign recognition—is instituted
through declarations of rights and other such communicative action.[91] From
Polar Whale's perspective, the *bios* or form of life proper to whales is similar to
human *bios* in that it includes the possibility of politics.

Ishmael's account of the whale, while alluding to political criteria, is
primarily grounded in moral concerns. If, as Lyell's account of extinction
suggested, there is no moral ground either for an interspecies ethic of protection, as Polar Whale would wish, or for Ahab's vengeful metaphysical
quest—"Sometimes I think there's naught beyond," he admits (178)—then,
as Ishmael interprets Ahab's quarter-deck speech, "with little external to constrain us, the innermost necessities of our being, these still drive us on" (179).
Locating the problem of extinction in the nature of species being, a question
that had also fascinated Edward Taylor and Cotton Mather (see Chapter 1),
Ishmael finds species responsible for their own fates. Yet, in so doing, he constructs a narrative in which whales belong to the world into the deep future
while humans do not.

Where Melville considers the question of belonging in a global and
abstract way, poising the ultimate fate of the whale kind against that of humankind, Indigenous Pacific coast whaling peoples such as the Makah consider
the question locally and politically. This is not only because they work through
institutional frameworks—including the tribal council, the U.S. judicial system, and the International Whaling Commission—but also because they too
affirm the personhood of whales. A similar sense of cross-species relations as
social interaction informs Great Plains Indigenous peoples' relation to buffalo, as we will see in the next chapter. As Hogan puts it, speaking generally
for a Native American account of the relations between humans and animals,
"In the traditional and historic past, we recognized the sovereignty of other
species, animal and plant. We had treaties with the animals shaped by mutual
respect and knowledge of the complex workings of the world, and these were
laws the [U.S.] legal system can't come close to."[92] Along with the profession
of nonhuman species' sovereignty, the arrangement necessarily allowed for
the harvest of some animals and plants for human consumption. A modern
treaty would have to regulate not only hunting, but also other more significant
environmental threats to the gray whale species' flourishing.[93] Coté and the

pro-whaling Makah see whales and humans as still bound by the traditional treaties that have always regulated species' (including humankind's) belonging, although now regulated additionally by scientifically informed agencies such as NOAA and the IWC, yet protected by intergovernmental agreements such as the Treaty of Neah Bay. Hogan, of course, does not advocate abrogating the Treaty of Neah Bay, but she does advocate making the guarantee of whaling rights in Article 4 of the treaty irrelevant by granting whales exceptional status. That is, she wants a new treaty between humans and animals. This new treaty would stand on the exceptionalism that structures the human/animal distinction, retaining salmon's and halibut's status as killable fish, but incorporating whales into the human exception.

CHAPTER 4

Buffalo Commons, Buffalo Nation

In the summer of 1869, the commanding general of the U.S. Army William Tecumseh Sherman proposed, "half in jest and half in earnest," a military campaign against the buffalo. "The quickest way to compel the Indians to settle down to civilized life," Sherman remarked, "was to send ten regiments of soldiers to the Plains, with orders to shoot buffaloes until they become too scarce to support the redskins."[1] Although the army was never in a position to undertake such an action (ten regiments amounted to a third of the entire army in 1869), unofficially it encouraged the extermination of the buffalo by aiding market hunters, allowing them to use army forts as depots to store and ship hides.[2] Some Indigenous accounts describe this market-hunting complex as "a war between the buffalo and the white men."[3] In a little over a decade, hunters brought the buffalo to the brink of extinction, with massive consequences for the people of the buffalo.

White activists who worked to preserve the bison from extinction during the late nineteenth century, such as Joel Asaph Allen, William T. Hornaday, and George Bird Grinnell, linked their fate to the "civilization" of Indigenous Great Plains peoples.[4] They blamed white market hunters and Plains peoples alike for wasteful hunting practices that decimated the bison. They also blamed the bison themselves: their supposedly "sluggish nature" and "intense stupidity" apparently prevented them from adapting to increased hunting pressure, as Melville had suggested whales had done.[5] Since bison were unable to save themselves, preservationists argued, humans would have to save them either physically through domestication or, as Hornaday would propose, virtually in museums. Plains peoples took a different approach to the buffalo's survivance, more along the lines indicated by Melville's and Indigenous whaling peoples' regard for the whale's personhood. They regarded buffalo as persons, a position which implies that the extermination of the buffalo was an act of genocide.[6] In the late nineteenth century, they responded through traditional story and

memoir to the preservationists' misunderstanding of their historical relation to the buffalo. By the late twentieth century, they materially restored human-buffalo interaction as a social relation through tribal buffalo projects.

Both the whites' and the Indigenous Americans' relations to the buffalo, like Nantucket and Makah whalers' relations to the whale, centered on violence—but with important differences in the ordering of that violence. The question for the persistence of whales, buffalo, and many other species remains: What kind of violence is sustainable?

Preservationism's Moral Narrative

Although the near extinction of the bison involved multiple causal factors—including drought, predation, disease, and changing land use patterns as well as market hunting—nineteenth-century preservationists focused largely on two factors, the actions of human hunters and the bison's nature in the light of evolutionary biology.[7] The first phase of preservationist writing—contemporary with the publication of Lyell's *Principles of Geology*, which as we have seen outlined an amoral logic of competitive extermination—linked the bison with Indigenous Great Plains peoples in a narrative of retreat in the face of civilization. George Catlin, who traveled the Plains from 1831 through 1837, assumed that the bison, "whose myriads were once spread over the whole country, from the Rocky Mountains to the Atlantic Ocean," had "fled, like the Indian, towards the 'setting sun;' until their bands have crowded together, and their limits confined to a narrow strip of country on this side of the Rocky Mountains."[8] Prevalent through the nineteenth century, this narrative of retreat linking the fate of the bison and Indigenous peoples oscillated between celebration and lament. Sometimes lament settled into the complacency registered in William Cullen Bryant's "The Prairies," a poetic meditation on the Illinois landscape in the early 1830s, depopulated of both bison and humans:[9]

> Thus change the forms of being. Thus arise
> Races of living things, glorious in strength,
> And perish, as the quickening breath of God
> Fills them, or is withdrawn. The red man too—
> Has left the blooming wilds he ranged so long,
> And, nearer to the Rocky Mountains, sought
> A wider hunting-ground.
> . . . .

    In these plains
The bison feeds no more. Twice twenty leagues
Beyond remotest smoke of hunter's camp,
Roams the majestic brute, in herds that shake
The earth with thundering steps.[10]

The narrative of retreat became fixed in the popular imagination—for example, through the wide distribution of John Gast's allegorical painting *American Progress*. Here, buffalo and Indigenous Plains peoples retreat before advancing settler-colonists led by the spirit of liberty, who carries a book and unfurls telegraph wire as she goes.

    Sometimes, however, writers targeted Native Americans as agents of the buffalo's disappearance, as Catlin did when he criticized the "profligate waste" of a May 1832 buffalo hunt near Fort Pierre in present-day South Dakota (256). Hunting during a season when the skins would not be good for robes and the fort was well furnished with fresh meat, a Sioux party had brought *"fourteen hundred fresh buffalo tongues"* to the fort to trade for whiskey,

Figure 2. George A. Crofutt, chromolithograph after John Gast,
American Progress (1872). Library of Congress Prints
and Photographs Division.

leaving the rest of the animals' remains on the plains to rot (256, italics in original). Catlin's account of this hunt became iconic and was cited by most activist writers, usually qualified with the observation that the waste by subsequent white hunters was just as bad if not worse.

While Catlin blames white traders and the consumers who demand the luxury of buffalo robes more than he blames the Indian hunters, he imagines both the material extinction of the bison and the cultural extinction of the Indians as inevitable:[11] "It is truly a melancholy contemplation for the traveller in this country, to anticipate the period which is not far distant, when the last of these noble animals, at the hands of white and red men, will fall victims to their cruel and improvident rapacity; leaving these beautiful green fields, a vast and idle waste, unstocked and unpeopled for ages to come, until the bones of the one and the traditions of the other will have vanished, and left scarce an intelligible trace behind" (256). Catlin will have none of Bryant's metaphysical rationalizing on the changing "forms of being," however. Rather, he recasts complacent assessments ironically, in a passage that is omitted in modern editions of Catlin's writings: "It may be that *power* is *right*, and *voracity* a *virtue*; and that these people, and these noble animals, are *righteously* doomed to an issue that *will* not be averted. It can easily be proved—we have a civilized science that can easily do it, or anything else that may be required to cover the iniquities of civilized man in catering for his unholy appetites" (260, italics in original).[12] The "voracity" of "civilized man," which Bryant had overlooked and Lyell had characterized as inherent in humankind's species being, Catlin evaluates according to the Christian criteria of vice and virtue.

In response, Catlin proposes a practical preservationist program for both buffalo and Plains peoples, which includes an educational component. He argues that capital from the fur trade ought to be "invested in machines for the manufacture of *woolen robes*, of equal and superior value and beauty" to buffalo robes in order to change consumers' behavior (263, italics in original). Freed from the pressure of overhunting, the buffalo could be returned to its historical role of supplying Plains peoples efficiently with the necessities and "all the luxuries of life which they desire" (262). This natural economy could, "by some great protecting policy of government," be "preserved in [its] pristine beauty and wildness, in a *magnificent park*, where the world could see for ages to come, the native Indian in his classic attire, galloping his wild horse, with sinewy bow, and shield and lance, amid the fleeting herds of elks and buffaloes. What a beautiful and thrilling specimen for America to preserve and hold up to the view of her refined citizens and the world, in future

ages! A *nation's Park*, containing man and beast, in all the wild and freshness of their nature's beauty!" (262, italics in original). Henry David Thoreau may have been thinking of this passage when, in *The Maine Woods*, he similarly proposed the designation of nature preserves "in which the bear and the panther, and even some of the hunter race, may still exist, and not be 'civilized off the face of the earth.'"[13]

Catlin's project in the *Letters and Notes on the Manners, Customs, and Condition of the North American Indian* is preservationist, oscillating between the assumption that Native Americans as a "race" are "rapidly passing away from the face of the earth" and the promotion of what he understood to be the remedy of cross-cultural understanding, for he became "fully convinced, from a long familiarity with these people, that the Indian's misfortune has consisted chiefly in our ignorance of their true native character and disposition, which has always held us at a distrustful distance from them; inducing us to look upon them in no other light than that of a hostile foe" (3, 9). The logic of this pedagogical program shapes Catlin's sometimes anthropomorphic treatment of the buffalo as well, from the "amusement" he finds in the "curious manoeuvres" of recently born calves to the valiant effort of an injured old bull in fighting off an attack by wolves (255). Chasing away the wolves, Catlin addresses the bull directly—"Now is your time, old fellow, and you had better be off"—remarking that "though blind and nearly destroyed, there seemed evidently to be a recognition of a friend in me, as he straightened up, and, trembling with excitement, dashed off at full speed" (258). Despite these humanizing efforts, however, Catlin's overall assessment of the buffalo's fate is not hopeful. As with his educational project regarding the Native Americans, he does not seem confident that his writings will alter the behavior of "their fellow-man, whose cupidity, it is feared, will fix no bounds on the Indian's earthly calamity, short of the grave" (10). Thus, while both Catlin and Lyell locate the problem of extinction with respect to Euro-American "civilization," Catlin does not posit civilization as the natural realization of humankind's species being as an extirpating force, as does Lyell, but rather as an exception to the natural primitive state. He offers the noble savage figure, economically bound to its animal partner the buffalo, as a sustainable counterexample to civilization's rapacity.

At the time Catlin wrote, market hunting was undertaken primarily by Native Americans during the winter months when the robes were prime—hence his outrage at the Sioux hunt of May 1832, which was conducted out of season. Seasonal market hunting at this level was probably sustainable in climate-favorable periods, according to a recent estimate, enhanced by lightly

hunted buffer zones between warring nations where game especially flourished.[14] A drought beginning in the mid-1840s, however, combined with disease, predation, and most importantly a change in hunting technologies and
practices threatened the extinction of the buffalo by the mid-1880s.[15] Traditionally, Plains peoples understood the buffalo as autochthonous, migrating
seasonally from underground where they originated. The buffalo were of the
earth and so could not become extinct, although populations could fluctuate, as
in the drought cycles that occurred during 5000–2500 BCE and 500–1300 CE.[16]
Indigenous stories of the scarcity of buffalo may preserve historical memories
of these drought cycles (as for example in the Blackfoot stories transcribed by
George Bird Grinnell that will be discussed later in this chapter). When this
worldview was confronted by the technologically more powerful market culture, the irreversible decline of the buffalo was inevitable.[17]

A key factor was the westward extension of the railroads following the
Civil War. New tanning processes and industrial expansion increased the
demand for hides, which sent hundreds of white hunters westward. Now val-
ued more for leather than for robes, the hides could be taken at any time of
the year. By 1872, when the Atchison, Topeka, and Santa Fe line established
a terminal near Fort Dodge, Kansas, three railroads through the middle of
the Plains effectively divided the buffalo into two large herds. Hide hunters soon reduced the southern herd to a scattered few in western Texas. The
northern herd, farther from transportation routes, was similarly reduced by
1883. Many who undertook the extermination were well aware of its consequences not only for the buffalo, but for the Indigenous peoples that the buffalo supported. The veteran hide hunter John Cook, for example, reflected on
a version of Lyell's logic of competitive extermination, collapsing Indigenous
Plains culture and the buffalo together as bound for extinction. Cook says
that as he went on a hunt, he sometimes asked himself,

> "What would you do . . . if you had been a child of this wonderfully
> prolific game region, your ancestors, back through countless ages,
> according to traditional history, having roamed these solitudes as free
> as the air they breathed? What would you do if some outside inter-
> loper should come in and start a ruthless slaughter upon the very soil
> you had grown from childhood upon, and that you believed you alone
> had all the rights by occupancy that could possibly be given one? Yes,
> what would you do?"
>
>   But there are two sides to the question. It is simply a case of sur-
> vival of the fittest. Too late to stop and moralize now.[18]

The decimation of the southern herd and threat to the northern herd by the mid-1870s invited a stronger, second wave of bison activism, beginning with the publication of Joel Asaph Allen's scientific monograph, *The American Bisons, Living and Extinct*, and his popular magazine articles, "The North American Bison and Its Extermination" and "The Extirpation of the Larger Indigenous Mammals of the United States." In *The American Bisons*, Allen undertook two projects. One was the taxonomic description and natural history of all species, extant (*Bison bison*, which he calls *Bison americanus*) and extinct (*Bison antiquus*, remains of which had been found at Big Bone Lick, and *Bison latifrons*). This project included an evolutionary narrative according to which significant morphological change could happen on a fairly short time scale. Allen's second project, a historical account of the geographical distribution of *Bison americanus*, included activist writing in favor of preservationist legislation. In his articles, Allen lobbied for the preservation of the remaining wild herds through protected lands, hunting seasons (linked to reproductive cycles rather than to quality of hides), and kill limits. He also proposed a complementary program of domestication. In the articles, he omitted the evolutionary narrative that had formed an important component of his book while more strongly emphasizing, as Catlin had done, the link between the bison and the Plains Native Americans. He linked the fate of the bison in turn to what he took to be key characteristics of its species being, notably the "sluggish nature" and "intense stupidity" that, he argued, made it an ideal candidate for domestication.[19]

In *The American Bisons*, Allen intervenes in the progress-of-civilization narrative that had informed earlier writing on the bison, according to which the bison and Native Americans had both retreated westward to become concentrated in great numbers on the Plains. Based on an extensive survey of primary literature from numerous locales east of the Mississippi, Allen argues that—as John Filson and other early observers had in fact documented—it was "more probable that [the bison] was *exterminated* rather than *driven out*" as European settlers encroached (117, italics in original). "The North American Bison" opens with this narrative, again to correct the causal narrative of both bison and Native Americans "alike fading away before the rapid advance of civilization—driven into the remoter wilds, as it is usually expressed, but, in reality, wiped out of existence"[20] The migration narrative proved to be tenacious, however, for while Allen refutes it in the case of *Bison americanus*, he retains it in his paleontological account of the lower Ohio River valley concerning the historical distribution of *Bison latifrons*. In effect giving scientific warrant to Bryant's poetic narrative in "The Prairies" of the replacement of

a more sophisticated Aboriginal culture by a lesser one, Allen hypothesizes that *Bison latifrons* coexisted in the early postglacial period with "mound-building peoples" (*American Bisons*, 235).[21] The latter were said to have been driven out by "ruder tribes" (235)—Bryant's "roaming hunter tribes." The latter peoples, Allen concluded, burned the woods to open up prairie environments in which *Bison latifrons* evolved into *Bison americanus*.

The rather short span of geological time in which Allen imagined the evolution of *Bison latifrons* into *Bison americanus* would seem to support the proposal in his magazine article for domestication as a complement to preservation. Here, he begins with a late eighteenth-century account by Albert Gallatin describing a mixed breed of bison and domestic cattle that was common in northwestern Virginia but "gradually became merged into the common domestic stock" of cattle as the bison were exterminated by hunters and could no longer "supply . . . the wild blood" necessary to continue the cross ("North American Bison," 222). He argues, however, not for a new cross-breed, but rather for the propagation of "an unmixed domestic race" of bison as both draft animal and meat animal: "Experience shows that even the first [domestic] generation are no more dangerous to handle than ordinary cattle" (222). If there was an implied analogy to the cultural domestication of Native Americans, however, Allen does not make it explicit in either the book or the article. Similarly, Allen's preservationist proposal that "certain portions of the public lands . . . be set aside as protected ground," unlike Catlin's and Thoreau's earlier proposals for reservations, does not include any provision for Native Americans (224).

Without such protection, Allen felt, the bison's "sluggish nature" doomed it to extinction (*American Bisons*, 67). The bison lacked the "sagacity that so effectually protects most wild animals" from human predation ("North American Bison," 219). Allen infers from the hide-hunter's technique of getting a "stand" that "the buffalo is endowed only with the smallest degree of instinct, and . . . this little seems rather to lead him into difficulties than out of them" ("North American Bison," 220). This view of the bison as maladapted persisted well into the twentieth century, as for example in a standard work by the eminent historian of the Great Plains Walter Prescott Webb. In Webb's view, "slow of gait, clumsy in movement," and having "relatively poor eyesight and little fear of sound," the bison "had few qualities save massive size and gregariousness, that fitted it to the Plains."[22]

Bison herds tend to follow a leader in moving from place to place, a large herd often following a single track. Successful hide-hunters, as Allen noted, developed the technique of identifying a group's leader and other more

dominant animals in order to shoot these animals first. Without leadership, the rest of the group would remain in place, "buffaloed," while the hunter shot them one by one, taking perhaps twenty or more animals before panic ensued.[23] This evolved trait of group leadership through general consent suggested to Allen a lack of emotion and even moral failing: "So indifferent are the buffaloes to the death of their companion, or so stupidly unconscious of what has befallen them, . . . they will not only stand and see them shot down around them, but the living have been known to playfully gore the dead, so little do they comprehend the situation" ("North American Bison," 220). Yet precisely these characteristics, which ostensibly marked the bison as among the least humanlike, least sentimental, and least sagacious of wild animals, made it the ideal subject for domestication according to Allen. More winter hardy and drought tolerant than domestic cattle, their "habits" were in other key respects "not far different" ("North American Bison," 220).

The next important preservationist writer, William T. Hornaday, presented an evolutionary narrative that is more complex than Allen's and added urgency to the ongoing moral discourse on the bison. In his book-length study, *The Extermination of the American Bison*, which was first published in the Smithsonian Institution's 1889 *Annual Report*, Hornaday splits the moral discourse into two narratives: in one narrative, bison act by means of their own extinction as avenging agents to punish Native Americans for wasteful hunting practices; in the other, bison become objects of the preserving agency of white American management. In a magazine article aimed at a popular audience, however, Hornaday reframes some of the Smithsonian report as a western adventure narrative and speaks less of environmental management than of personal emotional response. With its complex mix of guilt, lament, and pleasure, this article assembles in uncomfortable proximity emotions regarding the fact of extinction that are often separated and distributed.

In the Smithsonian report, Hornaday like Allen assumes a short evolutionary time scale. He similarly posits the innate stupidity of the bison but argues that through natural selection the few wild animals remaining are the swiftest and most cunning and that domestication would make them fat and sluggish and induce other bodily changes. Hornaday's sense of evolution is more teleological than Allen's in that he presents the bison as evolutionarily incomplete. Anticipating the concept of stabilizing selection, Hornaday contends that different subgroups were on their way toward fine-tuned adaptation to different environmental niches until modern humans intervened in the evolutionary process.[24] Bison had begun to adapt to predation from Native Americans deploying Paleolithic technologies (spears, arrows, buffalo jumps or traps),

but could not adapt to predation from (mostly white) hunters using firearms, despite the short time frame that Hornaday, like Allen, allows for evolutionary change.[25] "Had the bison remained for a few more centuries in undisturbed possession of his range," Hornaday argues, "it is almost certain that several distinctly recognizable varieties would have been produced."[26] Northern bison, for example, would have developed longer, denser hair similar to that of the musk ox. The "wood" or "mountain buffalo," a variety also noticed in Allen's and earlier explorers' accounts, seemed to provide a "distinct foreshadowing" of this evolutionary patterning, developing shorter manes, darker pelage, and "a degree of agility and strength unknown in his relative of the plain" (377, 409).

Like Allen, Hornaday gives an account of behavior that implies moral evaluation. The bison's "dullness of intellect was one of the important factors in his phenomenally swift extermination," Hornaday writes with a note of irritation: "He was provokingly slow in comprehending the existence and nature of dangers that threatened his life and, like the stupid brute that he was, would very often stand quietly and see two or three score, or even a hundred, of his relatives and companions shot down before his eyes, with no other feeling than one of stupid wonder and curiosity" (429–30). If Hornaday does not go so far as Allen to depict a bison "playfully gor[ing] the dead" while the herd is under attack, nevertheless he faults their lack of intelligence. He concludes that "the buffalo owes his extermination very largely to his own unparalleled stupidity" (465). However, he believes that hunting pressure, operating as a form of natural selection, has produced superior animals "who now represent the survival of the fittest" because they "have learned better wisdom" in becoming wary and elusive (431). These survivors have reached an evolutionary pinnacle, Hornaday opines, being "mentally as capable of taking care of themselves as any animals I ever hunted" (431). He characterizes this greater wariness and elusiveness as the disappearance of the herd instinct and the development of individualism: "When the herds were totally broken up, when the few survivors were scattered in every direction" because of intense hunting pressure, "it became a case of every buffalo for himself" (466). Species change resulting from selection pressure had moral implications, as the rugged individualist bison evolved to become an even match for the rugged individualist white hunter.

Another preservationist writing at the same time, George Bird Grinnell, emphasized morphological rather than behavioral response to hunting pressure, again within a very short evolutionary time scale.[27] In an essay for a popular audience published in *Scribner's Magazine* in 1892, Grinnell argued that within the past twenty years, the typical bison had become "a long-legged,

light-bodied beast, formed for running," thus "very different in appearance" as well as in "habits" from just a few generations prior.[28] Grinnell's account of the bison's vulnerability to hunters was more complex than Hornaday's or Allen's, naming different characteristics during different historical eras based on accounts from numerous Indigenous informants. Before the Plains peoples had horses, Grinnell reports, the bison's natural "curiosity" compelled a herd to follow a "caller" who possessed a powerful talisman and who "endeavored to attract their attention by moving about, wheeling round and round, alternately appearing and disappearing." Wanting "to discover what this strange creature might be," the herd followed the caller into a trap devised from a cut bank on one side and rocks, logs, and brush on the other (279). Here, they could easily be killed. When discussing hunting practices during the modern era, however, Grinnell like Hornaday and Allen emphasizes the bison's "lack of intelligence": "sluggish, . . . mild, inoffensive, and dull," bison were "slow to learn by experience." When "at last they learned" what threat was posed by hunters armed with rifles, it was too late (271).

Hornaday's observations of bison in captivity supplement his claims regarding selection pressure on wild animals. "Confinement and semi-domestication," Hornaday argues, "are destined to effect striking changes in the form of *Bison americanus*" (394–95)—whereas Grinnell, by contrast, emphasizes the potential for improving range cattle through cross-breeding (274–76). To Hornaday, bison confined in New York's Central Park Zoo and the National Museum's collection of live animals in Washington, DC, seem "almost like another species" compared to their wild counterparts—for example, exhibiting "shortness of body and lack of muscle" (395). Hornaday claims to have observed other morphological changes as well that could not so easily be attributed to mere diet and exercise. He focuses on the eye, a feature that bears implications for soul as well as body: "In no feature is the change from natural conditions to captivity more easily noticeable than in the eye. In the wild buffalo, the eye is always deeply set, well protected by the edge of a bony orbit, and perfect in form and expression. The lids are firmly drawn around the ball, the opening is so small that the white portion of the eyeball is entirely covered, and the whole form and appearance of the organ is as shapely and pleasing in expression as the eye of a deer" (395). In many of the captive animals, by contrast, "various muscles which support and control the eyeball seem to relax and thicken, and the ball protrudes far beyond its normal plane, showing a circle of white all around the iris, and bulging out in a most unnatural way" (395). Although the eye is the proverbial window to the soul, Hornaday does not explicitly consider the resemblance of these captive bison's eyes, with an

unusual amount of white surrounding the iris, to the expression of fear in many large mammals. The animals might be perpetually frightened. Yet, otherwise, he posits a Lamarckian sense of the inheritance of acquired traits—for example, speculating that the tendency of captive animals to "'hump up' the back" in an attitude of "dejection and misery . . . will eventually become a permanent habit" (396).

If hunting pressure produced wily, individualist, aesthetically pleasing bison who were nonetheless doomed to extinction given the pressures of hunting and habitat loss, whereas captivity produced small, sluggish, deformed, and dejected animals, then specimens of animals perfect in body and soul had to be preserved immediately for scientific and aesthetic reasons. The logic was similar to the program of salvage ethnography often identified with Franz Boas and Edward Curtis, which attempted during the same era to document authentic Native American cultures in the face of their supposed inevitable disappearance. Thus in 1886 the Smithsonian Institution sponsored a hunting expedition led by Hornaday to collect such specimens from the small herd that remained in eastern Montana. Hornaday's account of the expedition and his description of the resulting Buffalo Group of six stuffed carcasses that he prepared for display in the National Museum forms the conclusion of *The Extermination of the American Bison*.

Hornaday also packaged an account of the expedition as a two-part hunting narrative for a popular audience, published in *Cosmopolitan Magazine* in 1887. While the magazine narrative provides some of his book's documentary detail and evolutionary speculation, its baseline mode of western humor and adventure incorporates diverse and sometimes incongruous responses to the phenomenon of extinction. Some of the narrative interest comes from good-natured competition among hunters and much of the humor celebrates outdoorsmen's endurance, as when a camp's water hole dries up to become "so thick with mud and filth that we could drink it no longer, but had to take it in slices, in the manner of ice-cream."[29] But the article opens with a sarcastic tone, noting that the Montana legislature has "just rushed through a bill" to regulate the hunting of bison, a bill that is "only ten years behind its time!"[30] They might as well, Hornaday goes on to remark, regulate the hunting of mastodons and prohibit the interstate shipping of mastodon carcasses. Thus suggesting by analogy that the bison is already extinct, Hornaday can the more easily make his ironic confession: "We have been guilty of killing buffalo in the year of our Lord 1886"—guilty of killing but not of murdering, as he goes on to clarify (85). Hornaday killed the buffalo in order to save them from being "killed

Figure 3. Life Group of American Buffaloes in the Mammals Exhibit in the
United States National Museum, assembled by William T. Hornaday (1887).
Smithsonian Institution Archives, negative no. MNH-4323.

by the care-for-naught cowboys, who would leave them to decay, body and
soul, where they fell" (85, italics added). Hornaday's innocence of the charge of
"murder," the exonerating factor that differentiates his buffalo hunt from the
"cowboy's" buffalo hunt, is that he will make good "earthly use" of the "magnificent skin" and "beautiful head" (85). In so doing he will attempt to atone for
humankind's crime of exterminating the species. Hornaday carries his readers
along within familiar terms of romantic nature discourse: "Perhaps you think
a wild animal has no soul; but let me tell you it has" (85). Yet his next sentence
takes a surprisingly materialist turn: "Its skin is its soul, and when mounted by
skillful hands, it becomes comparatively immortal" (85). The fantasy is not so
much the transcendence of the body, as Donna Haraway has famously argued
of taxidermy displays presented in natural history museums, but rather the
immanence of the soul.[31] For Hornaday, who would go on to write an inno-
vative and influential manual on taxidermy, such "production of depth" was
accomplished by the artful "reproduction of the surface."[32]

After an engaging hunting narrative in which the reader might easily lose sight of the paradox of killing the last of a species in order to preserve it, Hornaday concludes by reinstating the essay's opening moral register in order to reassess the verdict. He tells the story of killing the largest bull the expedition had encountered—the very animal that would feature centrally in the mounted Buffalo Group that Hornaday prepared for the National Museum and would later take on iconic status as the model for the buffalo nickel.[33] Having wounded the bull and chased it until it faltered, Hornaday drew close to the "grandest quadruped [he had] ever beheld" and realized that "until this moment [he had] never had an adequate conception of the great American bison" (241). Contributing to the iconographic discourse that was emerging at the time, Hornaday compares this animal to "Bartholdi's statue of liberty," similarly "built on a grand scale" (242). Not content to take a "mental photograph" of the wounded animal before killing him, Hornaday takes out his field notebook and pencil and makes "a sketch from life with a vengeance" that would later serve as a guide for taxidermy (242). In this extended aesthetic response, Hornaday procrastinates what he knows he must do, kill the wounded animal (meanwhile prolonging the animal's suffering). Here, then, he reassesses the verdict rendered in the essay's opening page, grandly mapping that verdict onto the fate of the bison as a species and onto humankind's implication in that fate: "I had the great beast completely in my power, and I was obliged to be his executioner. He seemed to me like the very last one of his race, that he knew it as well as I, and he also was doomed. People will say this is all put on for effect, but I swear *I felt as if I was about to commit a murder*. With the greatest reluctance I ever felt about taking the life of an animal, I shot the noble beast through the lungs, and he fell down and died. . . . It seemed to me that I never saw an animal die harder" (242, italics added). The scene is a familiar one in literary hunting narratives: the moment, usually soon swept aside, of encounter with the animal-as-human, the claim of mutual recognition. Such an anthropomorphic moment is less emphatic in Washington Irving's *Tour on the Prairies*, a hunting narrative written prior to any recognition that the bison might be endangered: "Now that the excitement was over, I could not but look with commiseration upon the poor animal that lay struggling and bleeding at my feet. His very size and importance, which had before inspired me with eagerness, now increased my compunction. It seemed as if I had inflicted pain in proportion to the bulk of my victim, and as if there were a hundred-fold greater waste of life than there would have been in the destruction of an animal of inferior size."[34] Hornaday, however, narrates not only the killing of an animal but by synecdoche the killing of a species, and

this recognition foregrounds the questions of sovereignty and agency. With the animal's "last breath," Hornaday "exclaim[s] fervently: 'Thank Heaven! it's over, at last'" (242). The invocation to Heaven invites readers to hear an echo of Christ's last words on the cross, "It is finished" (John 19:30). This echo may contain Hornaday's plea, not merely for his own exoneration as an individual for killing this animal—whose soul would attain a measure of immortality in the Buffalo Group via the creative act of taxidermy—but for humankind's exoneration as a species burdened with the sin, perhaps the original sin, of exterminating another species.

Charles Lyell's means of exoneration, as we have seen, was to attempt to bypass such moral accounting entirely in an appeal to the nature of humankind's species being—which in this respect, he argued, was the same as every other species' being: amorally competitive. Hornaday, by contrast, admits guilt and in response develops a moral narrative that is bifurcated along racial lines. In this narrative, whites and Native Americans share the guilt of exterminating the bison but only whites have the capacity to atone. Hornaday contends that observers of both races predicted the "final extermination of the buffalo" some "forty years" ago, at the time when Catlin was writing (*Extermination of the American Bison*, 480). He claims that even with this foreknowledge, "the Indian tribes were not moved by a common impulse to kill sparingly" and exercise "reasonable economy"; rather they "killed wastefully, wantonly, and always about five times as many head as were necessary" (480). As a result, Hornaday reports with "grim satisfaction," now "many of the ex-slaughterers are almost starving for the millions of pounds of fat and juicy buffalo meat they wasted a few years ago. Verily, the buffalo is in a great measure avenged already" (480–81). This theme is evident in an 1883 painting by John Dare Howland, *A Western Jury*, which depicts a Plains Native American lying dead on the ground, surrounded by several intently staring bison.

Hornaday picks up this theme of "the buffalo [as] his own avenger" against these "remorseless slayers" as he introduces his proposal for the preservation of the species from complete extinction (527). Notwithstanding the unfavorable morphological changes that he had earlier suggested were brought on by captivity, Hornaday argues that the very small herd in the National Zoological Park in the District of Columbia ought to be supplemented as soon as possible through the capture of as many wild animals as possible, so as to prevent inbreeding. Such a program would "preserve fine living representatives" of the species "for centuries to come." In this way, Hornaday writes, "we might, in a small measure, *atone* for our neglect of the means which would have protected the great herds from extinction" (528, italics added).

Figure 4. John Dare Howland, *A Western Jury* (1883).
Autry Museum, Los Angeles; 88.108.32.

Hornaday's personal means of atonement was to save the skin-as-soul of the buffalo in the Buffalo Group exhibit that he prepared for the National Museum, the institution that later became the Smithsonian Museum of Natural History.[35] Six type specimens showing the animal's growth and development—male calf, male yearling, spike bull, adult bull, young cow, and adult cow—were "mounted with natural surroundings, and displayed in a superb [glass and] mahogany case," (546). Here, as a reporter for the Washington *Star* put it, the animals gained "immortality" (quoted on 547). The group was disassembled in 1955 but reassembled in 1996 at the Museum of the Northern Great Plains in Fort Benton, Montana.[36] Although it is displayed today as a historical artifact, in 1887 the Buffalo Group evoked authentic presence, according to the *Star*'s report: "It is as though a little group of buffalo that have come to drink at a pool had suddenly been struck motionless by some magic spell" (546). An engraved illustration for Hornaday's 1887 *Cosmopolitan* article completes the illusion by placing the same group in an expanded scene with the Montana mountains in the background, presenting the animals as if they are living in their natural habitat, thus representationally atoning for the guilt that Hornaday had confessed in the article's opening.

A year after Hornaday debuted the Buffalo Group, Albert Bierstadt com-
pleted his grand quasihistorical fantasy, *The Last of the Buffalo*. Here, on a
canvas measuring nearly six by ten feet, Bierstadt took up Hornaday's moral
narrative according to which bison avenged themselves on the Indigenous
peoples who had wastefully overhunted them. The painting's central action
depicts a horse and hunter, armed not with a rifle but the traditional lance,
locked in a death struggle with a powerful bull—the hunter trying to spear
the bull as the bull gores the hunter's horse and possibly his right leg. This
action links two horizontally cascaded temporalities. The middle third of the
canvas, depicting an endless herd filling a great valley, pulls the central hunter
and his cohort (less prominent at the middle right of the canvas) toward a
timeless past. Bierstadt's use of light, however, brings the hunter forward to
the present of the late nineteenth century, signified by the litter of skulls and
bones in the left foreground and by a dying animal in the center foreground
that looks accusingly at the viewer. This look, in conjunction with the painting's title, implicates the viewer in the carnage while the action—undertaken
by Indians wielding lances, bows, and clubs—shapes this implication as a
failure to stop the Indians from killing buffalo. The actual historical agents
of the buffalo's extirpation—rifle-bearing white market hunters and the
industrial apparatus they served—are nowhere to be seen. The buffalo are
shown to have taken some measure of vengeance by killing one of the Indian

Figure 5. Albert Bierstadt, *The Last of the Buffalo* (1888).
National Gallery of Art, Corcoran Collection
(Gift of Mary Stewart Bierstadt [Mrs. Albert Bierstadt]).

hunters, who lies face down with his horse behind a young bull whose horns are covered with blood. An article in the *New York Times* affirmed the painting's "truth" when it reported on the painting's reception in Paris. When the painting was rejected by the New York Union League Art Club for the American section of the 1889 Exposition Universelle in Paris, Bierstadt exhibited it instead through the Paris Salon.[37] The *Times* reported that it was frequently visited at a Paris gallery by Lakota members of Buffalo Bill's Wild West show, which performed in Paris in 1889. The Lakota Rocky Bear was particularly said to have praised Bierstadt for "giving breath and life to the glorious past of the redskin and to the buffalo, when the Indian was master of all he could survey." Inserting Rocky Bear into the painting's fictional temporalities by granting "the Indian" retrospective possession—making him oddly Crusoe-like with an allusion to William Cowper's poem on Alexander Selkirk—the *Times* attested to his "recognition of the truth of the scene" and his sensitivity to "its sentiment and poetry."[38]

From Buffalo Commons to Buffalo Nation

Despite the *Times*' handling of Rocky Bear's response to *The Last of the Buffalo*, Plains peoples themselves would have none of Hornaday's and Bierstadt's moral narratives of wasteful Indigenous hunting practices and justly inflicted vengeance. The Oglala Lakota holy man Black Elk, for example, unequivocally blamed the demise of the buffalo on the Wasichus or "fat-takers"—a name for Euro-Americans that Black Elk's amanuensis John Neihardt left untranslated in the main text of *Black Elk Speaks* and which bears literal significance in reference to the buffalo as food. Black Elk recalled that, in 1883, "the last of the bison herds was slaughtered by the Wasichus. . . . The Wasichus did not kill them to eat; they killed them for the metal that makes them crazy, and they took only the hides to sell. Sometimes they did not even take the hides, only the tongues; and I have heard the fire-boats came down the Missouri River loaded with dried bison tongues. You can see that the men who did this were crazy. Sometimes they did not even take the tongues; they just killed and killed because they liked to do that."[39] This account of extermination introduces a grim chapter in Black Elk's life, when he despaired of fulfilling his great vision, gave up curing the sick, and joined Buffalo Bill's Wild West show.[40] As one of Buffalo Bill's performers, Black Elk enacted for white Americans and Europeans the nostalgic adventure-fantasy of hunting the buffalo from horseback, a fantasy typically featured in preservationist

writing oriented toward a popular audience such as Hornaday's article for *Cosmopolitan* or Grinnell's article for *Scribner's*.

The impending extermination of the buffalo was central to Black Elk's great vision, a vision that he admitted he did not fully understand at the time, with tragic consequences. When Black Elk was nine years old—in 1871, when buffalo were still relatively plentiful on the Northern Great Plains—he had been given a vision of the future, when "the nation's hoop was broken like a ring of smoke that spreads and scatters" and the people are starving (38). Weeping with the force of this revelation, the young Black Elk saw that "there stood on the north side of the starving camp a sacred man who was painted red all over his body, and held a spear as he walked into the center of the people, and he lay down and rolled. And when he got up, it was a fat bison standing there, and where the bison stood a sacred herb sprang up right where the tree had been in the center of the nation's hoop" (38). Black Elk says that only later—after his stint as a performer in the Wild West show, after his Ghost Dance vision, after the massacre at Wounded Knee—did he come to realize "what this meant, that the bison were the gift of a good spirit, and were our strength, but we should lose them, and from the same good spirit we must find another strength" (39). This strength is indicated by the herb, which grows and blooms and "suddenly the flowering tree was there again at the center of the nation's hoop where the four-rayed herb had blossomed" (39). Unlike Allen or Hornaday, then, Black Elk sees nothing inherent in the buffalo themselves that led to their demise. The narrative pits gifts of the "good spirit" against the Wasichus' greed and craziness.

A subtler turn on Hornaday's racially bifurcated moral narrative is evident in some traditional Blackfoot narratives that were transcribed by Grinnell and published in 1892 as *Blackfoot Lodge Tales*. Some of these stories comment particularly on the claim, voiced by Hornaday and no doubt common among whites in the west, that the bison was "his own avenger" against the "remorseless [Indian] slayers" with their wasteful hunting practices.[41] Grinnell reports that he heard these stories during annual visits that had begun in 1888 when he acted as an ombudsman for the Blackfeet, working to resolve complaints they had against the U.S. government.[42] It is likely that the Blackfeet would have seen him as a favorably disposed listener who was well prepared to hear their accounts of the old days before the arrival of horses and white men, as inflected through their present-day experience of hardship and deprivation. Particularly in this context, the stories' themes of greed, deception, starvation, and vengeance provide a moral counter-discourse to Hornaday's narrative of the buffalo's vengeance-through-extinction and to other white narratives

that had circulated since Catlin's time depicting Native Americans as wasteful hunters. The archaeological record in fact suggests that the rate of "waste" at kill sites varied, likely according to season, perceived need, distance to camp, and so on.[43] In different cases, hunters may have butchered heavily, taking almost all parts of the animal for various uses, or they may have butchered lightly, taking only humps and tongues. They were sometimes motivated to kill in large numbers because they did not want any buffalo to escape from a hunt to warn other buffalo. Nineteenth-century Native American accounts of old-time hunting, however, tended to omit mention of such ostensibly wasteful practices.[44] Grinnell's Blackfoot informants, for example, indicated that market forces and white technology introduced a cultural change, saying that "when bows and arrows, and, later, muzzle-loading 'fukes' were the only weapons, no more buffalo were killed than could actually be utilized" (235).

Blackfoot retellings of traditional stories in the late nineteenth century context thus frame the question of waste not within the Euro-American context of sustainability—the context of the so-called "ecological Indian"—but rather within the Indigenous economic context of access and distribution.[45] In the first of these stories, which Grinnell titles "The Blackfoot Genesis," the relation between humans and buffalo is central to the creation and ordering of the Plains world, as accomplished by Na'pi or Old Man.[46] As Na'pi goes about creating the animals, birds, and plants, shaping the land, and showing the first people "how to get a living," he finds that the people were having difficulty because the buffalo possessed weapons (their horns and hooves) but the people did not (139). In one instance, "as the people were moving about, the buffalo saw them, and ran after them, and hooked them, and killed and ate them." Na'pi reflects: "This will not do. I will change this. The people shall eat the buffalo" (140). Having thus established the world's proper moral order, he demonstrates hunting techniques to various groups of people, such as how to build a pis'kun or buffalo trap and how to call the buffalo and lead them into it, an operation that is later made easier through the discovery of the power of I-nis'-kim, the buffalo stone (which Grinnell glosses as small ammonite fossils, 126). In Pawnee stories transcribed during the same era, the buffalo themselves, often guided by their master, Old Buffalo, are more active agents than in Grinnell's Blackfoot stories. The buffalo agree to be eaten after a race, a game, or a trial by combat between buffalo and humans.[47] Even so, as in the Blackfoot tales, these decisions made in ancient times established the current order of being. They function, in effect, as treaties between buffalo and humans.

In Blackfoot stories from the old days when they had no horses, the buffalo do sometimes disappear. Often, the disappearance is linked to human or humanlike greed, selfishness, or cruelty. In one instance, Na'pi discovers that Raven "has hidden all the buffalo and deer from the people" and punishes him by tying him over the smoke hole of a lodge (145). Another story from the time before horses, "Adventures of Bull Turns Round," links the question of just vengeance with the plenitude of buffalo. Wolf Tail's wife asks Wolf Tail's younger brother, Bull Turns Round, to kill "a beautiful strange bird" for her (24). Bull Turns Round kills the bird then leaves on a hunting trip. When the wife strokes her face with the bird, her face swells. The wife tells Wolf Tail, however, that "your younger brother has pounded me so that I cannot see" (24). When Bull Turns Round returns, Wolf Tail invites him on an eagle hunt and then pushes him over a cliff into a river, apparently killing him. However, an old man of the Under Water People saves Bull Turns Round. Although the old man has a great herd of buffalo, the Under Water People only eat leeches until Bull Turns Round marries one of the daughters and shows them how to cook and eat buffalo—a repetition of the motif from other stories in which Na'pi shows the people "how to get a living" (139). Here, the old man can resurrect the buffalo that have been eaten, as long as none of their bones have been broken. When Bull Turns Round wants to visit his father, the old man gives him a herd of buffalo and a means of punishing Wolf Tail and his wife. On returning home, Bull Turns Round discovers that "the people were starving, and some had died, for they had no buffalo" (27). The link between Wolf Tail's wife's deceit, Wolf Tail's crime of misguided revenge, and the disappearance of the buffalo is implicit, but clear. Bull Turns Round throws a bit of sinew given him by the old man into the fire, so that Wolf Tail and his wife "twisted up and died" like the sinew shriveling in the flames. Evildoers thus vanquished, Bull Turns Round points out the herd he has brought and says to the people, "There is food, go chase it" (28). The story associates injustice with the disappearance of the buffalo and the restoration of the social order through just vengeance with the presence of the buffalo.

The story of Kŭt-o'-yis, Clot of Blood, also set in the old days before horses, suggests an allegory pertinent to the late nineteenth-century context concerning relations among Plains peoples, white hunters and traders, and buffalo. This is a significant variant of an origin story common to other Plains nations, in which humankind arises from a clot of buffalo blood.[48] The Blackfoot story as told to Grinnell takes place well after the time of origins. An old man gives his son-in-law all his wealth, keeping only a small lodge for

himself and his aging wife. At first, the son-in-law treats them well, but then he begins to hoard the buffalo, which he has been keeping "hidden under a big log jam in the river" (29). The son-in-law makes the old man help him hunt the buffalo, "never killing wastefully," but often keeps all the meat for himself (29). If not for the resourcefulness of a younger daughter, who sometimes steals a bit of meat, the old man and his wife would starve. One time the old man manages to grab a clot of blood from the butchering, unbeknownst to the son-in-law. When his wife cooks this clot, it turns into a child, whom they name Kŭt-o'-yis. The child soon grows up, kills the mean son-in-law and daughter, and gives the old man access to the buffalo. After that, Kŭt-o'-yis journeys around the country, dispensing justice in a similar manner. In one camp he finds that the chief, a great bear, has been keeping all the fat meat for himself and letting the people have only a little lean meat. Kŭt-o'-yis kills the bear chief, gives the people access to all the buffalo meat and fat they need, and then journeys to another camp where the scenario is repeated with its chief, this time a snake. All told, Kŭt-o'-yis kills seven "bad animals and people" in this way (38), including two cannibals, Ai-sin'-o-ko-ki (Wind Sucker) and an unnamed "man-eater" (37). He resurrects some of the people that Wind Sucker has eaten by climbing into his gullet. Leading them in "the ghost dance" and singing "the ghost song," Kŭt-o'-yis kills Wind Sucker and leads the people out (36). Like other stories in which humankind originates from a clot of buffalo blood, this Blackfoot story shows the buffalo responsible for human flourishing. Here, they do so indirectly, by means of the culture hero Kŭt-o'-yis who is born from a clot of their blood. Told around the time of the massacre at Wounded Knee, the story's characterization of Kŭt-o'-yis as a ghost dancer would have resonated strongly with the revitalization movement that started with the prophet Wovoka among the Paiutes and caught on rapidly among many Plains peoples.[49] This episode of vengeance and resurrection thus follows the pattern of earlier episodes in which Kŭt-o'-yis punishes a villain for taking all the buffalo for himself and, to use Black Elk's term, for acting like a Wasichu or fat-taker.

While these particular Blackfoot stories often feature agents with greater-than-human or supernatural powers, they present a worldview in which human flourishing is the most important value. White preservationists, developing evolutionary as well as moral narratives, distributed agency among racially differentiated humans and the buffalo themselves. Black Elk's account (or in any case Neihardt's translation) does not animate the buffalo's agency but rather directs all blame toward the Wasichus. By contrast, in many traditional Plains stories, buffalo make decisions for themselves, often guided by

their master, Old Buffalo (as we saw in the case of mammoths and beavers in Chapter 2). Important among these decisions is the choice to give themselves as food for humans (as we saw of whales in Chapter 3). Yet the Blackfoot stories told to Grinnell from the late 1880s to the early 1890s, reflecting on the apparent extinction of the buffalo, say little regarding the agency of the buffalo themselves. Instead, the stories feature conflicts among human and quasihuman agents concerning access, distribution, and use of buffalo already given as "the gift of a good spirit," as Black Elk put it (39). In these Blackfoot stories, a morally ordered world allows buffalo and humans alike to flourish. In Black Elk's account, such a moral order is now no longer possible and the task is to find a replacement, an analogous gift.

I will not speculate on how, prior to 1840 or 1800—that is, prior to the decline of the buffalo caused by market-driven exploitation—traditional Blackfoot stories addressed scarcity or disappearance, caused for example by periodic drought cycles. As Peter Nabokov and other scholars have demonstrated, the telling of traditional stories is contextually inflected according to present occasion and circumstances.[50] We have seen that traditional stories told by Blackfoot narrators to the white ombudsman Grinnell during 1888–92, when the buffalo were all but extirpated, do feature this theme. In these stories, the scarcity or disappearance of buffalo is associated with deceit and/or greed. Buffalo themselves do not exhibit much agency nor are they assigned any portion of responsibility for their own persistence or disappearance—unlike the stories told by Hornaday regarding the bison's failures to evolve or adapt to drastic change in the capacity of their predators. Hornaday distributes agency among the bison and humans and gives Plains natives and white hunters equal blame but gives only whites the capacity to atone. In the Blackfoot stories, responsibility for persistence or disappearance is rather assigned to particular, deceitful or greedy human or humanlike agents. Whereas Hornaday's racially bifurcated moral narrative has Plains peoples bringing the buffalo's vengeance on themselves by means of extinction caused by the peoples' wasteful hunting practices—a narrative supported by other white cultural productions such as Howland's and Bierstadt's paintings—the Blackfoot stories imagine a reversal of the terms of blame and vengeance. The stories punish those who have killed too many buffalo, hoarded meat and hides, and left the people to starve. The analogy between these morally flawed Blackfoot actors and modern white exploiters is plain to see.

In recent times, Indigenous Plains peoples have attempted to reset the ecocultural order not by enacting vengeance, as the 1892 Blackfoot stories imagine, but rather through local restoration projects. The economic dimension

of those nineteenth-century stories speaks to these recent projects. At stake in the stories I have discussed is the agency of human or anthropomorphized actors in prohibiting or gaining access to buffalo as food. This question set the terms of the buffalo's survival into the twentieth century.

The predominant response by the U.S. government and private industry to the economic view of the buffalo registered in Grinnell's Blackfoot stories has been bison ranching. From this perspective, it seems that the survival of the bison as a species depends largely on the meat industry, which annually kills some 60,000 animals.[51] Even the small, government-managed "wild" herds in Yellowstone National Park, Custer State Park, and the National Bison Range are integrated with the meat industry as management plans require annual culling according to the parks' forage capacities and subsequent sale to ranchers or directly to meat processors.[52] The "Bison Sale" page on the National Bison Range's website shows a photograph of a bison in a metal chute waiting to be slaughtered.[53]

The resurgence of the buffalo did not depend wholly on commodification, however. In the twentieth century, the bison became an icon for a healthy prairie ecosystem, as for example in the controversial vision of a Buffalo Commons developed by the geographers Deborah and Frank Popper.[54] Initially a vague planning proposal addressing what the Poppers perceived as the depopulation and ecological degradation of the western Great Plains, the Buffalo Commons became a multivalent metaphor.[55] The Poppers' original proposal recommended government buyouts and relocation programs for ranchers and other white residents in an attempt to simulate the return of pre-nineteenth-century conditions. Even so, implications for Native American sovereignty were questionable: "In many areas," the Poppers wrote, "the distinctions between the present national parks, grasslands, grazing lands, wildlife refuges, forests, *Indian lands*, and their state counterparts will largely dissolve."[56] As "the world's largest historic preservation project, the ultimate national park"—something like the reservations for animals and Native Americans alike envisioned by Catlin and Thoreau—the Poppers' Buffalo Commons anticipates later "rewilding" projects such as those proposed by Dave Foreman and Paul Martin, neither of which is concerned with Indigenous sovereignty.[57] Similarly, in a Western novel, Richard Wheeler imagines a private foundation's attempt to accomplish such a project, focusing on the conflict with white ranchers and ignoring the Northern Cheyenne reservation located in the project's western sector. In one brief mention, "the tribes" are said to be upset because they are banned from hunting buffalo within the Commons.[58]

Contrasting with the idea of a Buffalo Commons are numerous tribal efforts to establish a Buffalo Nation.[59] The difference of figures is significant. A "common," as defined in English tradition, was not a parcel of otherwise unused land but rather a long-standing "right or privilege which one or more persons have, to take some part or portion of that which another person's lands, waters, woods, &c. produce," a right affirmed by continual usage, such as the right to pasture a given number of animals, the right to gather a certain amount of fuel, and the like.[60] In its liberal-individualist reformulation, however, a common was redefined as land itself or other resources, ungoverned by any traditionally allotted rights of commonage and available for expropriation. John Locke theorized this reformulation in the late seventeenth century, fantasizing a presocial state—which he claimed still existed in America—in which property could be expropriated from the commons by anyone "without any express Compact of the Commoners."[61] In order for Locke to formulate the commons in this way, he had to disregard the traditional definition of commons in British law, according to which a commons is not open land but rather the property of some manorial lord with rights of access traditionally allotted to tenants and other local residents. Since, for Locke, Indigenous Americans could not occupy the role of manorial lords, the American commons was ungoverned public land open to exploitation by anyone without others' consent. Such conditions of unrestrained exploitation could easily result in the "tragedy of the commons," in Garrett Hardin's famous phrase.[62] Such a tragedy is precisely what happened during the nineteenth century, because settler-colonists envisioned the American West as open land, rather than as traditional commons in which the Plains peoples were in effect commoners with certain accustomed rights. Working from the liberal-individualist reformulation of commons, whites organized bison hunting as an extractive industry, ignoring Indigenous management of this resource and drawing down what they viewed as the Great Plains' free, unclaimed natural capital. While the Poppers' original proposal called for the deprivatization of land without specifying what this would mean for reservation lands and without any plan for the management of rights and privileges, it invited "economic development based on wildlife" as free natural capital.[63]

The figure of a Buffalo Nation, by contrast, integrates the buffalo, and by extension the prairie ecosystem in which they flourish, into a social whole managed by humans on tribal lands, access to which is legally regulated. The figure presents buffalo themselves as having a culture, which means that ranching is a social interaction.[64] Thus the first step in many tribal buffalo projects is to gain the consent of the buffalo. As the primary organizer of Pte

Hca Ka, Inc., the Cheyenne River Sioux Reservation's buffalo project, Fred DuBray, remarked, "When I was first planning this project, one of the elders says something that stuck with me. . . . He says that before you bring the buffalo back you must ask the buffalo if they want to come back. There are other places where people are raising buffalo in feedlots, sawing their horns off. . . . Buffalo need a lot of room to develop in a herd situation. If they had to come back to standing around in a feedlot, then it's not realistic to think they would want to come back."[65] While this act of asking permission exemplifies the way traditional ecological knowledge can guide buffalo restoration projects, these projects are not nostalgic exercises. Rather, they recognize that traditional roles have shifted: where Plains peoples once depended on the buffalo to survive, now the buffalo depend on humans to survive. The terms of survival are determined by ranching practices, such as whether the buffalo are held in pens before slaughter, or whether, as with the Cheyenne River project, they are individually hunted without frightening them. Rituals such as rubbing tobacco on the animal's nose after the kill (not in some grandiose ceremonial manner but by crumpling a cigarette) mark a respectful relation.[66]

Indigenous preservation of the buffalo dates back to Salish, Lakota, and Red River Métis efforts to establish herds during the late 1870s and 1880s. Differing from better-publicized efforts by the white ranchers Charlie Goodnight and C. J. "Buffalo" Jones, these early projects had primarily preservationist rather than economic motives.[67] Several new tribal projects began in the wake of the Indian Self-Determination Act (1975) and flourished in the 1990s with the founding of the Intertribal Bison Cooperative in 1992 (renamed the Intertribal Buffalo Council in 2009). While the ITBC acts as a resource and sets standards, each tribe manages its own herd. This can lead to intratribal conflicts concerning economic issues, especially on reservations where a strong cattle-ranching culture developed during the twentieth century.[68] Pte Hca Ka, for example, was founded as a nonprofit corporation independent of tribal government and was reorganized in 1999 with the stated mission to "restore buffalo back to their ancient homeland in a manner which preserves and protects our cultural relationship."[69] Tribal government, however, expected more in the way of economic development and took over the corporation in 2001. Expanding operations to meet this economic goal, Pte Hca Ka became overextended and was forced to sell off much of its herd and close in 2007. It reopened in 2017 on a sustainable basis.[70] Other tribal buffalo projects persist, the vast majority using nonintensive management practices and affirming "spiritual/cultural" purposes as primary.[71] Bringing back the buffalo, writes Linda Hogan, "the people looked again for their human place

in the world." As another buffalo project organizer said, "We found that we, too, are just common people, like the squirrel and the sparrow."[72]

*   *   *

Tribal buffalo projects assume that the Great Plains were never the Lockean wilderness commons that white hunters, ranchers, and entrepreneurs imagined. Such a wilderness vision, characteristic of settler societies, was compatible with Lyell's logic of competitive extermination and the Lockean appropriation of "unoccupied lands."[73] Moreover, tribal buffalo projects do not take up the white preservationists' project of blame and atonement that culminated in Hornaday's Buffalo Group. They intervene in the historical fictions presented by Howland's *Western Jury* and Bierstadt's *Last of the Buffalo*. Countering these fictions, tribal projects assume a vision of relation that is also anthropocentric, but in a different way. As Fred DuBray said, "Buffalo are our relatives. We are obligated to take care of them."[74] Part of this care includes killing and eating them—a practice that by Euro-American logic would mark the buffalo as purely animal, objects of "a noncriminal putting to death," as Derrida puts it.[75] In traditional terms, however, the relation between humans and buffalo cannot be captured by the Western distinction between *zoe* or bare life and *bios* or organized life that structures the animal/human difference.[76] Rather, the practices of Buffalo Nation accord with the decision made by the buffalo themselves long ago, as recorded in many stories, when they agreed to be food for the people. The stories that the Blackfeet told Grinnell in the late 1880s, which anthropomorphize buffalo and other animals, assume this agreement. Thus they speak not only to the 1880s context but also to the economic conflicts that sometimes happen with modern buffalo projects. They tell the origins of the ecocultural relation between buffalo and humans while emphasizing the economic dimension of that relation. Killing some individual animals, in a context that promotes equitable access—such as distribution in school lunch programs—is part of the project of this particular species' survivance. The extinction theorist Thom van Dooren might call this an ethic of "violent-care," in which individuals are harmed for the conservation of the species.[77] As a practical case study, tribal buffalo husbandry complicates theorizing such as Timothy Morton's fantasy of escape from what he regards as the death-driven agricultural program that originated with the Neolithic revolution, for it is much more than a return to Paleolithic hunting.[78] Morton never quite gets to the point of what to eat. Tribal buffalo projects provide one local answer.

The Human Exception Revisited

In May 2019, a United Nations–sponsored assessment of global biodiversity concluded that the current rate of species extinction threatens a sustainable human future. The report, published by the Intergovernmental Science-Policy Platform on Biodiversity and Ecosystem Services (IPBES), found that around one million species are threatened and named the causes in descending order as "(1) changes in land and sea use; (2) direct exploitation of organisms; (3) climate change; (4) pollution and (5) invasive alien species."[1] As the IPBES chair Robert Watson interpreted the report, "The most important thing isn't necessarily that we're losing ... 1 million species—although that's important. . . . The bigger issue is the way it will affect human well-being." In order for the report to inspire action, Watson suggested, "we need to link it to human well-being, that's the crucial thing. Otherwise we're going to look like a bunch of tree-huggers."[2] The cochair of the assessment team Sandra Díaz stated that "biodiversity and nature's contributions to people are our common heritage and humanity's most important life-supporting 'safety net.' But our safety net is stretched almost to the breaking point."[3]

Biodiversity, as Ursula Heise has observed, is as much a cultural as a scientific question, an assessment of "what we value."[4] The IPBES report's core value, according to Watson, is humankind's flourishing—not merely our survival as "bare life," to use Giorgio Agamben's phrase, but our "human well-being."[5] In rhetorically differentiating this value of "human well-being" from (unspecified) values held by tree-huggers, Watson dismissed modern environmental activism's claim for the power of "biophilia," that is, the capacity for cross-species love that the conservation biologist Edward O. Wilson posits as a key feature of humankind's species being.[6] As the founder of conservation biology, Michael Soulé, puts it, "We only protect what we love."[7] While tree-huggers perform love for nonhumans, the Sixth Extinction enacts a refusal of that love through nonhumans' withdrawal of the material supports

of human life. The IPBES report is managerial rather than emotional, asserting the human exception in presenting "a wide range of illustrative actions for sustainability and pathways for achieving them . . . adopting integrated management and cross-sectoral approaches."[8] Using this managerial language, the assessment team recognizes that humans have always been environment shapers and will continue to be. Tree-hugging and other such expressions of love pose checks on that shaping.

Human well-being is the core theme of most of the extinction narratives examined in this book. Indigenous peoples of the Great Plains and the Pacific coast, as we have seen, promote the mutual flourishing of humans and certain animal species. In other contexts, Indigenous Americans and Euro-Americans affirmed that human flourishing depended on the extermination of certain harmful or unfit forms of life. Some looked to cooperative human effort while others believed that such favorable extinctions had been ordered by the "Creator of the universe."[9] Georges Cuvier and Charles Lyell removed this theological claim from the extinction debate—a claim that Joseph Nicolar retained and redirected for political reasons. Cuvier attributed species extinctions to climate changes caused, he thought, by global revolutions. Lyell, observing the results of settler-colonization and technological intensification, focused on humankind's capacity as an extinction-causing agent. Lyell asserted that this capacity was an inherent feature of humankind's species being, as it was in different ways of other species' beings. From this claim he drew a moral conclusion while claiming not to moralize. Anthropogenic extinctions would increase as "highly-civilized nations spread themselves over unoccupied lands," he argued, but since all extinctions are equally natural, "we have no reason to repine at the havoc committed."[10]

Measuring the "havoc committed" over the nearly two centuries since Lyell wrote, the IPBES report refutes his justification of humans as competitive independent actors, and rather encourages awareness of our enmeshment in a "life-supporting 'safety net'" comprising a million other species. The distance from Lyell to the IPBES report marks a familiar narrative of increasing environmental awareness over these two centuries, a shift from the claim of human mastery to the recognition of human dependence—a shift that environmental humanities scholarship has examined and helped produce. Human exceptionalism remains an issue, however, despite ecocriticism's repeated efforts to decenter human subjectivity, from Thoreauvian asceticism to deep ecology.[11] The perennial return of the decentering move in new guises (most recently, the new materialisms) signals the project's perpetual incompletion.[12]

I have been arguing instead throughout this book that the self-reflective recognition of a human/animal difference provides a necessary counter to both Lyellian apologies for human mastery and deep ecology's attempts to erase the human.[13] Some of the extinction or endangerment narratives examined here posit human mastery as the core feature of relations between humans and others. Some assume subordination to greater powers beyond the human that organize the world. Few appeal to biophilia. All take human flourishing as a primary value. Many of the most productive narratives, as we have seen, work at least loosely within the paradigm of treaties or agreements between humans and nonhumans.

The treaty form is grounded neither in mastery nor in love but in the recognition of sovereignty and mutual respect. In human diplomacy—whether the example case is the Treaty of Westphalia or the ancient confederation of the Haudenosaunee five nations—the treaty form developed in order to resolve histories of violent relations.[14] Similarly, treaties with animals are founded on histories of interspecies violence, as some traditional Indigenous stories explicitly indicate. According to an Anishnabe story, long ago the deer, moose, and caribou were captured by the crows. The Anishnabeg went to war against the crows to rescue the game animals, but the game animals did not want to be rescued. The crows, who merely fed on the remains of dead animals, did not harass them as the Anishnabeg had done. As the deer chief explained to the Anishnabe chief during a truce, "The crows have treated us better than you have ever treated us. . . . You have wasted our flesh, you have despoiled our haunts, you have desecrated our bones, you have dishonoured us and yourselves. Without you we can live. But without us, you cannot live." Without the game animals, the Anishnabeg would face extinction. The Anishnabe chief asked, "How shall we atone for your grief?" The deer chief answered, "Honor and respect our lives . . . in life and in death. Cease doing what offends our spirits." So the Anishnabeg negotiated an agreement with the game animals, witnessed by the crows, to organize and regulate interspecies violence. The treaty stipulated that the game animals would willingly allow themselves to be killed so long as the Anishnabeg observed certain "customs and practices" and paid respect through "prayers that expressed sorrow and heed and apology."[15]

Another Anishnabe story, however, shows animals organizing among themselves to resist human oppression. In council, they formed a multispecies treaty that pointedly excluded humans. During the negotiations, some animals argued for the extermination of humans altogether: "We have suffered enough. . . . The Anishnabeg have killed us; . . . and they have subjected us. Only with the death of man will these injustices cease." But the bear observed

that humans were "too strong, too many, and too cunning" to be exterminated outright. Rather, the bear advised, "to make it difficult for man to enslave us again, we will no longer speak the same language. . . . Let men learn to fend for themselves without our help." After the animals agreed among themselves (except for the dog, who was banished as a human-bonded traitor), humans could no longer understand the animals' language, but had to observe them closely "for knowledge of the world, life, and [themselves]."[16]

Stories from other traditions give varying yet similar accounts of the ordering of relations between hunter and hunted. In a Cherokee story, the animals also meet together to resist human oppression; they devise diseases to check the growth of the human population, which humans then learn to mitigate through their interactions with plants.[17] In some Pawnee stories, the buffalo agree to be eaten after a race, a game, or a trial by combat between buffalo and humans.[18] According to a Blackfoot story—as we saw in Chapter 4—long ago the buffalo ate humans, until the creator Na'pi reversed the relationship, decreeing that humans shall eat buffalo.

The common thread to all such stories is the recognition of violence as a significant component of interspecies relations. Any response to the Sixth Extinction ought to start from this recognition: not only a catalog of the "havoc committed" during the second, settler-colonial wave of extinctions but a reflection on how violence has been managed under other dispensations— including the aftermath of the Late Pleistocene wave of extinctions—so as to promote and sustain human flourishing. The Anishnabe, Cherokee, and Pawnee stories noted above even imagine human extinction, which is averted through both animals' limited, pragmatic generosity and humans' ingenuity. In Joseph Nicolar's story of the mammoth, human extinction remains an open question, as it does in the IPBES report. Some stories are optimistic about cross-species communication, as required by the treaty form, but others declare that it is to the animals' benefit *not* to speak a language that humans can understand. Such stories foreground the question of cross-species communication, a minimum precondition of treaties.

If "the animals can't speak for themselves," it may now be more urgent than ever that "we have to speak for them," as Linda Hogan and others argue, to reaffirm their treaties with humans.[19] Speaking for nonhumans, as we have seen, is also the premise of Bruno Latour's "parliament of things," in which cross-species communication is enabled by scientific "speech prostheses."[20] For Hogan, Indigenous peoples are the exceptional humans who can understand and translate animals for the rest of humankind; for Latour, scientists play that role.

While Hogan, Latour, and Aldo Leopold all use governmental figures to prescribe the relation between humans and nonhumans, their frames bear different, complementary implications. Hogan's reaffirmation of treaties implies distinct sovereignties, while Latour's parliament implies a single sovereignty within which, to use Leopold's language, humans and animals alike are "citizens."[21] Each anthropomorphic frame, governmental difference and governmental unity, is useful in its way. The IPBES report was assembled by scientists listening to and translating animals (and plants) for the rest of us humans. A treaty-oriented reading of the report would insist that if animals are not recognized as sovereign, they will cause harm to humans. The harm now will come not by way of animals' direct actions, for as the bear in the Anishnabe story observed, human power and cunning can resist attacks of force.[22] Rather, the harm will come much as the game animals withdrew from the Anishnabeg once long ago. The Anishnabeg faced extinction until they negotiated a treaty for the return of the deer, moose, and caribou, a treaty also affirmed by the crows. In the Sixth Extinction, the animals are withdrawing from our world on a much larger scale. While science will continue to document that withdrawal and investigate its immediate causes, the question remains whether we can now make effective treaties as the ancient Anishnabeg did. If not, with the animals' withdrawal, we will also, as Jefferson put it, "evanish by piece-meal."[23]

NOTES

Introduction

1. See "Woolly Mammoth on Verge of Resurrection, Scientists Reveal," *Guardian*, February 26, 2017, https://www.theguardian.com/science/2017/feb/16/woolly-mammoth-resurrection-scientists?CMP=share_btn_link. The team projected a window of two years, but as of summer 2020, no such creation had been announced.

2. Shapiro, *How to Clone a Mammoth*, 14.

3. Wray, *Rise of the Necrofauna*, 76.

4. The scientific literature on the current mass extinction event is substantial. For a judicious overview, see Barnosky et al., "Earth's Sixth Mass Extinction." The massive scope of anthropogenic extinctions is demonstrated in Ceballos, Ehrlich, and Dirzo, "Biological Annihilation." A focus on anthropogenic causes emerged in the 1980s, with some backlash in the 1990s; on the scientific debate from this era, see Leakey and Lewin, *Sixth Extinction*, 232–45. As a 2014 editorial in *Nature* observes, the extent of the crisis remains unknown because millions of earth's species, some threatened and some going extinct, remain uncatalogued ("Protect and Serve").

5. For convenience, I will often use "mammoth" throughout this book to refer to mammoths (*Mammuthus primigenius* and *M. columbi*) and mastodons (*Mammut americanum*).

6. On coral, see Kolbert, *Sixth Extinction*, 125–47. Although an insect extinction crisis is an important topic among biologists, the idea of an "insect apocalypse" has not gained much public attention; see Goulson, "Insect Apocalypse."

7. This is to delimit my use of the term within the larger domain of human exceptionalism, which includes a range of positions including Christian providentialism or millennialism, the modern secularist assumption that humanism is the only source of meaning, and classical and Marxist economics' configurations of the nonhuman world as mere resources. Thom van Dooren defines human exceptionalism broadly as the conceptualization of "humans as fundamentally set apart from all other animals and the rest of the 'natural' world" (*Flight Ways*, 5).

8. For example, Deborah Bird Rose observes that Aboriginal Australians hold the view of human exceptionalism as lack, positing that humans are the one creature that does not communicate directly with the original creative forces, the Dreaming beings (*Wild Dog Dreaming*, 139).

9. The limit case in the question of eating is cannibalism. Although Claude Lévi-Strauss demonstrated the imprecision of the definition ("We Are All Cannibals"), cannibalism considered as part of ritual sacrifice, mortuary custom, medical practice, and so on still maintains the human/animal distinction—it is permitted to eat other humans under these regulated conditions, but not otherwise—as do views of cannibalism as criminal or pathological. Herman Melville entertains the contrary—"Cannibals? who is not a cannibal?" (*Moby-Dick*, 327)—not to argue in favor of humans eating humans but to reflect on humans' practice of eating animals.

10. Bruno Latour posits this attempt to separate nature from culture as the defining operation of modernity (*We Have Never Been Modern*). While Latour argues that this has always been
an impossible project, anthropogenic climate change has confirmed the point. The problem has
been outlined in Kantian terms by Dipesh Chakrabarty ("Humanities in the Anthropocene").
On these terms, the legacy of the Enlightenment's conceptual separation of humankind's moral
and animal lives, based on the assumption that humankind's animal life could take care of itself,
is set against the recognition of the material entanglement of moral and animal life, as revealed
by various problems resulting from our species' ecological overshoot of planetary carrying
capacity including the extinction crisis.

11. Different accounts of the human/animal distinction have emerged in the Western tradition in response to different concerns. Colleen Boggs usefully divides the recent critical terrain into animal-rights activism, which works with the human/animal difference to argue that
humanlike subjectivity ought to be extended to some (but not all) animals, and poststructuralism,
which uses animals to deconstruct human subjectivity (*Animalia Americana*, 3–19). The former
has roots in utilitarianism while the latter engages with other aspects of the Enlightenment philosophical tradition. For example, Kant's claim that reflection on mental access to the concept of
the sublime, through which "we can become conscious of being superior to nature within us and
also nature outside us," emerges from his attempt to instantiate a universal moral sense specific
to humans (*Critique of the Power of Judgment*, 147). Dominick LaCapra cites Kant's move as a
canonical example of the insufficient problematization of the human/animal difference (*History
and Its Limits*, 156). Wittgenstein's famous proposition that "if a lion could talk, we could not
understand him" emerges from an investigation into the nature of language and the limits of communicability (*Philosophical Investigations*, 223). Cary Wolfe deconstructs such linguistic accounts
of the human/animal difference by way of biosemiotics, which investigates the signifying processes
that organize all life (*Animal Rites*, 44–94). Heidegger's claim that animals are "poor in world"
emerges from an attempt to specify humankind's unique historical essence or destiny; see Calarco,
Zoographies, 15–53. Giorgio Agamben follows the undoing of Heidegger's project through the
biopolitical "assumption of the burden—and the 'total management'—of biological life, that is,
of the very animality of man" (*Open*, 77). A recent turn in the articulation of the human/animal
difference is the coinage of "human-animal studies," which draws on the work of Donna Haraway
(especially *When Species Meet*) to "[think] about animals as inseparable from human lives" and
explore "cross-species entanglements" (McHugh, *Love in a Time of Slaughters*, 8).

12. In the first two chapters, which focus on accounts of the remains of Pleistocene
megafauna through the nineteenth century, the archive consists primarily of Indigenous oral
narratives, historical narratives, and scientific narratives. In the nineteenth century, the novel
expanded its reach beyond domestic interiors and opened itself to the possibility of addressing environmental concerns. Thus novels such as Cornelius Mathews's *Behemoth* and especially
Melville's *Moby-Dick*, with its extensive use of natural history materials and field observation,
became part of the archive of endangerment and extinction narratives.

13. M. R. O'Connor entertains the idea that the Sixth Extinction is a hyperobject (*Resurrection Science*, 221–22). On the general concept, see Morton, *Hyperobjects*.

14. The discovery of extinction as geohistorical fact has been told numerous times, often as
a component of the discovery of geological time. Martin Rudwick gives an especially thorough
account in *Bursting the Limits of Time* (239–87).

15. On the mammoth's cultural symbolism, see Semonin, *American Monster*; and Sayre,
"Mammoth." Mathew Chrulew suggests that the mammoth is the totem animal of postmodernity,

its extinction in the transition from Pleistocene to Holocene resonating with current ecological crises ("Hunting the Mammoth").

16. Starbuck would take exception to my characterization of the white whale's behavior as moral. Recall that he reproaches Ahab for wanting to take "vengeance on a dumb brute" that, as he (Starbuck) sees it, acts from "blindest instinct" rather than from a moral basis (Melville, *Moby-Dick*, 178). Arguing that morality is an evolved trait shared by at least some animals, Marc Bekoff and Jessica Pierce posit the usefulness of anthropomorphism in humans' everyday and scientific understandings of animals (*Wild Justice*, 40–43).

17. Svenning, "Future Megafaunas," G76.

18. LaDuke, *All Our Relations*, 143.

19. Many Indigenous nations' sacred traditions, however, emphasize autochthonous origins over migration. Gerald Vizenor plays with this point in his 1984 film *Harold of Orange*: when asked by a white philanthropist what he thinks of the Bering land bridge migration theory, the trickster Harold replies, "Which way?" Such mismatches raise the question of the chronological reach and continuity of oral traditions over several millennia, a question that will be taken up in Chapter 2.

20. Araujo et al., "Bigger Kill Than Chill."

21. In addition to Araujo et al., "Bigger Kill Than Chill," see Barnosky et al., "Causes of Late Pleistocene Extinctions"; Flannery and Burney, "Fifty Millennia of Catastrophic Extinction"; Koch and Barnosky, "Late Quaternary Extinctions"; Leakey and Lewin, *Sixth Extinction*, 171–94; P. Martin, "Prehistoric Overkill"; P. Martin, *Twilight of the Mammoths*, 165–78; and Sandom et al., "Global Late Quaternary Megafaunal Extinctions." Human causation does not mean killing every last one of the mammoths by hunting, but rather killing enough over many generations to bring the reproduction rate below the mortality rate. The correlation is less robust for Europe until ten thousand years ago. Not enough data exists for Asia. The correlation does not hold for Africa, where presumably the coevolution of hominids and megafauna sorted the matter out long before the advent of anatomically modern humans. Correlation is not causation, however; thus the debate continues. See Haynes, ed., *American Megafaunal Extinctions*.

22. Craig Womack (Creek-Cherokee), for example, argues against eating animals except in case of true necessity ("There Is No Respectful Way to Kill an Animal"). I will revisit this question in Chapters 3 and 4.

23. One might wish to hear more, for example, about Indigenous stories associated with the remains of the megatherium that were first transported to Europe from the River Luján in Argentina in 1788; see Pimentel, *Rhinoceros and the Megatherium*, 138–39. Rose, in *Wild Dog Dreaming*, provides a model, incorporating Aboriginal Australian knowledge in her study of the endangerment of the dingo.

24. H. G. Wells speculated that "the legends of ogres and man-eating giants that haunt the childhood of the world" originated in Cro-Magnons' encounters with Neanderthals ("Grisly Folk," 618).

25. A significant amount of work has been published since Roy Harvey Pearce's *The Savages of America*. The present study will cite, for example, Elmer, *On Lingering and Being Last*; and O'Brien, *Firsting and Lasting*.

26. Gerald Vizenor, in *Manifest Manners*, first used the term "survivance" in this context, reviving and revising a technical legal term to indicate continuance into the future.

27. See TallBear, "Shepard Krech's *The Ecological Indian*"; and Nasady, "Transcending the Debate." Nasady observes that Indigenous peoples have sometimes deployed the image for

political ends ("Transcending the Debate," 314–15). One such instance is Joseph Nicolar's *Life and Traditions of the Red Man*, which will be discussed in Chapter 2; see Kolodny, "Rethinking the 'Ecological Indian.'"

28. Krech, *Ecological Indian*. On the disequilibrist view of ecosystem dynamics, see Botkin, *Discordant Harmonies*.

29. For a review of arguments, see Kelly and Prasciunas, "Did the Ancestors of Native Americans Cause Animal Extinctions?" Indigenous rights under the IWC convention will be discussed further in Chapter 4.

30. See Steadman, "Prehistoric Extinctions of Pacific Island Birds." On the extinction of the moa specifically, see A. Anderson, *Prodigious Birds*, 171–87. While this history ought to have no bearing on the question of present-day Maori sovereignty, accounts of the extinction were used in Victorian-era anthropological narratives that rationalized colonization; see Armstrong, "Moa Citings."

31. The term seems to have been popularized by Leakey and Lewin in *Sixth Extinction*. See also Kolbert, *Sixth Extinction*; and Glavin, *Sixth Extinction*.

32. Counting anthropology among the humanities, titles include Mark Barrow Jr., *Nature's Ghosts*; Thom van Dooren, *Flight Ways*; Deborah Bird Rose, *Wild Dog Dreaming*; Ursula Heise, *Imagining Extinction*; Deborah Bird Rose, Thom van Dooren, and Matthew Chrulew, eds., *Extinction Studies*; and Susan McHugh, *Love in a Time of Slaughters*.

33. McHugh, in *Love in a Time of Slaughters*, shows how some contemporary novels return to nineteenth- and twentieth-century scenes of mass killing in order to revitalize traditional knowledges based on cross-species interdependence.

34. As Cary Wolfe argues, the concepts of extinction, endangered species, and the like create a sense of human responsibility because they are human constructs ("Condors at the End of the World").

35. Latour, *We Have Never Been Modern*. The blending of human and geophysical agencies that is the topic of so much Anthropocene discourse (e.g., Chakrabarty, "Climate of History") gives the lie to the Moderns' impossible project, as diagnosed by Latour, of attempting to settle politics by purifying nature from culture.

36. Ursula Heise names the ideal of "multispecies justice" but does not elaborate a program (*Imagining Extinction*, 167). One might take the position that in a "broken" or resource-depleted world, calculations regarding survival become inevitable; see Mulgan, *Ethics for a Broken World*. Although Mulgan's speculations focus only on human politics, they might be extrapolated to our relations with nonhumans. Often the preservation of a species requires the sacrifice of individuals; for example, the preservation of the Kirtland's warbler requires the killing of thousands of brown-headed cowbirds annually. On practical problems and inevitable judgments in conservation biology, see Kareiva and Levin, eds., *Importance of Species*. One alternative to a "multispecies justice" program would be an emphasis on companion species, those species that are most closely and for the most part positively entangled with humans, as explored for example by Donna Haraway in *When Species Meet*. Such an approach need not concern itself explicitly with questions of biodiversity and extinction. Haraway's interest in human companion species (e.g., racing pigeons, sheep, dogs) persists, sometimes reckoning these relations' impacts on other species, in *Staying with the Trouble*.

37. This approach is exemplified by Rose, van Dooren, and Chrulew, eds., *Extinction Studies*; and van Dooren, *Flight Ways*.

38. van Dooren, *Flight Ways*, 27.

39. Heise, *Imagining Extinction*, 5.

40. Less ostensibly evaluative projects in response to environmental crisis, such as Haraway's *Staying with the Trouble*, nevertheless maintain a prescriptive dimension, in Haraway's case an exhortation to refuse both techno-optimist and cynical-despairing "futurisms" in favor of a present-oriented "partial recuperation and getting on together" (4, 10).

41. Leopold, *Sand County Almanac*, viii, hereafter documented parenthetically. As Greg Garrard points out, environmental science has rendered Leopold's assumption of "stability" in nature problematic (*Ecocriticism*, 80). Thus, for example, Daniel Botkin argues that a new understanding of Leopold's keyword "harmony" is needed in order for his ethic to remain relevant (*Discordant Harmonies*, 191).

42. The project was announced in Latour, *We Have Never Been Modern*, 142–45, and continued in works such as *Politics of Nature* and *Facing Gaia*.

43. Latour proposes that we regard the sciences as "speech prostheses" for nonhumans (*Politics of Nature*, 66). Literary imaginations of animal speech have focused primarily on domestic animals: a horse in Anna Sewell's *Black Beauty* (1877) or a dog in Margaret Marshall Saunders's *Beautiful Joe* (1894). Elizabeth Young explores the latter's "first-dog" voice in *Pet Projects*.

44. Hogan, "First People," 10.

45. Simpson, "Looking After Gdoo-naaganinaa," 33. For other examples, see Borrows, *Recovering Canada*, 16–20; Craft, *Breathing Life into the Stone Fort Treaty*, 70; and Noble, "Treaty Ecologies," 316–17. Throughout, I will use different spellings—Nishnaabeg, Anishinaabeg, Anishnabeg—following my sources.

46. Hogan, "First People," 11.

47. On E. O. Wilson's hopes for biophilia, see *Future of Life*, 129–48. Wilson posits that biophilia and its antithesis, biophobia, are inherent human capacities that can be nurtured or discouraged. On Soulé, see Tonino, "We Only Protect What We Love."

48. Agamben, *Means Without End*, 111. Agamben's assertion that sovereignty functions as a "guardian who prevents the undecidable threshold between violence and right . . . from coming to light," thus sealing off questions of justice, is an apt distillation of his engagement in *Homo Sacer* with Carl Schmitt's account of sovereignty (*Means Without End*, 112). Although Agamben does not explicitly extend this investigation of sovereignty to his critique of the human/animal difference in *The Open*, the implication seems clear.

49. See, for example, van Doren, ed., *Indian Treaties Printed by Benjamin Franklin*.

50. Extending Rob Nixon's *Slow Violence* to nonhumans, we might differentiate between fast violence such as direct killing and slow violence such as habitat degradation.

51. On the Anthropocene's distinctive geological signature, see Zalasiewicz et al., "Stratigraphy of the Anthropocene."

52. Critiques of the Anthropocene concept, of course, point out that the responsibility for the fossil fuel economy, one of the Anthropocene's largest markers, lies not with all humans but with particular groups; see Malm and Hornborg, "Geology of Mankind?"

53. For example, hominins have used fire to shape their environments for some 400,000 years; for a summary overview, see Scott, *Against the Grain*, 37–43.

54. On the interventions required to produce "wilderness," see Cronon, "Trouble with Wilderness."

55. In addition to *We Have Never Been Modern*, see Latour, "Will Non-Humans Be Saved?"; Latour, "'Compositionist Manifesto'"; and Latour, "Agency at the Time of the Anthropocene."

Beyond Latour, see also Philippe Descola's work in comparative ontology, *Beyond Nature and Culture*.

56. Descola, *Beyond Nature and Culture*, for example, maps four ontologies deriving from differential stances with respect to humans and nonhumans using the universal categories of interiority and physicality.

57. The final sentence of the first (1859) edition of *On the Origin of Species* reads, "There is grandeur in this view of life, with its several powers, having been originally breathed into a few forms or into one; and that, whilst this planet has gone cycling on according to the fixed law of gravity, from so simple a beginning endless forms most beautiful and most wonderful have been, and are being, evolved" (Darwin, *On the Origin*, 490). For the second (1860) edition, Darwin revised the sentence to read, ". . . having been originally breathed *by the Creator* into a few forms or into one" (*On the Origin*, 2nd ed., 490, italics added).

58. See, for example, Glavin, *Sixth Extinction*, 277–84.

59. Morton, *Hyperobjects*, 201, 198. Morton refines this line of thought, differentiating "mindfulness" as a neoliberal, anthropocentric activity from "awareness" as the ground of Marxist-anarchist solidarity with nonhumans, in *Humankind*, 175–89.

60. Aristotle, *Poetics*, 5.

61. Frye, *Anatomy of Criticism*, 33.

62. Isabelle Stengers argues that capitalism "doesn't speak about humans" at all but rather must be understood as a "machine" that must be resisted, irrespective of human "greed" and "self-interest" (*In Catastrophic Times*, 52).

63. Capitalism is the culprit for Ashley Dawson (*Extinction*), Naomi Klein (*This Changes Everything*), and Jason Moore (*Capitalism*). Justin McBrien argues that the very name Anthropocene renders the extinction crisis inherent to human nature, thus displacing the true cause, capitalism ("Accumulating Extinction"). Christophe Bonneuil and Jean-Baptiste Fressoz have similarly argued that "Capitalocene" implies a better explanatory heuristic for global environmental degradation generally than does "Anthropocene," while nevertheless stressing the need for local, differential analysis (*Shock of the Anthropocene*, 222–52). This general line of thinking derives from Marx's claim that alienated labor estranges humankind from the rest of nature. Yet estrangement is already assumed in Marx's exceptionalist theorization of species being, according to which humankind, even prior to capitalism, is the only species capable of conceptualizing itself *as* a species. See *Economic and Philosophic Manuscripts*, 74–77.

64. Morton dates the beginning of the Sixth Extinction specifically to the Neolithic revolution, which he calls the Severing, with the initiation of "the death-driven agricultural program" that extends human life at the cost of nonhuman life (*Humankind*, 18).

65. Wright, *Short History of Progress*; Scranton, *Learning to Die in the Anthropocene*; Ghosh, *Great Derangement*.

66. Chakrabarty, "Climate of History," 212, 220.

67. Sale, *After Eden*.

68. The claims for genetic mutation are summarized by Yuval Harari in *Sapiens* (20–39).

69. For an overview, see Sykes, *Kindred*.

70. Wright, *Short History of Progress*, 30.

71. Scott, by contrast, argues for the gradual and uneven development of agriculture and other domestications within hunting and gathering cultures, rather than a turn to agriculture as a last resort, *Against the Grain*, 1–67.

72. Compare, for example, Rose's elaboration of "ecological existentialism," which posits that "there is no predetermined essence of humanity" yet recognizes that humankind is "thoroughly entangled" with other species (*Wild Dog Dreaming*, 43, 44).

73. Molyneux, "Discourse Concerning the Large Horns," 501, 502, italics in original.

74. Jefferson, *Notes on the State of Virginia*, 56.

75. Focusing on Algonquian languages, Daryl Baldwin, Margaret Noodin, and Bernard Perley argue that extinction is an invasive concept that arrived with European colonizers ("Surviving the Sixth Extinction"). Indigenous language analogs include "killed off," "wiped out," or "dead," and in the case of languages no longer spoken, "sleeping."

76. Cuvier, *Essay on the Theory of the Earth*, 166.

77. See Barrow, *Nature's Ghosts*, 47–107.

78. Lyell, *Principles of Geology*, 1:164.

79. Lyell, *Principles of Geology*, 2:150.

80. Lyell, *Principles of Geology*, 2:156.

81. Lyell, *Principles of Geology*, 2:156.

82. Agamben would characterize this as an operation of the "anthropological machine" that produces the human/animal difference (*Open*, 29).

83. Derrida, "'Eating Well,'" 112.

84. See, for example, Marean, "How *Homo sapiens* Became the Ultimate Invasive Species."

85. Sahlins, *Western Illusion of Human Nature*.

86. On Amerindian perspectivism, see Viveiros de Castro, *Cannibal Metaphysics*; and Danowski and Viveiros de Castro, *Ends of the World*, 61–74.

87. Danowski and Viveiros de Castro, *Ends of the World*, 70.

88. Kohn, *How Forests Think*, 1, italics in original.

89. As noted above, Heise, in *Imagining Extinction*, catalogs the range of responses more finely to differentiate among elegy, tragedy, comedy, epic, encyclopedia, and other forms. Even so, elegy and comedy (the latter in the form of techno-futurist happily-ever-afters) predominate. Mick Smith, in "Environmental Anamnesis," intervenes in the elegiac mode by working with Freud's distinction between mourning and melancholia, arguing that melancholic narratives of human moral failing overwrite a species' uniqueness; redemptive moments of wonder, Smith argues, short-circuit these melancholic narratives to enable mourning the species as such.

90. R. Clifton Spargo posits that this sense of death's injustice forms the ethical basis of elegy's aesthetic reflection (*Ethics of Mourning*). I do not claim that mourning is uniquely human. Van Dooren argues that Hawaiian crows, for example, mourn the loss of their loved ones (*Flight Ways*, 122–44). If so, there is no reason to claim that crows have no sense of justice in this regard. Justice is one of three moral categories examined in Bekoff and Pierce, *Wild Justice*.

91. Clive Hamilton uses the term "anticipatory mourning" (*Requiem for a Species*, 212). Haraway's speculative fiction performs another kind of future elegy, in which "symbionts," humans into whom genes of endangered animals have been spliced, become living memorials after the extinction of their associated animals (*Staying with the Trouble*, 143–68).

92. Even in the case of the passenger pigeon, regret was not universal. Reporting the death of the last passenger pigeon in captivity in the Cincinnati Zoo in 1914, the *New York Evening World* opined that "we have good cause to rejoice that nature did not fit him to adapt himself

to civilization and stay with us like the grasshopper." See "The Last Passenger Pigeon," *New York Evening World*, September 7, 1914, 8, Library of Congress, Chronicling America: Historic American Newspapers, https://chroniclingamerica.loc.gov/.

93. Max Cavitch, for example, explores ways in which elegy mitigates grievances against the past through the building of present- and future-oriented allegiances (*American Elegy*).

94. See Haraway, *Staying with the Trouble*.

95. Arnold Krupat, in *"That the People Might Live,"* argues that although, strictly speaking, there is no formal Native American equivalent to the Western tradition of elegy, its functional equivalent, the expressive response to death that offers consolation, is oriented to the revitalization and maintenance of community rather than, as in Western elegy, an individual's psychic healing. The Haudenosaunee condolence ceremony and the Tlingit potlatch are among Krupat's primary examples.

96. Lin, *What Is Missing?* In her earliest conception of the project, Lin intended to link the monitoring of endangered species to climate and habitat indicators; see *Boundaries*, 12:03. As the project developed, first in sculpture and then as a website, monitoring gave way to memorialization. The website enables users to locate historical extinctions by place or time—each clickable dot embeds information—and to associate these extinctions with their own experiences by inviting them to "share a memory about something you, or your parents or grandparents, have personally witnessed diminish or disappear from the natural world" ("Share a Memory"). Clint Wilson reads the sculptural component of Lin's project as a multisensory investigation into cross-species relations ("Sacrificial Structures," 94–96).

97. Robinson, *Green Mars*, 76. This novel is the second in Robinson's Mars trilogy, a multigenerational saga of interplanetary colonization. Robinson's fiction was important in the formulation of the Mars Society; see Zubrin, *Entering Space*, 120. See also Newitz, *Scatter, Adapt, and Remember*. For a skeptical survey of geoengineering solutions, see Hamilton, *Requiem for a Species*, 159–89.

98. See, for example, Barrow's history of the development of biodiversity conservation in response to extinction events (*Nature's Ghosts*). Rafi Youatt, in *Counting Species*, surveys challenges and prospects for the future. See also Heise on biodiversity conservation narratives (*Imagining Extinction*, 55–86). On de-extinction, see, for example, O'Connor, *Resurrection Science*; Shapiro, *How to Clone a Mammoth*; and Wray, *Rise of the Necrofauna*.

99. Paul Martin coined the phrase "resurrection ecology"; see *Twilight of the Mammoths*, 200–211. See also Shapiro, *How to Clone a Mammoth*; and the Long Now Foundation's Revive and Restore project website, http://reviverestore.org/. O'Connor, *Resurrection Science*, gives an objective but ultimately critical account based on eight case studies. So far, scientists have been more successful at manipulating genomes than at managing populations and landscapes, which would be necessary to ensure the survival of resurrected animals in the wild; see Donlan, "De-Extinction." On DNA preservation efforts, see Kolbert's discussion of the Frozen Zoo and Frozen Ark projects (*Sixth Extinction*, 259–61).

100. For example, Paul Martin's plan to repopulate spaces in the American West with living analogues of Late Pleistocene fauna; see *Twilight of the Mammoths*, 179–99. Gordon Sayre argues that Martin's proposal should be understood in a colonialist context in which mourning for extinct fauna echoes "America's imperial mourning over the vanishing Indian" ("Mammoth," 83). Kim Stanley Robinson develops an elaborate fictional restoration ecology narrative, in which whole biomes of plants and animals that had become extinct in the wild have been raised

for some three hundred years off-planet and then reintroduced all at once. This "Reanimation," as his characters call it, has "led to the recreation of [Earth's] landscapes both physical and political" (Robinson, *2312*, 552).

101. For example, Svenning, "Future Megafaunas." Unless rewilding projects encompass areas large enough to support carnivores as well as herbivores, however, such projects are doomed to fail, as in the Netherlands' experimental Oostvaardersplassen, where large numbers of herbivores must be killed by humans or starve to death; see Faure, "Man and Beast."

102. "Why Efforts to Bring Extinct Species Back." Mark Avery makes a similar point in the course of his book-length elegy on the passenger pigeon (*Message from Martha*, 228–29). De-extinction efforts open the possibility of the patenting and commercial exploitation of newly created organisms. See Dawson, "Biocapitalism and De-Extinction"; and Regalado, "Stealthy De-Extinction Startup."

103. International Whaling Commission, *International Convention for the Regulation of Whaling*, 1. The moratorium takes the form of annual catch limits, which have been set at zero since 1985–86, with exceptions for subsistence whaling by some Indigenous peoples (see Chapter 3), but could be increased if stocks permit. Norway and Iceland take whales within their Exclusive Economic Zones under objection or reservation to the moratorium. See International Whaling Commission, "Commercial Whaling."

104. Claire Colebrook examines the recent emergence of the postapocalyptic mode as a response to this question. She argues that in its focus on survival, this mode represses the question of whether we ought to survive. See *Death of the Posthuman*, 185–207. Reflecting more generally on this normative question of what ought to survive, however, Colebrook contends that its very formulation is a consequence of the formation of the Western, rational, calculating subject; see "Lives Worth Living."

105. Some speculative realists such as Ray Brassier argue that the fact of extinction completes the Enlightenment disenchantment of the world—"everything is dead already"—and that the resulting nihilism is liberating (*Nihil Unbound*, 223).

106. I take the number from Raup, *Extinction*, 4.

107. James Lovelock, who coined this name for the earth as a living, self-sustaining being in 1974, now imagines Gaia as a nurturing mother turned vengeful at humankind's abuses; see *Revenge of Gaia*. By contrast, Stengers presents an image of Gaia as utterly indifferent to humankind; see *In Catastrophic Times*, 43–50. There is a utilitarian argument as well, according to which, based on a calculus of suffering, the human species ought not exist; see Benatar, *Better Never to Have Been*.

108. Weisman, *World Without Us*.

109. Zalasiewicz, *Earth After Us*.

110. R. Martin, "Fossil Thoughts."

111. Freud, *Reflections*, 41.

Chapter 1

1. On Cuvier and the consolidation of the extinction concept, see Rudwick, *Bursting the Limits of Time*, 246–75. I use *kind of life* in this chapter to register the fact that the concept of species as designating a group or class of creature sharing certain distinguishing characteristics remained in flux until it was consolidated by Enlightenment taxonomies such as Linnaeus's (and even then remained in debate). *Form of life* might be more appropriate if not for Giorgio

Agamben's use of that phrase specifically to indicate human life beyond *zoe* or bare life. See Agamben, *Means Without End*, 3–12.

2. The shift from openness to skepticism is mapped by Stephen Toulmin in *Cosmopolis*, and Jorge Cañizares-Esguerra in *How to Write the History of the New World*. Cañizares-Esguerra positions his argument specifically against Walter Mignolo, *Darker Side of the Renaissance*.

3. For an overview of Mexican and Andean fossil legends recorded by sixteenth-century Spanish historians, see Mayor, *Fossil Legends*, 73–89.

4. Díaz del Castillo, *Discovery and Conquest*, 229, hereafter documented parenthetically.

5. A. P. Maudslay's translation closely follows the original, in which the Tlaxcalans had been told by their ancestors that they fought and killed the giants "porque eran muy malos y de malas maneras." See Díaz del Castillo, *Historia verdadera de la conquista*, 135.

6. At the time of Cortés's arrival in 1519, the Aztec Triple Alliance of Tenochtitlan, Texcoco, and Tlacopan, under the rule of Moctezuma II, dominated central Mexico, controlling all territories surrounding two unconquered city-states, Tlaxcala and Teotitlan.

7. José de Acosta's account incorporates the work of Durán and Juan de Tovar, whom Acosta had met in Mexico before returning to Spain to write the *Natural and Moral History of the Indies*. On Acosta's use of Tovar's manuscripts and Tovar's method of working with Indigenous codices and informants, see Cañizares-Esguerra, *How to Write the History of the New World*, 73–75. Durán evidently used some of Tovar's manuscripts; see Bernal, introduction to Durán, *Aztecs*, xxvi–xxix. He also worked with local informants and some of this work was in turn used by Tovar; see Acosta, *Natural and Moral History*, 10.

8. Acosta, *Natural and Moral History*, 384–85, hereafter documented parenthetically.

9. Durán, *Aztecs*, 12, hereafter documented parenthetically.

10. Walter Stephens argues that giants in the European imagination were universally conceptualized as evil through the late medieval era (*Giants in Those Days*). Jeffrey Jerome Cohen argues that in European stories, giants' monstrosity functioned as an uncanny other, defining the limits of masculinity (*Of Giants*). Mayor speculates on the fossil origins of classical Greek and Roman hero legends (*First Fossil Hunters*, 104–56).

11. See Acosta, *Natural and Moral History*, 359. Durán is not so ethnographically precise as Acosta but he also records the Nahua's categorization of the Aboriginal inhabitants of Mexico as nomadic hunter-savages; see *Aztecs*, 11.

12. Durán speculates that the Indigenous people are descended from the ten tribes of Israel who were taken captive by the Assyrians (*Aztecs*, 3). Acosta does not insist on this point and is more interested in the route of migration. He was perhaps the earliest to propose the idea of a land link in the arctic region between Asia and the Americas (*Natural and Moral History*, 63). Classical climatology, which Acosta examines critically, posited the Torrid Zone as a global tropical belt too hot and dry to support much life, like the Sahara Desert (*Natural and Moral History*, 75–98).

13. Acosta understood Indigenous Mesoamerican writing as pictographic, which he judged to be inferior to alphabetic writing (*Natural and Moral History*, 334–42). Durán refers to preconquest "paintings" which his informants interpreted for him (e.g., *Aztecs*, 4).

14. On seasonality, see Clendinnen, *Aztecs*, 91, 111, 116, 200, 202. On the war of attrition thesis, see Hassig, *War and Society*, 145–46.

15. See Acosta, *Natural and Moral History*, 293–94, 415, 426.

16. Harris, *Cannibals and Kings*, 127–66.

17. See Marshall Sahlins's critique of Harris's functionalist reduction ("Culture as Protein," 45–53).

18. David Hodell et al., in "Climate Change on the Yucatan Peninsula," correlate oxygen isotope research with Aztec and Maya chronicles to present evidence for a fifteenth-century Little Ice Age in Mesoamerica.

19. Clendinnen also states that early frosts had stunted the maturing maize (*Aztecs*, 135–36). The memory was preserved, for example, in the phrase for suffering hunger, "being one-rabbited"; see Sahagún, *Primeros Memoriales*, 186.

20. Acosta does not mention the famine; see *Natural and Moral History*, 413–15. Durán narrates the innovation of the flower wars prior to the famine, though the chronology remains unclear; see *Aztecs*, 141–48. Caroline Dodds Pennock gives an earlier date for the origin of the flower wars (*Bonds of Blood*, 19).

21. Damrosch, "Aesthetics of Conquest."

22. Clendinnen, *Aztecs*, 262.

23. Clendinnen, *Aztecs*, 74–75. See the extensive treatment of the agricultural-sacrifice complex in Mesoamerican religion by Enrique Florescano in *Myth of Quetzalcoatl*, especially 116–93.

24. Clendinnen, *Aztecs*, 263. See also Carrasco, *City of Sacrifice*, 164–87.

25. On the Nahua distinction between a "flowery war" and an "angry war," see Hicks, "'Flowery War' in Aztec History."

26. The giants' appetitive qualities resonate with Jeffrey Jerome Cohen's reading of medieval English giant legends in *Of Giants*.

27. See de la Vega, *Incas*, 273–74.

28. Cieza de León, *Travels*, 189, hereafter documented parenthetically. On the excavation of the bones, see Zárate, *Discouerie and Conquest*, sig. Cii v.

29. Zárate also records their enormous appetites and their fishing (*Discouerie and Conquest*, sig. Cii r).

30. "Como les faltasen mujeres y las naturales no les cuadrasen por su grandeza, o porque sería vicio usado entre ellos, por consejo y inducimiento del maldito demonio, usaban unos con otros el pecado nefando de la sodomía, tan gravísimo y horrendo" (Cieza de León, *La Crónica del Perú*, 163). Markham found this sentence to be "unfit for translation" and omitted it; see Cieza de León, *Travels*, 190.

31. Again, Markham refused to translate "sodomía," supplying ellipses instead.

32. Acosta, *Natural and Moral History*, 60; Zárate, *Discouerie and Conquest*, sig. Cii r.

33. Mayor, *Fossil Legends*, 77. I discuss the question of the preservation of ancestral memory in Indigenous American narratives more fully in Chapter 2.

34. Here, I use Clovis loosely as a term to indicate a culture equipped with mammoth-killing technologies such as large flaked spear points. While archaeological evidence suggests that other peoples may have inhabited the Americas prior to the advent of Clovis, Clovis technology spread rapidly. See Waters and Stafford, "Redefining the Age of Clovis."

35. Aldo Leopold asserts to the contrary that the "Cro-Magnon who slew the last mammoth thought only of steaks" and concludes that mourning extinctions is a modern phenomenon (*Sand County Almanac*, 110).

36. On the possibility that the fire from the heavens might refer to the strike of a comet, see the discussion of the Younger Dryas scenario in Chapter 2.

37. Bender, *Culture of Extinction*, 125–39. Timothy Morton is among the latest to follow this line, positing that the Neolithic revolution instituted the "death-driven agricultural program" that alienates us from nonhuman beings (*Humankind*, 18).

38. See, for example, Sahlins's critique in *Stone Age Economics* of anthropologists' bourgeois assumptions in describing Paleolithic economies as impoverished.

39. Rappaport, *When Geologists Were Historians*, 105–35.

40. Molyneux, "Discourse Concerning the Large Horns," 489.

41. Hooke, *Posthumous Works*, 317.

42. See W. B. Hunter, "Plastic Nature."

43. Hooke, *Posthumous Works*, 321. Buffon would use a similar line of reasoning in his study of climate change: "In Civil History, one consults documents, studies old medals, deciphers antique inscriptions, to determine the epochs of human revolution and to establish the dates of moral events. Likewise, in natural history, one must rummage through the Earth's archives, pull ancient monuments from the entrails of the Earth, reassemble their remains, and put together in a body of evidence all the indications of physical change that can allow us to reach back into the different ages of Nature" (*Epochs of Nature*, 3).

44. Hooke, *Posthumous Works*, 327.

45. Hooke, *Posthumous Works*, 327.

46. Hooke, *Posthumous Works*, 285; see also the engraving, facing page 286, fig. 1.

47. As late as 1745, naturalists were still considering the Roman occupation as the explanation for elephant-like fossils found in England. See Rappaport, *When Geologists Were Historians*, 118.

48. J. Ewan and N. Ewan, *John Banister*, 332–33.

49. Clayton, "Continuation," 942–43. This John Clayton is not to be confused with the better-known botanist of the same name, a distant relation, whom Thomas Jefferson cites in Query VI of *Notes on the State of Virginia*.

50. Molyneux included accounts of South American giants gathered from sixteenth-century Spanish sources prominently in "An Essay Concerning Giants." Note that Hooke was evidently unaware of these American fossils.

51. Stiles, *Extracts*, 82, italics in original.

52. Stiles, *Extracts*, 82.

53. Stanford, "Giant Bones," 50, 51.

54. Stiles, *Extracts*, 82.

55. E. Taylor, *Minor Poetry*, 211–16.

56. Stiles, *Extracts*, 83, ellipses in original.

57. E. Taylor, *Minor Poetry*, 215.

58. On Taylor's use of Native American sources, see Morris, "Geomythology," 707–9. Stories of Maushops are collected in Simmons, *Spirit of the New England Tribes*, 172–209.

59. Only later in the eighteenth century would whale populations decline off the New England coast. Sturgeon remained abundant in the Hudson River well into the nineteenth century.

60. Simmons, *Spirit of the New England Tribes*, 199–201.

61. E. Taylor, *Minor Poetry*, 213.

62. Molyneux, "Essay Concerning Giants," 488.

63. E. Taylor, *Christographia*, 114–15.

64. E. Taylor, *Minor Poetry*, 211.

65. E. Taylor, *Minor Poetry*, 212.

66. E. Taylor, *Minor Poetry*, 212, 214.

67. Taylor knew alchemy through Paracelsian medicine. See Gordon-Grube, "Medicinal Cannibalism"; and Clack, *Marriage of Heaven and Earth*, 13–39. On alchemy and New England

Puritanism, see Woodward, *Prospero's America*. Of particular interest here are the homology between the alchemical refinement of metals and the purification of the soul and alchemy's projects of recovering primordial wisdom that had been lost with Adam's fall and discerning the interaction of visible and occult forces. Similarities in imagery between the prologue to the Claverack poem and Meditation 2.47 were first noted by Lawrence L. Sluder ("God in the Background," 268).

68. E. Taylor, *Poems*, 167.

69. E. Taylor, *Christographia*, 187.

70. E. Taylor, *Minor Poetry*, 213.

71. Bennett, *Vibrant Matter*, 91.

72. E. Taylor, *Christographia*, 187. The *OED* records the first use of *vitalism* in 1822 and *vitalist* in 1860.

73. Latour, *We Have Never Been Modern*. On the modernist project of de-animation, see also Latour, "Agency at the Time of the Anthropocene," 13–15.

74. As Amy Morris observes, arguments such as Hans Sloane's 1727 refutation of the idea that fossil teeth and bones were remains of giants speak to the persistence of the idea ("Geomythology," 714).

75. Mather, *Biblia Americana*, 1:582, italics in original. In all subsequent quotations from Mather, italics are in the original unless otherwise stated.

76. Mather, *Biblia Americana*, 1:588, 591.

77. The full text of Mather's letter to Woodward, November 17, 1712, is given in Levin, "Giants in the Earth." The quoted passage is at 767. Mather mistakenly transcribes the citation to Augustine as book 5, chapter 4; see Levin, 766.

78. Members of the Royal Society were not likely to be impressed by Mather implicitly positioning himself as a father of the New England church. The summary of Mather's letter published in the *Philosophical Transactions* in 1714 criticizes Mather for not including a drawing of the teeth and bones in question and dismisses the central claim, assuming that they are "the Bones and Teeth of some large Animals, . . . which, for some Reasons, [Mather] judges to be Human." The letter is reproduced in Stanford, "Giant Bones" (51–52, quotation taken from 51).

79. Mather, *Biblia Americana*, 1:597.

80. Mather, *Biblia Americana*, 1:586.

81. Mather, *Biblia Americana*, 1:594.

82. Morris, "Geomythology," 711. On the epistemological status of Indigenous knowledge in transatlantic natural history and colonial Europeans' ambivalent position, see Parrish, *American Curiosity*, especially 215–58.

83. Mather, *Biblia Americana*, 1:594n158.

84. Mather cites Acosta but includes no details beyond the reported size of the teeth and bones (*Biblia Americana*, 1:598). He may have known the 1604 English translation, *The Naturall and Morall Historie of the East and West Indies*.

85. Joseph Dudley to Cotton Mather, July 10, 1706, transcribed in Stanford, "Giant Bones," 50.

86. Mather, *Biblia Americana*, 1:665. The full commentary runs from 625 to 666.

87. On Burnet, see Gould, *Time's Arrow, Time's Cycle*, 20–59. On Burnet's reception in England and North America, see Semonin, *American Monster*, 49–61. John Woodward, secretary of the Royal Society to whom Mather addressed his letter on giants, particularly objected to Burnet's apparent removal of the intervening hand of God in his explanation of the flood.

88. Mather, *Biblia Americana*, 1:633.

89. Mather, *Biblia Americana*, 1:584.

90. Mather, *Biblia Americana*, 1:595.

91. On Leeuwenhoek, see Ruestow, "Images and Ideas."

92. W. B. Hunter, "Plastic Nature," 209.

93. Mather, *Christian Philosopher*, 117.

94. Mather, *Angel of Bethesda*, 28.

95. Mather, *Angel of Bethesda*, 30.

96. Mather, *Angel of Bethesda*, 30–31.

97. Mather, *Angel of Bethesda*, 30, 31.

98. Mather, *Angel of Bethesda*, 32.

99. Maturana and Varela, "Autopoiesis."

100. Žižek, *Less Than Nothing*, 120; see also 653. As a way out of this bind, Pier Luigi Luisi suggests the term "co-emergence," which is not used by Maturana and Varela ("Autopoiesis: A Review," 55). This focus on co-emergence could mitigate Donna Haraway's critique of autopoiesis as inattentive to the symbiotic character of all life. Haraway favors the term "sympoiesis"; see *Staying with the Trouble*, especially 58–98.

101. Cudworth, *True Intellectual System*, 1:234.

102. Cudworth, *True Intellectual System*, 1:234; Latour, "Compositionist Manifesto," 482, italics in original.

103. Maturana and Varela, "Autopoiesis," 122–23.

104. On Mather's rhetorical use of proto-germ theory during the Boston inoculation controversy, see Silva, *Miraculous Plagues*, 151–65.

105. Mather, *Angel of Bethesda*, 47.

106. Mather, *Angel of Bethesda*, 47. Inoculation could prepare the Nishmath-Chaijim for this onslaught much in the way that preparation helped the soul to receive grace; see Silva, *Miraculous Plagues*, 156.

107. Mather, *Biblia Americana*, 1:597.

108. Hooke, *Posthumous Works*, 327.

Chapter 2

1. The expedition was traveling from eastern Canada to New Orleans via the Ohio River. For details, see Mayor, *Fossil Legends*, 1–15. Mayor, working with a contemporary Abenaki informant, identifies the warriors as Abenaki. However, an officer's journal indicates that the group was predominantly Haudenosaunee, though it included a few Abenakis among Algonquian speakers of various nations; see J. F. H. Claiborne, "Journal of the Chickasa War," 72–73. Thanks to Gordon Sayre for directing me to this source.

2. Buffon, *Des époques de la nature*, 2:91; translated as "father-of-oxen" (Buffon, *Epochs of Nature*," 141), or as "grandfather of the buffalo" (Mayor, *Fossil Legends*, 13). The upper Hudson River valley is a significant repository of mammoth and mastodon fossils; see, for example, Semonin, *American Monster*, 15–19, 176–78, 315–16.

3. Subsequently collected remains found their way, often by circuitous routes, into other repositories of curiosity, including the private collections of Benjamin Franklin and other members of the Royal Society, the Royal Society's museum, the Tower of London, the American Philosophical Society, the great hall at Thomas Jefferson's Monticello, Charles Willson Peale's

Philadelphia Museum, and P. T. Barnum's American Museum. See Semonin, *American Monster*; and Rudwick, *Bursting the Limits of Time*, 263–71.

4. On Buffon, Cuvier, and the debate over Pleistocene fossils, see Rudwick, *Bursting the Limits of Time*, 246–75.

5. According to the Myaamia (Miami) scholar David Baldwin, none of the known Algonquian languages (the language family of most of the Big Bone Lick storytellers cited here, including Joseph Nicolar) has a solid equivalent for the concept of species extinction; the nearest equivalents would be dormancy or absence. See Baldwin, Noodin, and Perley, "Surviving the Sixth Extinction," 210–13.

6. On the debate over the premise that American nature was degenerate, see Gerbi, *Dispute of the New World*.

7. Jefferson, *Notes on the State of Virginia*, 43–44, 55.

8. Peale, *Historical Disquisition*, 2:577.

9. Barton, *Discourse*, 59–60, italics in original.

10. See Daston and Park, *Wonders and the Order of Nature*.

11. The homonym of *naturalist* as one who studies natural history (a standard eighteenth-century usage) and as one who holds a naturalistic (that is, materialistic) ontology may cause some terminological confusion. However, this confusion underscores the confusion of the students of natural history who excoriated Native Americans' supernaturalism while adhering to their own supernaturalism.

12. On water monsters, see Mayor, *Fossil Legends*, 9, 12–13.

13. Bartram, *Correspondence*, 563.

14. Bartram, *Correspondence*, 566.

15. It is not clear where the interview took place. Wright resided in Lenape County, outside of Philadelphia. However, it is unlikely that Bartram would have written to him unless he were in a location where he could meet someone who knew about the bones. Mayor thus places him at Fort Pitt in 1762; see *Fossil Legends*, 53.

16. Bartram, *Correspondence*, 569. As we saw in Chapter 1, stories of humanlike giants among New England Algonquian peoples cited mammoth teeth or bones as evidence. See also Stanford, "Giant Bones."

17. On Haudenosaunee raids into the Carolina Piedmont in the late seventeenth and early eighteenth century, see Merrell, *Indians' New World*, 5, 41–42, 78. One wonders whether this speaker had taken part in Longueuil's expedition; he would have been about fifty-seven at the time.

18. Winterbotham, *View of the American United States*, 3:139. On the emergence of the story of separate creations in the Ohio River valley in the mid-eighteenth century, see Dowd, *Spirited Resistance*, 30; and Cave, *Prophets of the Great Spirit*, 13–14.

19. Mather, *Biblia Americana*, 1:597.

20. Jefferson, *Notes on the State of Virginia*, 44. A version of the Lenape story, evidently deriving from Jefferson's text but stylistically embellished so as to sound more "Indian," was published in *American Museum* in 1790 and reprinted in Peale's *Historical Disquisition*, in *Selected Papers*, 2:577–78. On the composition of the 1781 delegation to Charlottesville and Jefferson's address, see Jefferson, *Papers*, 6:60.

21. Jefferson, *Notes on the State of Virginia*, 56.

22. E. J. W. Barber and P. Barber, *When They Severed the Earth*, 6–11.

23. Deloria, *Red Earth, White Lies*. Dismissing scientific techniques such as radiocarbon dating, Deloria claims that paleontologists work with a falsely expanded chronology. Deloria's postflood chronology encompasses three thousand years and places Indigenous Americans and dinosaurs in the same environment.

24. Echo-Hawk, "Ancient History," 273. See also Echo-Hawk, "Oral Traditions and Indian Origins"; and Bruchac, "Earthshapers and Placemakers." Peter Nabokov's comprehensive study of Native American historical narration leaves the question open (*Forest of Time*, 72–75).

25. On the hypothesis that a comet caused the Younger Dryas phase, see Dalton, "Blast from the Past?"

26. Archaeological evidence of human coexistence with mammoths and other extinct megafauna was discovered in France by Jacques Boucher de Perthes beginning in the 1830s; see Grayson, "Nineteenth-Century Explanations," 25–27. Clovis artifacts were first discovered, in association with mammoth remains, at Blackwater Draw (Texas and New Mexico) in the 1930s.

27. For overviews, see Krech, *Ecological Indian*, 29–43; and Mithen, *After the Ice*, 246–57.

28. Barton, *Discourse*, 60.

29. Latour, "Compositionist Manifesto," 482.

30. W. Hunter, "Observations on the Bones," 45.

31. On Buffon's theories of extinction and climate change, see Semonin, *American Monster*, 111–35; C. Cohen, *Fate of the Mammoth*, 94–100; and Rudwick, *Bursting the Limits of Time*, 139–50. Buffon explained the absence of elephants from tropical South America by arguing that they were stopped by a mountain barrier north of the isthmus of Panama. On Cuvier, see C. Cohen, *Fate of the Mammoth*, 105–21; and Rudwick, *Bursting the Limits of Time*, 353–88. On Breyne, see C. Cohen, *Fate of the Mammoth*, 70–73.

32. Peale, *Historical Disquisition*, 2:579.

33. Filson, *Discovery, Settlement, and Present State of Kentucke*, 34, 36.

34. On Turner's western career, see Semonin, *American Monster*, 306–7.

35. Turner, "Memoir on the Extraneous Fossils," 518.

36. Nabokov, in *Forest of Time*, argues that Native American historical narration—be it legend, myth, or folktale—is always oriented toward the present of the telling. The modal approach to the narration of environmental agency that I am suggesting here owes much to Hayden White's *Metahistory*.

37. On revitalization in the Ohio River valley, see Dowd, *Spirited Resistance*, 27–35; Richter, *Facing East*, 180–81, 193–99; and Cave, *Prophets of the Great Spirit*, 11–44.

38. On such "masters of the game" in Algonquin territory, see C. Martin, *Keepers of the Game*. On the Great Beaver, see also Brooks, *Common Pot*, 14–24; and Bruchac, "Earthshapers and Placemakers," 70–73. In citing Martin, I do not agree with his thesis that the Algonquins overhunted the beaver to take revenge for their supposed causing of diseases. Rather, Krech's account of Algonquin belief seems more plausible, according to which the beaver would always return, if treated with respect, no matter how many were killed; see *Ecological Indian*, 300n56.

39. Kenny, "Journal," 180.

40. As the Ottawa leader Pontiac explained the Lenape prophet Neolin's vision, the Master of Life told Neolin that he had sent the game animals away as punishment for the peoples' dependence on the whites and would bring them back when the people returned to the old ways and followed his teachings (Pontiac, *Journal*, 22–32). In Neolin's vision, the Master of Life acts

as master of the game; in the Haudenosaunee Big Bone Lick story, the creator spirit controls the giant buffalo, a master-of-the-game figure.

41. On the Revolutionary War context, see A. F. C. Wallace, *Jefferson and the Indians*, 62–66.

42. Jefferson, *Notes on the State of Virginia*, 44.

43. Jefferson, *Notes on the State of Virginia*, 55.

44. Jefferson, "Memoir on the Discovery of Certain Bones," 255–56. The remains were discovered in a cave in western Virginia by workers digging nitrous deposits for a saltpeter works. The animal was soon classified by Cuvier as a species of giant ground sloth.

45. Jefferson to John Adams, April 11, 1823, in *Writings*, 15:427.

46. God disappeared or receded into a nebulous figure of ultimate cause that did not intervene in nature, as wonders were reduced to the regular order of nature; see Daston and Park, *Wonders and the Order of Nature*.

47. Darwin, *On the Origin*, 1st ed. (1859), 490, italics added.

48. Owen, *History of British Fossil*, 270.

49. Darwin, *On the Origin*, 2nd ed. (1860), 490.

50. Among Darwin's contemporaries, Richard Owen explicitly posited "intelligence evoking means adapted to the end," theoretically traceable back to a "great First Cause, which is certainly not mechanical" (*Palaeontology*, 414).

51. Wallace, *Geographical Distribution of Animals*, 1:150.

52. Parkinson, *Organic Remains*, 3:xiv. This volume's frontispiece derives from Big Bone Lick, depicting "The back grinding tooth of the MAMMOTH or MASTODON of the Ohio." Parkinson is better known as the author of *An Essay on the Shaking Palsy* (1817), the disease later named after him.

53. W. Hunter, "Observations on the Bones," 45.

54. Wells, "Grisly Folk," 607.

55. Cuvier, *Essay on the Theory of the Earth*, 96, 166.

56. On Agassiz's speculative analogy to the human body, see Irmscher, *Louis Agassiz*, 65. Buffon presented his theory of global cooling in *The Epochs of Nature*.

57. Agassiz, *Geological Sketches*, 208.

58. Agassiz, *Geological Sketches*, 210.

59. Wallace, *Geographical Distribution of Animals*, 1:150–51.

60. Darwin to Wallace, June 5, 1876, in *More Letters*, 13.

61. Grayson, "Nineteenth-Century Explanations," 15–20.

62. On Mathews and the founding of Young America, see P. Miller, *Raven and the Whale*, 85–87. On Young America's expansionist politics, see Rogin, *Subversive Genealogy*, 71–75.

63. The genesis of the Mound Builder fiction is analyzed by Gordon Sayre in "Mound Builders." Probably the best known example of the Mound Builder fiction is William Cullen Bryant's much-anthologized 1834 poem "The Prairies."

64. See Watts, *Colonizing the Past*, 95–137; on Mathews's *Behemoth*, see Watts, 109–16.

65. Mathews, *Behemoth*, 4, hereafter documented parenthetically. Mathews supplied extensive notes on both archaeological finds that he supposed supported the Mound Builder fiction and accounts of several discoveries of mammoth remains. He also reprinted the Lenape story first printed by Jefferson (*Behemoth*, 163–64).

66. Miller speculates on the novel's influence on Melville (*Raven and the Whale*, 82–83). The mammoth's vengeance here seems to foreshadow Moby Dick's behavior.

67. Mathews, *Behemoth*, 106; Melville, *Moby-Dick*, 70.

68. Peale displayed the painting alongside the rearticulated skeleton in his Philadelphia museum. Mathews notes the discovery and display of these remains in Peale's museum (*Behemoth*, 177). On the exhumation and Peale's painting, see Rigal, *American Manufactory*, 89–113.

69. Sayre argues that, notwithstanding the novel's ending, symbolically the Mound Builders and the mammoth are both conflated with the "vanishing Indian" ("Mammoth," 78).

70. Cusick, *Sketches*, 19, hereafter documented parenthetically.

71. Haudenosaunee print culture emerged at the same time as whites' attempts to expropriate land intensified; see Radus, "Printing Native History." On the political context and the response of Haudenosaunee activists such as Red Jacket and Cusick, see Konkle, *Writing Indian Nations*, 224–87. On the publication history of the *Sketches*, see Round, *Removable Type*, 188–90, 210–16.

72. Cusick's verb tenses are not always consistent. English was not his first language.

73. Lyell, *Principles of Geology*, 2:155.

74. Lyell, *Geological Evidences*, 189. Archaeological work by Jacques Boucher de Perthes persuasively demonstrated that humans and the Pleistocene megafauna were contemporaneous. Boucher de Perthes was a catastrophist, however, who attributed the Late Pleistocene extinctions to a great deluge. When his stratigraphic evidence was correlated by archaeologists working at other sites, his chronology gained credence but his causal explanation did not. See Grayson, "Nineteenth-Century Explanations," 24–26.

75. Owen, *Palaeontology*, 399, hereafter documented parenthetically.

76. A. R. Wallace, *World of Life*, 262, hereafter documented parenthetically.

77. The Penobscots formed part of the confederation of eastern Algonquians known as the Wabanaki, who shared a language, Abenaki.

78. Quoted in Kolodny, "Rethinking the 'Ecological Indian,'" 5–6.

79. Nicolar, *Life and Traditions of the Red Man*, 95, hereafter documented parenthetically. On the political and economic context, see Kolodny, "Summary History of the Penobscot Nation," 1–34.

80. Klose-kur-beh (or Gluskap, Gluska'be) is a Wabanaki trickster-creator similar to the Anishinaabe Nanabozho or the Winnebago Wakjankaga; on Wakjankaga, see Radin, *Trickster*. As Kolodny observes, Nicolar's Klose-kur-beh is less deceitful and lewd than other Wabanaki versions; see introduction to Nicolar, *Life and Traditions of the Red Man*, 48.

81. "The Great Mastodon" was one of the exhibits in the Anthropological Building of the Columbian Exposition of 1893. Photographs were circulated by publishers such as Keystone or the American Stereoscopic Company; e.g., "The Great Mastodon, Anthropological Building, World's Columbian Exposition. Smithsonian Institution," Identifier number 1996.0009. KU71140, Keystone-Mast Collection, UCR/California Museum of Photography, University of California at Riverside, *Online Archive of California*, accessed November 24, 2020, https://oac .cdlib.org/ark:/13030/kt6m3nc30t/?brand=oac4. The Exposition also included a Penobscot Village exhibit; see Kolodny, "Introduction," 37.

82. See, for example, Wabanaki stories collected in Leland, *Algonquin Legends*, 19, 29; and Alger, *In Indian Tents*, 111–12. These stories concern Gluskap's downsizing of Moose, Squirrel, Bear, and Beaver to make them less threatening to humans. They do not mention the mammoth, nor do they broach the topic of extinction.

83. Eastman, *Indian Boyhood*, 192, 193.

84. Deloria, *Red Earth, White Lies*, 154–78.

85. Kelly Wisecup identifies a metaphorical dimension as well, the "interpretive fog" of English treaty writing and settler-colonial bureaucracies ("'Meteors, Ships, Etc.'").

86. Quoted in Brooks, *Common Pot*, 20–21.

87. Jefferson, "Memoir on the Discovery of Certain Bones," 256.

Chapter 3

1. Curtis, *North American Indian*, 11:37. This is taken from a story of the origin of whaling told by a whale hunter from Clayoquot village to George Hunt, a Tlingit-English ethnologist who often worked with Franz Boas. Like other early anthropologists, Curtis used the name given to these peoples by Captain James Cook, Nootka.

2. Curtis, *North American Indian*, 11:23.

3. Willie Sport, quoted in Ćoté, *Spirits of Our Whaling Ancestors*, 34.

4. On the sinking of the *Essex*, see N. Philbrick and T. Philbrick, eds., *Loss of the Ship "Essex"*; and N. Philbrick, *In the Heart of the Sea*.

5. The whale chief did not eat of the whale he killed (see Curtis, *North American Indian*, 11:18) but would receive meat and oil in potlatches held by other chiefs. On landing ceremonies and whaling chiefs' potlatches, see Coté, *Spirits of Our Whaling Ancestors*, 34–41.

6. Coté, *Spirits of Our Whaling Ancestors*, 69–114.

7. Melville, *Moby-Dick*, 500, hereafter documented parenthetically.

8. In chapter 104 on the fossil record of whales, Melville drew on the latest paleontological findings, including Richard Owens's famous identification of the Zeuglodon as a seagoing mammal. See Vincent, *Trying-Out*, 346–51. Jennifer Baker argues that such scientific investigations establish the ground for Ishmael's experience of awe and wonder ("Dead Bones and Honest Wonders"). In contrast to recent appropriations of the term "deep time" in literary criticism, here I return to John McPhee's original definition of the term as time preceding human existence. See Gould, *Time's Arrow, Time's Cycle*, 3.

9. Jefferson to John Adams, April 11, 1823, in *Writings*, 15:427. He did, as noted in Chapter 2, eventually accept the fact of extinction.

10. Jefferson, *Notes*, 55.

11. Quoted in Hornaday, *Extermination of the American Bison*, 387–88.

12. See Barrow, *Nature's Ghosts*, 47–107.

13. Lyell, *Principles of Geology*, 1:164.

14. Lyell, *Principles*, 2:156.

15. Lyell, *Principles*, 2:156.

16. On the quarterdeck scene as political allegory, see, for example, Pease, "Melville and Cultural Persuasion," 384–417.

17. See Semonin, *American Monster*.

18. See R. Webb, *On the Northwest*. In 1937 the marine biologist Johan Hjort proposed a managerial approach to the pattern, assuming an equilibrist ecological model and arguing that "the efficiency and magnitude of whaling operations must not be indefinitely increased but kept at a level corresponding to the reproductive abilities of the stock of whales, if whaling is ever to be made a lasting human activity." See Hjort, "Story of Whaling," 28.

19. Crèvecoeur, *Letters from an American Farmer*, 110–11.

20. "Whale Fishery," 115, italics in original.

21. M. E. Bowles, "Some Account of the Whale-Fishery of the N. West Coast and Kamschatka," *Polynesian* (Honolulu), October 4, 1845, 83. Bowles signed himself as an officer of the

Rhode Island whale ship *Jane* in "She Would Have Him: A Temperance Tale" (*Friend* [Honolulu], November 1, 1845, 161), accessed November 24, 2020, https://hmha.missionhouses.org/items/show/982.

22. M. E. Bowles, "The Sea Elephant: A Page from My Journal," *Friend* (Honolulu), May 1, 1845, 66, accessed November 24, 2020, https://hmha.missionhouses.org/items/show/970.

23. Cheever, *Whale and His Captors*, 107–9. On Melville's use of this book, see Vincent, *Trying-Out*, 131, 212–13, 256, 260, 266–67, 292, 323–24. Mark Bousquet identifies this book as marking a change in the national attitude toward whales from commercial exploitation to conservation ("Cruel Harpoon and the Honorable Lamp").

24. Montgomery, "Pelican Island," 2:19–20.

25. Montgomery, "Pelican Island," 2:18, 19.

26. "Polar Whale's Appeal," *Friend* (Honolulu), October 15, 1850, 82–83, accessed November 24, 2020, https://hmha.missionhouses.org/items/show/1133. All subsequent quotations are taken from these pages.

27. On this first polar whaling expedition, see Dolin, *History of Whaling*, 226–31. The Anadir Sea is now known as the Bering Sea.

28. Latour, *Politics of Nature*, 66–68.

29. "Memorials of the Cherokee Indians," 165, 164, 167, 168.

30. Dolin, *History of Whaling*, 84.

31. See, for example, Cary Wolfe's critique of the sacrificial logic of humanism in *Animal Rites*.

32. As critics have remarked, Melville questions the human/animal difference throughout *Moby-Dick*, frequently anthropomorphizing animals and zoomorphizing humans. See, e.g., Eric Wilson, "Melville, Darwin, and the Great Chain of Being," 131–50; Schultz, "Melville's Environmental Vision in *Moby-Dick*," 97–113; Buell, *Writing for an Endangered World*, 205–14; and Armstrong, "*Moby-Dick* and Compassion," 19–37.

33. Recent movements of the small remaining population of right whales (a baleen species) have become unpredictable, sometimes vexing conservation biologists' efforts to track them. See O'Connor, *Resurrection Science*, 94–99, 118–19.

34. Chase, *Narrative*, 13–73.

35. Melville's annotations are reproduced in Philbrick and Philbrick, eds., *The Loss of the Ship "Essex."*

36. Philbrick and Philbrick, eds., *Loss of the Ship "Essex,"* 4.

37. Chase, *Narrative*, 29–30.

38. Jefferson, *Notes*, 67–68. On Jefferson's Logan as a figure for lastness, see Elmer, *On Lingering*, 118–46. On the resonance of Ahab and the "vanishing Indian" motif, see Dimock, "Ahab's Manifest Destiny."

39. Lawrence, *Studies in Classic American Literature*, 159.

40. Melville, "Benito Cereno," 90.

41. Melville quotes from Jeremiah 31:15. The allusion suggests that it is doubtful whether the *Rachel* ever finds the missing whaleboat; she does, however, later rescue the *Pequod*'s lone survivor Ishmael.

42. On traditional biblical time scales such as the 6,000-year chronology popularized by James Ussher's *Annals of the World*, five thousand years ago is a reasonable date for the flood. Genesis 7:6 reports Noah's age at the time as six hundred years.

43. On Miller's influence on U.S. literature, see Scharnhorst, "Images of the Millerites," 19–36. Robert Levine focuses on Poe and Hawthorne in *Race, Transnationalism* (63–81). Thomas Beebee discusses Hawthorne and locates Melville's Ahab in millennial discourse as a "hybrid messiah" in *Millennial Literatures* (49–55, 109–15). On Miller's influence in Great Britain, see Corfield, *Time and the Shape of History*, 120.

44. Melville, "Hawthorne and His Mosses," 1415, 1417.

45. See W. Miller, *Evidence from Scripture and History*, 7.

46. Poe, *Poetry and Tales*, 361.

47. Hawthorne, *Tales and Sketches*, 742.

48. Hawthorne, *Tales and Sketches*, 746.

49. Hawthorne, *Tales and Sketches*, 905.

50. Quoted in Watters and Dugger, "Hunt for Gray Whales," 332, italics added.

51. Harrison, "Sea Level," 167.

52. Hogan, "Silencing Tribal Grandmothers," italics added.

53. Hogan, "Silencing Tribal Grandmothers."

54. Harrison, "Sea Level," 166–67.

55. The IUCN Red List of Threatened Species currently lists the gray whale (*Eschrichtius robustus*) as "regionally extinct" in European coastal waters but globally a species of "least concern" (accessed November 24, 2020, https://www.iucnredlist.org/species/8097/12885185, https://www.iucnredlist.org/species/8097/50353881).

56. Coté, *Spirits of Our Whaling Ancestors*. Devoting less attention to whaling per se, Ann M. Tweedie also locates the 1999 hunt within a larger program of Makah cultural revitalization; see *Drawing Back Culture*, 6–8, 138–41.

57. Treaty of Neah Bay, 1855, Article 4, Governor's Office of Indian Affairs, State of Washington.

58. Reid, *Sea Is My Country*, 154, 262–63; Coté, *Spirits of Our Whaling Ancestors*, 120–21. On the problematic concept of a resource commons, see the discussion of the Buffalo Commons in Chapter 4.

59. International Whaling Commission, *International Convention for the Regulation of Whaling* (December 2, 1946), 2, resource 3607.

60. The moratorium takes the form of annual catch limits, which have been set at zero since 1985–86, with exceptions for Aboriginal subsistence whaling, but could be increased if stocks permit. See International Whaling Commission, "Commercial Whaling" and "Aboriginal Subsistence Whaling."

61. Reid, *Sea Is My Country*, 176. Concern that exploitative hunting by "the civilized whaler" would lead to the California gray whale's extinction was voiced as early as 1874; see Scammon, *Marine Mammals*, 33.

62. Coté, *Spirits of Our Whaling Ancestors*, 69–114.

63. Coté, *Spirits of Our Whaling Ancestors*, 15–16. A recent print by Art Thompson (Ditidaht/Nuu-chah-nulth/Cowichan), "Not a Good Day," integrates the three actors in this story, depicting a whale diving, surrounded by Thunderbird on one side and Lightning Serpent on the other, twined around a harpoon shaft; reproduced in Coté, *Spirits of Our Whaling Ancestors* (107). The line bound to the harpoon head follows the curves of Lightning Serpent's body. The print thus aligns human whalers with Thunderbird and their weapons with Lightning Serpent.

64. Coté, *Spirits of Our Whaling Ancestors*, 164, 171–72.

65. *Annual Report of the International Whaling Commission 1998*, 78, italics added.

66. Reid, *Sea Is My Country*, 1–2.

67. For a review of legal proceedings from the treaty era through the 1999 hunt and its immediate aftermath, see Bradford, "Save the Whales."

68. National Oceanic and Atmospheric Administration, "Draft Environmental Impact Statement on the Makah Tribe Request to Hunt Gray Whales."

69. Hopper, "Whale Wars Group vs. Makah." This argument came from Catherine Pruett, executive director of Sea Shepherd Legal.

70. Charlotte Coté, email message to the author, March 17, 2018.

71. See Gaard, "Tools for a Cross-Cultural Feminist Ethics," 14. The Creek-Cherokee scholar Craig Womack takes a similar position in a recent essay, "There Is No Respectful Way to Kill an Animal," although he does not refer to the Makah hunt.

72. Deloria, "Self-Determination," 122.

73. Bradford, "Save the Whales," 212.

74. National Oceanic and Atmospheric Administration, "Draft Environmental Impact Statement," ES-6, ES-7.

75. Coté, *Spirits of Our Whaling Ancestors*, 204.

76. Coté, *Spirits of Our Whaling Ancestors*, 193–207.

77. Quoted in Coté, *Spirits of Our Whaling Ancestors*, 202.

78. Slogan quoted in Nasady, "Transcending the Debate," 291.

79. "Makah Whaling."

80. Coté, *Spirits of Our Whaling Ancestors*, 204.

81. Quoted in Coté, *Spirits of Our Whaling Ancestors*, 139.

82. See Bowechop (Makah), "Contemporary Makah Whaling," 414. The accounts are consistent in Coté, *Spirits of Our Whaling Ancestors*; Reid, *Sea Is My Country*; and Sullivan, *Whale Hunt*. Literary critics, however, have ignored the mismatch between the actual beliefs and conditions of the Makah hunt and Hogan's representations of these beliefs and conditions. See, for example, McHugh, *Love in a Time of Slaughters*, 74–91.

83. Hogan, *People of the Whale*, 78, hereafter documented parenthetically.

84. In September 2007, five Makahs, frustrated with the protracted legal process, organized a second hunt and killed a gray whale. The Coast Guard intervened, however, and the whale was never towed to shore. The Makah performed sacred songs over the dying whale as it sank. The Tribal Council denounced the hunt. Even so, the negative publicity from the unauthorized hunt did not help the Makah's case. See Coté, *Spirits of Our Whaling Ancestors*, 183–88.

85. Harrison, "Sea Level," 167.

86. Coté, Reid, Bowechop, and Sullivan all provide similar accounts of the facts of the hunt that contravene these claims. Sullivan reports, for example, that the gun was a single-action rifle used for hunting elephants, as recommended by an expert veterinarian (that is, not a "machine gun" as charged by Hogan) (*Whale Hunt*, 211). As Bowechop points out, the .577 caliber bullet inflicted less pain than the traditional method, in which sealskin floats were attached to the harpoon line to tire out the whale and keep it from diving ("Contemporary Makah Whaling," 416).

87. Harrison, "Sea Level," 168.

88. Hogan, "Silencing Tribal Grandmothers." Coté does not mention Hogan. It is quite possible that, since *Spirits of Our Whaling Ancestors* was published in 2010, she was not aware

of Hogan's novel. McHugh concedes that a distinction between killing whales and killing fish remains "a lingering problem" in Hogan's novel (McHugh, *Love in a Time of Slaughters*, 92).

89. In the first chapter of *Principles of Geology*, Lyell warns against confusing geology with cosmogony and identifies Charles Hutton as the first to draw a clear distinction; see 1:4.

90. Latour, *Politics of Nature*, 66.

91. Agamben, *Homo Sacer*, 127.

92. Hogan, "Silencing Tribal Grandmothers."

93. A much greater threat than closely regulated hunting is posed, for example, by pollution from the salt mining industry that impacts one of the gray whales' mating and birthing grounds, the Laguna Ojo de Liebre in Baja California. See Sullivan, *Whale Hunt*, 185.

Chapter 4

1. "Buffalo Campaign," 705.

2. David Smits, in "The Frontier Army and the Destruction of the Buffalo," reviews the evidence. The destruction of the buffalo as a means of pacifying Plains peoples would have been consistent with the total-war strategy that had characterized Sherman's March to the Sea and Carolinas Campaign, which effectively ended Confederate resistance.

3. Old Lady Horse (Kiowa), "The Last Buffalo Herd," quoted in Hubbard, "Buffalo Genocide," 301.

4. I will use *bison* and *buffalo* interchangeably in this chapter, generally following my sources.

5. Allen, *American Bisons, Living and Extinct*, 67.

6. Hubbard, "Buffalo Genocide."

7. Andrew Isenberg's history takes all these factors into account (*Destruction of the Bison*). See also Flores, "Bison Ecology"; and Krech, *Ecological Indian*, 123–49. John Barnard focuses on the displacement of bison by settler-colonists' cattle ("Bison and the Cow").

8. Catlin, *Letters and Notes*, 1:261, hereafter documented parenthetically.

9. Based on Bryant's visit to Illinois in 1832, the poem curiously avoids all mention of the state's last Indigenous territorial struggle, the Black Hawk War, which took place during that year.

10. Bryant, "Prairies," 164.

11. On the pervasive nineteenth-century narrative of Native American extinction, see, for example, Dippie, *Vanishing American*; Sheehan, *Seeds of Extinction*; Maddox, *Removals*; Elmer, *On Lingering and Being Last*; and O'Brien, *Firsting and Lasting*.

12. Compare Catlin, *North American Indians*, 262, which does not print this passage.

13. Thoreau, *Maine Woods*, 712.

14. On the potential for the sustainability of the pre-1840s Plains complex, see Isenberg, *Destruction of the Bison*, 83–84. Others, however, argue that even the buffalo-hunting culture which developed after the widespread adoption of horses but prior to repeating rifles (i.e., circa 1750–1850) may not have been sustainable in the long term. See Flores, "Bison Ecology"; and Lewis, *Green Delusions*, 65. On buffer zones, see Flores, "Bison Ecology," 476; and P. Martin and Szuter, "War Zones."

15. The historical information in this paragraph is taken largely from Isenberg, *Destruction of the Bison*.

16. On the Plains peoples' assumptions of the bison's autochthonous origin, see Krech, *Ecological Indian*, 148–49. On drought cycles, see Flores, "Bison Ecology," 469.

17. A little-remarked feature of this market culture was the U.S. government's effort to privatize Native Americans' access to buffalo by assigning particular hunting grounds to particular tribes in exchange for safe passage of white settlers bound for the west coast. See Flores, "Wars over Buffalo."

18. Cook, *Border and the Buffalo*, 115.

19. Allen, *American Bisons*, 67, hereafter documented parenthetically.

20. Allen, "North American Bison," 215, hereafter documented parenthetically.

21. As discussed in Chapter 2, Mound Builders occupied an important place in the nineteenth-century white American imagination. See Sayre, "Mound Builders"; and Watts, *Colonizing the Past*, 95–137.

22. W. P. Webb, *Great Plains*, 44.

23. See, for example, a buffalo hunter's use of this term in John Williams's thoroughly researched historical novel, *Butcher's Crossing* (131).

24. On stabilizing selection, see Schmalhausen, *Factors of Evolution*.

25. Recent science also describes *Bison bison* as a human artifact that evolved (e.g., becoming smaller and developing mixed-sex herding behavior) in response to human predation and environmental management by means of fire, but on a longer time scale. See Flannery, *Eternal Frontier*, 221–27.

26. Hornaday, *Extermination of the American Bison*, 377, hereafter documented parenthetically.

27. The editor of *Forest and Stream* magazine from 1876 to 1911, Grinnell used the magazine's pages to mount a preservationist campaign. See Punke, *Last Stand*, 124–39.

28. Grinnell, "Last of the Buffalo," 282, hereafter documented parenthetically.

29. Hornaday, "Passing of the Buffalo.—II," 231, hereafter documented parenthetically.

30. Hornaday, "Passing of the Buffalo.—I," 85, hereafter documented parenthetically.

31. See Haraway, "Teddy Bear Patriarchy."

32. Young, *Pet Projects*, 104. Young argues that Hornaday saw the taxidermist as "an all-powerful male creator" (103).

33. The image of this bull's head is also featured on the National Park Service's ranger badge and the Department of Interior's official seal. See Shell, Introduction, xviii.

34. Irving, *Tour on the Prairies*, 191.

35. Hornaday developed innovations in taxidermy, such as discarding much of the animal's skeleton and replacing it with a hollow wooden manikin, to present the ideal form of the animal. See Herron, "Stuffed," 65–67.

36. The Hornaday Smithsonian Buffalo and Dean and Donna Strand Western Art Gallery, Fort Benton, Montana Museums and Heritage Complex, accessed November 24, 2020, http://fortbentonmuseums.com/the-museums/hornaday-smithsonian-buffalo/. On the rediscovery and assembly of the Buffalo Group, see Coffman, *Reflecting the Sublime*.

37. On the painting's reception, see Cash et al., eds., *Corcoran Gallery of Art*, 170–72.

38. "French Talk of the Time," *New York Times*, October 1, 1889, 9, quoted in Cash et al., eds., *Corcoran Gallery*, 172. The first lines of Cowper's poem on Selkirk read, "I am monarch of all I survey, / My right there is none to dispute" (*Poems of William Cowper*, 1:403).

39. Black Elk and Neihardt, *Black Elk Speaks*, 213, hereafter documented parenthetically.

40. Although Black Elk was in Paris at the time Bierstadt's *Last of the Buffalo* was on exhibit, we do not know if he accompanied his compatriot Rocky Bear in visiting the gallery. For the chronology, see DeMallie, ed., *Sixth Grandfather*, 7–11, 245–51.

41. Hornaday, *Extermination of the American Bison*, 527.

42. See Grinnell, *Blackfoot Lodge Tales*, 293–94, hereafter documented parenthetically. Among other actions, Grinnell successfully lobbied for the removal of a corrupt Indian Affairs agent from the Blackfoot reservation. See Punke, *Last Stand*, 228, 269.

43. Krech briefly reviews the archaeological evidence of ostensibly wasteful kills, recognizing that waste is a concept imposed by Western values (*Ecological Indian*, 143–45).

44. Krech, *Ecological Indian*, 142–49.

45. Similar conflicts of context and values occur perpetually at the intersection of capitalist economies with subsistence economies, as for example in Alaska today. See Council of Athabascan Tribal Governments, *Survival Denied*.

46. While "Blackfoot Genesis" is chronologically the first of these stories, Grinnell placed it late in *Blackfoot Lodge Tales* with other stories about Na'pi, after "Stories of Adventure" and "Stories of Ancient Times."

47. For example, Dorsey, *Pawnee Mythology*. See "Buffalo Wife and Corn Wife," 62–68; and "Cannibal Witch and the Boy Who Conquered the Buffalo," 72–82.

48. For a summary of the story, shared by Utes and Lakotas, see Zontek, *Buffalo Nation*, 3.

49. On the Ghost Dance, see Andersson, *Lakota Ghost Dance*; Kehoe, *Ghost Dance*; and Black Elk and Neihardt, *Black Elk Speaks*, 230–62.

50. See Nabokov, *Forest of Time*, esp. 58–104.

51. U.S. Department of Agriculture, *USDA Livestock Slaughter 2018 Summary*, 65. Barnard argues that the marketing of buffalo as an ecologically sustainable alternative to beef cattle gives a green veneer to American food culture, which still privileges ranching and beef consumption ("Bison and the Cow," 389–93).

52. See, for example, the account of the annual buffalo roundup and auction at Custer State Park, which are open to the public ("Buffalo Auction," South Dakota Game, Fish & Parks, accessed November 24, 2020, https://gfp.sd.gov/buffalo-auction/). The National Park Service devotes much of its Bison Management FAQ page to answering questions about culling and shipping to meat processors ("Questions and Answers About Bison Management," National Park Service, accessed November 24, 2020, https://www.nps.gov/yell/learn/management/bison-management-faqs.htm). The Custer State Park herd in South Dakota numbers roughly 1,300 ("Custer State Park Buffalo Roundup," South Dakota Department of Tourism, accessed November 24, 2020, https://www.travelsouthdakota.com/things-do/events/custer-state-park-buffalo-roundup). Ironically, there is a small herd at Big Bone Lick State Park, site of the mammoth fossils discussed in Chapter 2. This herd is managed by periodic sales. See "Why Is This Kentucky Historic Site Offering Four Bison for Sale?," *Lexington Herald Leader*, February 4, 2019, https://www.kentucky.com/news/politics-government/article225506485.html.

53. See "Bison Sale," National Bison Range, accessed November 24, 2020, https://www.fws.gov/refuge/National_Bison_Range/Resource_Management/bison_sale.html.

54. Popper and Popper, "Great Plains."

55. Responding to criticism, the Poppers insisted that the idea should be viewed as an inspirational metaphor and not as a particular plan ("Buffalo Commons"). For an overview of the controversy, see Braun, "Ecological and Un-Ecological Indians."

56. Popper and Popper, "Great Plains," 18, italics added.

57. Popper and Popper, "Great Plains," 18. Dave Foreman focuses primarily on setting aside interlinked wilderness areas following the Rockies from British Columbia to New Mexico, with the primary goal of reestablishing large predators (*Rewilding North America*). Paul Martin

imagines re-creating, as nearly as can be accomplished with living species, analogues to Late Pleistocene ecosystems (*Twilight of the Mammoths*). As Dolly Jørgensen argues, rewilding discourse often erases human history and interactions with an ecosystem ("Rethinking Rewilding").

58. Wheeler, *Buffalo Commons*, 324.

59. The Ojibwe environmental activist Winona LaDuke uses "Buffalo Commons" when discussing the reception of the Poppers' proposal by white ranchers and "Buffalo Nation" for tribal projects (*All Our Relations*, 138–62).

60. Cruise, *Digest of the Laws of England*, 3:82.

61. Locke, *Two Treatises*, 304.

62. Hardin, "Tragedy of the Commons." For a critique outlining the way in which such formulations strip away the complex cultural forces that defined rights and responsibilities in actual, historical commons, see Nixon, "Neoliberalism, Genre, and 'The Tragedy.'" On Indigenous North Americans' traditional management of commons, see Greer, *Property and Dispossession*, 27–64.

63. Popper and Popper, "Buffalo Commons," 495.

64. See Braun, *Buffalo Inc.*, 48–60, 62.

65. Quoted in Matt Kelley, "Indians Work to Restore Buffalo on Tribal Lands," *Associated Press*, January 10, 1993. For other such instances, see Zontek, *Buffalo Nation*, xiii.

66. This image comes from Braun, *Buffalo Inc.*, 4. Zontek, *Buffalo Nation*, 86, summarizes the ceremonial dimension of many tribes' killing and butchering practices.

67. See Zontek, *Buffalo Nation*, 33–70.

68. From a broad survey, Krech concludes that conflicts between those who favor economic development (often those in tribal government) and those who place greater value on spiritual and ecological matters are "not uncommon" in Indian country ("Beyond the Ecological Indian," 20).

69. Quoted in Braun, *Buffalo Inc.*, 120.

70. On the closing, see Braun, *Buffalo Inc.*, 161–75, 235–37. On reopening, see "Pte Hca Ka: Buffalo Herd Vital to CRST People, Past, Present and Future," *West River Eagle* (Eagle Butte, SD), January 10, 2018, https://www.westrivereagle.com/articles/pte-hca-ka-buffalo-herd-vital -to-crst-people-past-present-and-future/.

71. Based on a 2003 survey of thirty-five tribes in Zontek, *Buffalo Nation*, 171–75. A recent ITBC document posted on the National Congress of American Indians website lists sixty-two member tribes ("Intertribal Buffalo Council Presentation," National Congress of American Indians, accessed November 24, 2020, http://www.ncai.org/conferences-events/ncai-events/Land _and_Natural_Resources_Committee_-_Inter_Tribal_Buffalo_Council_Presentation.pdf).

72. Hogan, "First People," 18, 19.

73. Lyell, *Principles of Geology*, 2:156.

74. Quoted in Braun, *Buffalo Inc.*, 81.

75. Derrida, "'Eating Well,'" 112.

76. See Agamben, *Open*.

77. van Dooren, "Care"; van Dooren, *Flight Ways*, 87–122.

78. Morton, *Humankind*.

Reprise

1. "Nature's Dangerous Decline 'Unprecedented'; Species Extinction Rates 'Accelerating,'" United Nations Sustainable Development Goals, May 6, 2019, https://www.un.org

/sustainabledevelopment/blog/2019/05/nature-decline-unprecedented-report/. See also the Intergovernmental Science-Policy Platform on Biodiversity and Ecosystem Services (IPBES) media release, accessed November 24, 2020, https://www.ipbes.net/news/Media-Release-Global -Assessment. Note that not all species are threatened by trends identified in the IPBES report. For example, ocean warming and acidification favor the proliferation of jellyfish; see Gershwin, *Stung!*

2. "One Million Species Face Extinction, U.N. Panel Says. And Humans Will Suffer as a Result," *Washington Post*, May 6, 2019, https://www.washingtonpost.com/climate-environment /2019/05/06/one-million-species-face-extinction-un-panel-says-humans-will-suffer-result/ ?utm_term=.6cd8c0cbf010.

3. "Nature's Dangerous Decline 'Unprecedented.'"

4. Heise, *Imagining Extinction*, 5.

5. Agamben differentiates *zoe* or bare life from *bios* or form-of-life/political life in *Means Without End* (3–12), and develops this differentiation extensively in *Homo Sacer*.

6. See E. O. Wilson, *Future of Life*, 129–48. Wilson posits that biophilia and its antithesis, biophobia, are inherent capacities that can be nurtured or discouraged.

7. Quoted in Tonino, "We Only Protect What We Love." Among the proponents of cross-species love as a response to the extinction crisis are Rose, *Wild Dog Dreaming*; and McHugh, *Love in a Time of Slaughters*.

8. IPBES media release.

9. Parkinson, *Organic Remains*, 3:xiv.

10. Lyell, *Principles of Geology*, 2:156.

11. On Thoreauvian asceticism, see Buell, *Environmental Imagination*, 143–79.

12. Matthew Taylor argues that the new materialisms "risked revivifying the very anthro-pocentrism they ostensibly challenged" and retain hierarchical, even eugenic implications ("Life's Return," 475).

13. That is, following the likes of Val Plumwood, in *Feminism and the Mastery of Nature*, I have argued for self-aware difference rather than deep ecology's holism or human mastery's dualism.

14. David Cusick's history, discussed in Chapter 2, spends less time on the "war [that] broke out among the Five Nations" during the time of the Onondaga chief Atotharo and the peaceful resolution of the "chain of alliance" than do some other histories of the confederation, probably for strategic reasons in its argument against preemption, but that episode is still crucial (*Sketches*, 22, 23).

15. Johnston, *Ojibway Heritage*, 56–57. The Anishinaabe legal scholar John Borrows retells this story working from two sources, Johnston and the Anishinaabe storyteller John Nadjiwan (*Recovering Canada*, 18–20). Paul Nasady argues that the claim that animals give themselves to hunters ought to be taken not metaphorically, as anthropologists typically do, but rather as a literal account of the world ("Gift of the Animal").

16. Johnston, *Ojibway Heritage*, 51–52.

17. "Origin of Disease and Medicine," in Mooney, *History, Myths, and Sacred Formulas of the Cherokees*, 250–52.

18. In Dorsey, *Pawnee Mythology*, see "Buffalo Wife and Corn Wife," 62–68; and "The Can-nibal Witch and the Boy Who Conquered the Buffalo," 72–82.

19. Sarah James (Gwichin), quoted in Hogan, "First People," 19. Hogan would not want to be taken as implying a hierarchy in which humans are superior to animals because animals lack language. (For a philosophical critique of the latter position, see Wolfe, *Animal Rites*, 44–94.)

Consistent with the claim that animals are capable of engaging in treaties, Hogan assumes a difference of language rather than a lack.

20. Latour, *Politics of Nature*, 66.

21. Leopold, *Sand County Almanac*, 204.

22. Viral pandemics such as AIDS or COVID-19 put even this claim of human power in question. I oversimplify here as well by discounting direct action taken by animals or plants, as invasive species, to disrupt other animals or plants important to human purposes—cause five as listed in the IPBES report.

23. Jefferson, "Memoir on the Discovery of Certain Bones," 256.

BIBLIOGRAPHY

Acosta, José de. *Natural and Moral History of the Indies.* Ed. Jane E. Mangan. Trans. Frances López-Morillas. Durham, NC: Duke University Press, 2002.

Agamben, Giorgio. *Homo Sacer: Sovereign Power and Bare Life.* Trans. Daniel Heller-Roazen. Stanford, CA: Stanford University Press, 1998.

———. *Means Without End: Notes on Politics.* Trans. Vincenzo Binetti and Cesare Casarino. Minneapolis: University of Minnesota Press, 2000.

———. *The Open: Man and Animal.* Trans. Kevin Attell. Stanford, CA: Stanford University Press, 2004.

Agassiz, Louis. *Geological Sketches.* Boston: Ticknor and Fields, 1866.

Alger, Abby L. *In Indian Tents: Stories Told by Penobscot, Passamaquoddy and Micmac Indians.* Boston: Roberts Brothers, 1897.

Allen, Joel Asaph. *The American Bisons, Living and Extinct.* 1876. Rpt. New York: Arno, 1974.

———. "The Extirpation of the Larger Indigenous Mammals of the United States." *Penn Monthly* 7 (1876): 794–806.

———. "The North American Bison and Its Extermination." *Penn Monthly* 7 (1876): 214–24.

Anderson, Atholl. *Prodigious Birds: Moas and Moa-Hunting in Prehistoric New Zealand.* Cambridge: Cambridge University Press, 1989.

Anderson, Nancy K., and Linda S. Ferber. *Albert Bierstadt: Art and Enterprise.* New York: Brooklyn Museum, in association with Hudson Hills Press, 1990.

Andersson, Rani-Henrik. *The Lakota Ghost Dance of 1890.* Lincoln: University of Nebraska Press, 2009.

Annual Report of the International Whaling Commission 1998. Cambridge: Red House, 1999. Accessible at https://iwc.int/documents.

Araujo, Bernardo B. A., Luiz Gustavo R. Oliveira-Santos, Matheus S. Lima-Ribeiro, José Alexandre F. Diniz-Filho, and Fernando A. S. Fernandez. "Bigger Kill Than Chill: The Uneven Roles of Humans and Climate on Late Quaternary Megafaunal Extinctions." *Quaternary International* 431 (2017): 216–22.

Aristotle. *Poetics.* Trans. Malcolm Heath. New York: Penguin Books, 1996.

Armstrong, Philip. "Moa Citings." *Journal of Commonwealth Literature* 45 (2010): 325–39.

———. "*Moby-Dick* and Compassion." *Society and Animals* 12 (2004): 19–37.

Avery, Mark. *A Message from Martha: The Extinction of the Passenger Pigeon and Its Relevance Today.* London: Bloomsbury, 2014.

Baker, Jennifer Jordan. "Dead Bones and Honest Wonders: The Aesthetics of Natural Science in Moby-Dick." In *Melville and Aesthetics,* ed. Samuel Otter and Geoffrey Sanborn, 85–101. New York: Palgrave Macmillan, 2011.

Baldwin, Daryl, Margaret Noodin, and Bernard C. Perley. "Surviving the Sixth Extinction: American Indian Strategies for Life in the New World." In *After Extinction*, ed. Richard Grusin, 201–33. Minneapolis: University of Minnesota Press, 2018.

Barber, Elizabeth Wayland, and Paul T. Barber. *When They Severed the Earth from the Sky: How the Human Mind Shapes Myth*. Princeton, NJ: Princeton University Press, 2004.

Barnard, John. "The Bison and the Cow: Food, Empire, Extinction." *American Quarterly* 72 (2020): 377–401.

Barnosky, Anthony D., Paul L. Koch, Robert S. Feranec, Scott L. Wing, and Alan B. Shabel. "Assessing the Causes of Late Pleistocene Extinctions on the Continents." *Science* 306, no. 5693 (2004): 70–75.

Barnosky, Anthony D., Nicholas Matzke, Susumu Tomiya, Guinevere O. U. Wogan, Brian Swartz, Tiago B. Quental, Charles Marshall, Jenny L. McGuire, Emily L. Lindsey, Kaitlin C. Maguire, Ben Mersey, and Elizabeth A. Ferrer. "Has Earth's Sixth Mass Extinction Already Arrived?" *Nature* 471, no. 7336 (March 3, 2011): 51–57.

Barrow, Mark, Jr. *Nature's Ghosts: Confronting Extinction from the Age of Jefferson to the Age of Ecology*. Chicago: University of Chicago Press, 2009.

Barton, Benjamin Smith. *A Discourse on Some of the Principal Desiderata in Natural History*. Philadelphia: Denham and Town, 1807.

Bartram, John. *The Correspondence of John Bartram, 1734–1777*. Ed. Edmund Berkeley and Dorothy Smith Berkeley. Gainesville: University Press of Florida, 1992.

Beebee, Thomas. *Millennial Literatures of the Americas, 1492–2002*. New York: Oxford University Press, 2009.

Bekoff, Marc, and Jessica Pierce. *Wild Justice: The Moral Lives of Animals*. Chicago: University of Chicago Press, 2009.

Benatar, David. *Better Never to Have Been: The Harm of Coming into Existence*. Oxford: Clarendon Press, 2006.

Bender, Frederic L. *The Culture of Extinction: Toward a Philosophy of Deep Ecology*. New York: Humanity Books, 2003.

Bennett, Jane. *Vibrant Matter: A Political Ecology of Things*. Durham, NC: Duke University Press, 2010.

Bernal, Ignacio. Introduction to *The Aztecs: The History of the Indies of New Spain*, by Fray Diego Durán, xxi–xxxii. New York: Orion, 1964.

Black Elk and John G. Neihardt. *Black Elk Speaks: Being the Life Story of a Holy Man of the Oglala Sioux as Told Through John G. Neihardt*. 1932. Rpt. Lincoln: University of Nebraska Press, 1988.

Boggs, Colleen. *Animalia Americana: Animal Representations and Biopolitical Subjectivity*. New York: Columbia University Press, 2013.

Bonneuil, Christophe, and Jean-Baptiste Fressoz. *The Shock of the Anthropocene: The Earth, History and Us*. Trans. David Fernbach. Brooklyn, NY: Verso, 2016.

Borrows, John. *Recovering Canada: The Resurgence of Indigenous Law*. Toronto: University of Toronto Press, 2002.

Botkin, Daniel. *Discordant Harmonies: A New Ecology for the Twenty-First Century*. New York: Oxford University Press, 1990.

Bousquet, Mark. "The Cruel Harpoon and the Honorable Lamp: The Awakening of an Environmental Consciousness in Henry Theodore Cheever's *The Whale and His Captors*." *Interdisciplinary Studies in Literature and Environment* 19 (2012): 253–73.

Bowechop, Janine. "Contemporary Makah Whaling." In *Coming to Shore: Northwest Coast Ethnology, Traditions, and Visions*, ed. Marie Mauzé, Michael Harkin, and Sergei Kan, 407–19. Lincoln: University of Nebraska Press, 2004.

Bradford, William. "Save the Whales vs. Save the Makah: Finding Negotiated Settlements to Ethnodevelopmental Disputes in the New Economic Order." *St. Thomas Law Review* 13 (2000): 155–220.

Brassier, Ray. *Nihil Unbound: Enlightenment and Extinction*. New York: Palgrave Macmillan, 2007.

Braun, Sebastian Felix. *Buffalo Inc.: American Indians and Economic Development*. Norman: University of Oklahoma Press, 2008.

———. "Ecological and Un-Ecological Indians: The (Non)portrayal of Plains Indians in Buffalo Commons Literature." In Harkin and Lewis, eds., *Native Americans and the Environment*, 192–208.

Brooks, Lisa. *The Common Pot: The Recovery of Native Space in the Northeast*. Minneapolis: University of Minnesota Press, 2008.

Bruchac, Margaret. "Earthshapers and Placemakers: Algonkian Indian Stories and the Landscape." In *Indigenous Archaeologies: Decolonizing Theory and Practice*, ed. Claire Smith and H. Martin Wobst, 56–80. New York: Routledge, 2005.

Bryant, William Cullen. "The Prairies." In *American Poetry: The Nineteenth Century*, ed. John Hollander, 1:162–65. New York: Library of America, 1993.

Buell, Lawrence. *The Environmental Imagination: Thoreau, Nature Writing, and the Formation of American Culture*. Cambridge, MA: Harvard University Press, 1995.

———. *Writing for an Endangered World: Literature, Culture, and Environment in the U.S. and Beyond*. Cambridge, MA: Harvard University Press, 2001.

"A Buffalo Campaign." *Army Navy Journal*, June 26, 1869, 705.

Buffon, Georges-Louis Leclerc, Comte de. *Epochs of Nature*. Trans. and ed. Jan Zalasiewicz, Anne-Sophie Milon, and Mateusz Zalasiewicz. Chicago: University of Chicago Press, 2018.

———. *Des époques de la nature*. In *Oeuvres complètes de Buffon avec les supplemens*, 2:71–184. Paris: P. Duménil, 1836. Biodiversity Heritage Library. https://www.biodiversitylibrary.org/.

Calarco, Matthew. *Zoographies: The Question of the Animal from Heidegger to Derrida*. New York: Columbia University Press, 2008.

Cañizares-Esguerra, Jorge. *How to Write the History of the New World: Histories, Epistemologies, and Identities in the Eighteenth-Century Atlantic World*. Stanford, CA: Stanford University Press, 2001.

Carrasco, David. *City of Sacrifice: The Aztec Empire and the Role of Violence in Civilization*. Boston: Beacon Press, 1999.

Cash, Sarah, Emily Dana Shapiro, and Lisa Strong, eds. *Corcoran Gallery of Art: American Paintings to 1945*. Washington, DC: Corcoran Gallery, 2011.

Catlin, George. *Letters and Notes on the Manners, Customs, and Condition of the North American Indian*. Vol. 1. New York: Wiley and Putnam, 1842.

———. *North American Indians*. Ed. Peter Matthiessen. 1989. New York: Penguin Books, 2004.

Cave, Alfred A. *Prophets of the Great Spirit: Native American Revitalization Movements in Eastern North America*. Lincoln: University of Nebraska Press, 2006.

Cavitch, Max. *American Elegy: The Poetry of Mourning from the Puritans to Whitman*. Minneapolis: University of Minnesota Press, 2007.

Ceballos, Gerardo, Paul Ehrlich, and Rodolfo Dirzo. "Biological Annihilation via the Ongoing Sixth Mass Extinction Signaled by Vertebrate Population Losses and Declines." *PNAS* 114 (July 10, 2017). https://doi.org/10.1073/pnas.1704949114.

Chakrabarty, Dipesh. "The Climate of History: Four Theses." *Critical Inquiry* 35 (2009): 197–222.

———. "Humanities in the Anthropocene: The Crisis of an Enduring Kantian Fable." *New Literary History* 47 (2016): 377–97.

Chase, Owen. *Narrative of the Most Extraordinary and Distressing Shipwreck of the Whale-Ship "Essex."* In *The Loss of the Ship "Essex," Sunk by a Whale,* ed. Nathaniel Philbrick and Thomas Philbrick, 13–73. New York: Penguin Books, 2000.

Cheever, Henry T. *The Whale and His Captors; or, The Whaleman's Adventures and the Whale's Biography.* New York: Harper and Brothers, 1850.

Chrulew, Matthew. "Hunting the Mammoth, Pleistocene to Postmodern." *Journal for Critical Animal Studies* 9 (2011): 32–47. http://www.criticalanimalstudies.org/wp-content/uploads /2009/09/3.-Chrulew-M-Issue-1-2-Hunting-the-Mammoth-pp-32-47.pdf.

Cieza de León, Pedro de. *La Crónica del Perú.* 3rd ed. Madrid: Espasa-Calpe, 1962.

———. *The Travels of Pedro de Cieza de León, A.D. 1532–50, Contained in the First Part of His Chronicle of Peru.* Trans. Clements R. Markham. London: Hakluyt Society, 1864.

Clack, Randall A. *The Marriage of Heaven and Earth: Alchemical Regeneration in the Works of Taylor, Poe, Hawthorne, and Fuller.* Westport, CT: Greenwood Press, 2000.

Claiborne, J. F. H. "Journal of the Chickasa War." In *Mississippi as a Province, Territory, and State,* vol. 1, *1880,* 64–85. Rpt. Baton Rouge: Louisiana State University Press, 1964.

Clayton, John. "A Continuation of Mr. John Clayton's Account of Virginia." *Philosophical Transactions* 17 (1693): 941–48.

Clendinnen, Inga. *Aztecs: An Interpretation.* New York: Cambridge University Press, 1991.

Coffman, Douglas. *Reflecting the Sublime: The Rebirth of an American Icon.* Fort Benton, MT: River and Plains Society, 2013.

Cohen, Claudine. *The Fate of the Mammoth: Fossils, Myth, and History.* Trans. William Rodarmor. Chicago: University of Chicago Press, 2002.

Cohen, Jeffrey Jerome. *Of Giants: Sex, Monsters, and the Middle Ages.* Minneapolis: University of Minnesota Press, 1999.

Colebrook, Claire. *Death of the Posthuman: Essays on Extinction.* Vol. 1. Critical Climate Change Series. Ann Arbor, MI: Open Humanities Press, 2014. http://openhumanitiespress.org /books/download/Colebrook_2014_Death-of-the-PostHuman.pdf.

———. "Lives Worth Living: Extinction, Persons, Disability." In *After Extinction,* ed. Richard Grusin, 151–71. Minneapolis: University of Minnesota Press, 2018.

Cook, John R. *The Border and the Buffalo: An Untold Story of the Southwest Plains.* Topeka, KS: Crane, 1907.

Cooper, James Fenimore. *The Pioneers.* 1823. Rpt. New York: Penguin, 1988.

———. *The Prairie.* 1827. Rpt. San Francisco: Rinehart, 1950.

Corfield, Penelope. *Time and the Shape of History.* New Haven, CT: Yale University Press, 2007.

Coté, Charlotte. *Spirits of Our Whaling Ancestors: Revitalizing Makah and Nuu-chah-nulth Traditions.* Seattle: University of Washington Press, 2010.

Council of Athabascan Tribal Governments. *Survival Denied: Stories from Alaska Native Families Living in a Broken System.* Seattle, WA: Alliance for a Just Society, 2013. http:// allianceforajustsociety.org/wp-content/uploads/2013/03/Survival-Denied2.pdf.

Cowper, William. *The Poems of William Cowper*. Vol. 1. Ed. John D. Baird and Charles Ryskamp. Oxford: Clarendon Press: 1980.

Craft, Aimée. *Breathing Life into the Stone Fort Treaty: An Anishnabe Understanding of Treaty One*. Saskatoon, SK: Purich, 2013.

Crèvecoeur, J. Hector St. John de. *Letters from an American Farmer*. Oxford: Oxford University Press, 1997.

Cronon, William. "The Trouble with Wilderness; or, Getting Back to the Wrong Nature." In *Uncommon Ground: Rethinking the Human Place in Nature*, ed. William Cronon, 69–90. New York: Norton, 1995.

Cruise, William. *A Digest of the Laws of England Respecting Real Property*. Vol. 3. 2nd ed. London: J. Butterworth and Son, 1818. https://archive.org.

Cudworth, Ralph. *The True Intellectual System of the Universe: Wherein All the Reason and Philosophy of Atheism Is Confuted, and Its Impossibility Demonstrated; With a Treatise Concerning Eternal and Immutable Morality*. Trans. John Harrison. Vol. 1. London: T. Tegg, 1845.

Curtis, Edward S. *The North American Indian*. Vol. 11. Norwood, MA: Plimpton Press, 1916.

Cusick, David. *David Cusick's Sketches of the Ancient History of the Six Nations*. New York: Cooley and Lathrop, 1828. Rpt. ed. Paul Royster. Lincoln: Faculty Publications 24, University of Nebraska Libraries, 1993. https://digitalcommons.unl.edu/libraryscience/24.

Cuvier, Georges. *Essay on the Theory of the Earth, With mineralogical notes and an account of Cuvier's geological discoveries by Robert Jameson and with observations on the geology of North America by Samuel L. Mitchel*. New York: Kirk and Mercein, 1818.

Dalton, Rex. "Blast from the Past?" *Nature* 447 (May 17, 2007): 256–57.

Damrosch, David. "The Aesthetics of Conquest: Aztec Poetry Before and After Cortés." *Representations* 132 (1991): 101–20.

Danowski, Déborah, and Eduardo Viveiros de Castro. *The Ends of the World*. Cambridge: Polity Press, 2017.

Darwin, Charles. *More Letters of Charles Darwin*. Ed. Francis Darwin and A. C. Seward. London: John Murray, 1903.

———. *On the Origin of Species by Means of Natural Selection*. London: John Murray, 1859.

———. *On the Origin of Species by Means of Natural Selection*. 2nd ed. London: John Murray, 1860.

Daston, Lorraine, and Katharine Park. *Wonders and the Order of Nature, 1150–1750*. New York: Zone Books, 2001.

Dawson, Ashley. "Biocapitalism and De-Extinction." In *After Extinction*, ed. Richard Grusin, 173–200. Minneapolis: University of Minnesota Press, 2018.

———. *Extinction: A Radical History*. New York: OR Books, 2016.

Deloria, Vine, Jr. "Self-Determination and the Concept of Sovereignty." In *Native American Sovereignty*, ed. John Wunder, 118–24. New York: Routledge, 1999.

———. *Red Earth, White Lies: Native Americans and the Myth of Scientific Fact*. New York: Scribner, 1995.

DeMallie, Raymond J., ed. *The Sixth Grandfather: Black Elk's Teachings Given to John Neihardt*. Lincoln: University of Nebraska Press, 1984.

Derrida, Jacques. "'Eating Well,' or the Calculation of the Subject: An Interview with Jacques Derrida." In *Who Comes After the Subject?*, ed. Eduardo Cadava, Peter Connor, and Jean-Luc Nancy, 96–119. New York: Routledge, 1991.

Descola, Philippe. *Beyond Nature and Culture*. Trans. Janet Lloyd. Chicago: University of Chicago Press, 2013.

Díaz del Castillo, Bernal. *The Discovery and Conquest of Mexico, 1517–1521*. Trans. A. P. Maudslay. New York: Harper, 1928.

———. *Historia verdadera de la conquista de la Nueva España*. Ed. Joaquín Ramírez Cabañas. Mexico: Alianza Editorial Porrúa, 1955.

Dimock, Wai Chee. "Ahab's Manifest Destiny." In *Macropolitics of Nineteenth-Century Literature: Nationalism, Exoticism, Imperialism*, ed. Jonathan Arac and Harriet Ritvo, 184–212. Philadelphia: University of Pennsylvania Press, 1991.

Dippie, Brian. *The Vanishing American: White Attitudes and U.S. Indian Policy*. Middletown, CT: Wesleyan University Press, 1982.

Dolin, Eric Jay. *The History of Whaling in America*. New York: Norton, 2007.

Donlan, Josh. "De-Extinction in a Crisis Discipline." *Frontiers of Biogeography* 6 (2014): 25–28. https://doi.org/10.21425/F5FBG19504.

Dorsey, George A. *The Pawnee Mythology. Part I*. Washington, DC: Carnegie Institution, 1906.

Dowd, Gregory Evans. *A Spirited Resistance: The North American Indian Struggle for Unity, 1745–1815*. Baltimore: Johns Hopkins University Press, 1992.

Durán, Diego. *The Aztecs: The History of the Indies of New Spain*. Trans. Doris Heyden and Fernando Horcasitas. Introduction by Ignacio Bernal. New York: Orion, 1964.

Eastman, Charles. *Indian Boyhood*. New York: McClure, Phillips, 1902.

Echo-Hawk, Roger. "Ancient History in the New World: Integrating Oral Traditions and the Archaeological Record in Deep Time." *American Antiquity* 65 (2000): 267–90.

———. "Oral Traditions and Indian Origins: A Native American Perspective." In *Exploring Ancient Native America: An Archaeological Guide*, by David Hurst Thomas, 41–42. New York: Macmillan, 1994.

Elmer, Jonathan. *On Lingering and Being Last: Race and Sovereignty in the New World*. New York: Fordham University Press, 2008.

Ewan, Joseph, and Nesta Ewan. *John Banister and His Natural History of Virginia, 1678–1692*. Urbana: University of Illinois Press, 1970.

Faure, Valentine. "Man and Beast." *Nation*, August 24, 31, 2020, 12–17.

Filson, John. *The Discovery, Settlement, and Present State of Kentucke*. 1784. Ann Arbor, MI: University Microfilms, 1966.

Flannery, Timothy. *The Eternal Frontier: An Ecological History of North America and Its Peoples*. New York: Grove Press, 2001.

Flannery, Timothy, and David Burney. "Fifty Millennia of Catastrophic Extinction After Human Contact." *Trends in Ecology and Evolution* 20 (2005): 395–401.

Flores, Dan. "Bison Ecology and Bison Diplomacy: The Southern Plains from 1800 to 1850." *Journal of American History* 78 (1991): 465–85.

———. "Wars over Buffalo: Stories Versus Stories on the Northern Plains." In Harkin and Lewis, eds., *Native Americans and the Environment*, 152–69.

Florescano, Enrique. *The Myth of Quetzalcoatl*. Trans. Lysa Hochroth. Baltimore: Johns Hopkins University Press, 1999.

Foreman, Dave. *Rewilding North America: A Vision for Conservation in the 21st Century*. Washington, DC: Island Press, 2004.

Freud, Sigmund. *Reflections on War and Death*. Trans. A. A. Brill and Alfred B. Kuttner. New York: Moffat, Yard, 1918.

Frye, Northrop. *Anatomy of Criticism: Four Essays*. Princeton, NJ: Princeton University Press, 1957.

Gaard, Greta Claire. "Tools for a Cross-Cultural Feminist Ethics: Exploring Ethical Contexts and Contents in the Makah Whale Hunt." *Hypatia* 16 (Winter 2001): 1–26.

Garrard, Greg. *Ecocriticism*. 2nd ed. New York: Routledge, 2004.

Gerbi, Antonello. *The Dispute of the New World: The History of a Polemic, 1750–1900*. Trans. Jeremy Moyle. Pittsburgh, PA: University of Pittsburgh Press, 1973.

Gershwin, Lisa-ann. *Stung! On Jellyfish Blooms and the Future of the Ocean*. Chicago: University of Chicago Press, 2013.

Ghosh, Amitav. *The Great Derangement: Climate Change and the Unthinkable*. Chicago: University of Chicago Press, 2016.

Glavin, Terry. *The Sixth Extinction: Journey Among the Lost and Left Behind*. New York: St. Martin's Press, 2006.

Gordon-Grube, Karen. "Evidence of Medicinal Cannibalism in Puritan New England: 'Mummy' and Related Remedies in Edward Taylor's 'Dispensatory.'" *Early American Literature* 28 (1993): 185–221.

Gould, Stephen Jay. *Time's Arrow, Time's Cycle: Myth and Metaphor in the Discovery of Geological Time*. Cambridge, MA: Harvard University Press, 1987.

Goulson, Dave. "The Insect Apocalypse and Why It Matters." *Current Biology* 29 (October 7, 2019): R942–95.

Grayson, Donald K. "Nineteenth-Century Explanations of Pleistocene Extinctions: A Review and Analysis." In *Quaternary Extinctions: A Prehistoric Revolution*, ed. Paul S. Martin and Richard G. Klein, 5–39. Tucson: University of Arizona Press, 1984.

Greer, Allan. *Property and Dispossession: Natives, Empires, and Land in Early Modern North America*. Cambridge: Cambridge University Press, 2018.

Grinnell, George Bird. *Blackfoot Lodge Tales: The Story of a Prairie People*. 1892. Rpt. Lincoln: University of Nebraska Press, 1962.

———. "The Last of the Buffalo." *Scribner's Magazine* 12 (1892): 267–86.

Hamilton, Clive. *Requiem for a Species: Why We Resist the Truth About Climate Change*. London: Earthscan, 2010.

Harari, Yuval. *Sapiens: A Brief History of Humankind*. New York: HarperCollins, 2015.

Haraway, Donna. *Staying with the Trouble: Making Kin in the Chthulucene*. Durham, NC: Duke University Press, 2016.

———. "Teddy Bear Patriarchy: Taxidermy in the Garden of Eden." In *Primate Visions: Gender, Race, and Nature in the World of Modern Science*, 26–58. New York: Routledge, 1989.

———. *When Species Meet*. Minneapolis: University of Minnesota Press, 2007.

Hardin, Garrett. "The Tragedy of the Commons." *Science* 162 (December 13, 1968): 1243–48.

Harkin, Michael, and David Rich Lewis, eds. *Native Americans and the Environment: Perspectives on the Ecological Indian*. Lincoln: University of Nebraska Press, 2007.

Harris, Marvin. *Cannibals and Kings: Origins of Cultures*. New York: Vintage Books, 1977.

Harrison, Summer. "Sea Level: An Interview with Linda Hogan." *Interdisciplinary Studies in Literature and Environment* 18 (2011): 161–77.

Hassig, Ross. *War and Society in Mesoamerica*. Berkeley: University of California Press, 1992.

Hawthorne, Nathaniel. *Tales and Sketches*. New York: Library of America, 1982.

Haynes, Gary, ed. *American Megafaunal Extinctions at the End of the Pleistocene*. Dordrecht: Springer, 2009.

Heise, Ursula. *Imagining Extinction: The Cultural Meaning of Endangered Species*. Chicago: University of Chicago Press, 2016.

Herron, John. "Stuffed: Nature and Science on Display." In *Rendering Nature: Animals, Bodies, Places, Politics*, ed. Marguerite S. Shaffer and Phoebe S. K. Young, 48–69. Philadelphia: University of Pennsylvania Press, 2015.

Hicks, Frederic. "'Flowery War' in Aztec History." *American Ethnologist* 6 (1979): 87–92.

Hjort, Johan. "The Story of Whaling: A Parable of Sociology." *Scientific Monthly* 45 (1937): 19–34.

Hodell, David A., Mark Brenner, Jason H. Curtis, and Roger Medina-González. "Climate Change on the Yucatan Peninsula During the Little Ice Age." *Quaternary Research* 63 (2005): 109–21.

Hogan, Linda. "First People." In *Intimate Nature: The Bond Between Women and Animals*, ed. Linda Hogan, Deena Metzger, and Brenda Peterson, 6–19. New York: Fawcett, 1998.

———. *People of the Whale*. New York: Norton, 2009.

———. "Silencing Tribal Grandmothers—Traditions, Old Values at Heart of Makah's Clash over Whaling." *Seattle Times*, December 15, 1996.

Hooke, Robert. *The Posthumous Works of Robert Hooke*. London, 1705. Eighteenth Century Collections Online.

Hopper, Frank. "Whale Wars Group vs. Makah: Who Decides If Traditions Are Authentic?" *Indian Country Today*, June 23, 2015. https://indiancountrytoday.com/archive/whale-wars-group-vs-makah-who-decides-if-traditions-are-authentic-DdpgR5qsAkivgO5VckxK0g.

Hornaday, William Temple. *The Extermination of the American Bison*. 1889. Rpt. Washington, DC: Smithsonian Institution Press, 2002.

———. "The Passing of the Buffalo.—I." *Cosmopolitan* 4 (1887): 85–98.

———. "The Passing of the Buffalo.—II." *Cosmopolitan* 4 (1887): 231–43.

Hubbard, Tasha. "Buffalo Genocide in Nineteenth-Century North America." In *Colonial Genocide in Indigenous North America*, ed. Andrew Woolford, Jeff Benevenuto, and Alexander Laban Hinton, 292–305. Durham, NC: Duke University Press, 2014.

Hunter, William. "Observations on the Bones, Commonly Supposed to Be Elephants Bones, Which Have Been Found Near the River Ohio in America." *Philosophical Transactions* 58 (1768): 34–45.

Hunter, William B., Jr. "The Seventeenth Century Doctrine of Plastic Nature." *Harvard Theological Review* 43 (1950): 197–213.

International Whaling Commission. "Aboriginal Subsistence Whaling." Accessed December 2, 2020. https://iwc.int/aboriginal.

———. "Commercial Whaling." Accessed December 2, 2020. https://iwc.int/commercial.

———. *International Convention for the Regulation of Whaling*. Washington, DC, 1946. Accessed December 2, 2020. https://archive.iwc.int/pages/view.php?ref=3607&k.

Irmscher, Christoph. *Louis Agassiz: Creator of American Science*. Boston: Houghton Mifflin, 2013.

Irving, Washington. *A Tour on the Prairies*. 1834. Rpt. New York: Pantheon, 1967.

Isenberg, Andrew. *The Destruction of the Bison: An Environmental History, 1750–1920*. Cambridge: Cambridge University Press, 2000.

Jefferson, Thomas. "A Memoir on the Discovery of Certain Bones of a Quadruped of the Clawed Kind in the Western Parts of Virginia." *Transactions of the American Philosophical Society* 4 (1799): 246–60.

———. *Notes on the State of Virginia*. Ed. Frank Shuffelton. New York: Penguin Books, 1999.

———. *Papers of Thomas Jefferson*. Ed. Julian P. Boyd et al. Vols. 6 and 29. Princeton, NJ: Princeton University Press, 1950–.

———. *The Writings of Thomas Jefferson*. Ed. Andrew A. Lipscomb and Albert Ellery Bergh. Vol. 15. Washington, DC: Jefferson Memorial Association, 1903.

Johnston, Basil. *Ojibway Heritage*. New York: Columbia University Press, 1976.

Jørgensen, Dolly. "Rethinking Rewilding." *Geoforum* 65 (2015): 482–88.

Kant, Immanuel. *Critique of the Power of Judgment*. Ed. Paul Guyer. Cambridge: Cambridge University Press, 2000.

Kareiva, Peter, and Simon Levin, eds. *The Importance of Species: Perspectives on Expendability and Triage*. Princeton, NJ: Princeton University Press, 2003.

Kehoe, Alison Beck. *The Ghost Dance: Ethnohistory and Revitalization*. New York: Holt, Rinehart, and Winston, 1989.

Kelly, Robert L., and Mary M. Prasciunas. "Did the Ancestors of Native Americans Cause Animal Extinctions in Late-Pleistocene North America? And Does It Matter If They Did?" In Harkin and Lewis, eds., *Native Americans and the Environment*, 95–122.

Kenny, James. "Journal of James Kenny, 1761–63." Ed. John W. Jordan. *Pennsylvania Magazine of History and Biography* 37 (1913): 1–47, 152–201. https://archive.org/details/pennsylvaniamaga37histuoft.

Klein, Naomi. *This Changes Everything: Capitalism vs. the Climate*. New York: Simon and Schuster, 2014.

Koch, Paul, and Anthony Barnosky. "Late Quaternary Extinctions: State of the Debate." *Annual Review of Ecology, Evolution, and Systematics* 37 (2006): 215–50.

Kohn, Eduardo. *How Forests Think: Toward an Anthropology Beyond the Human*. Berkeley: University of California Press, 2013.

Kolbert, Elizabeth. *The Sixth Extinction: An Unnatural History*. New York: Henry Holt, 2014.

Kolodny, Annette. Introduction to Nicolar, *Life and Traditions of the Red Man*, 35–88.

———. "Rethinking the 'Ecological Indian': A Penobscot Precursor." *Interdisciplinary Studies in Literature and Environment* 14 (2007): 1–23.

———. "A Summary History of the Penobscot Nation." In Nicolar, *Life and Traditions of the Red Man*, 1–34.

Konkle, Maureen. *Writing Indian Nations: Native Intellectuals and the Politics of Historiography, 1827–1863*. Chapel Hill: University of North Carolina Press, 2004.

Krech, Shepherd, III. "Beyond the Ecological Indian." In Harkin and Lewis, eds., *Native Americans and the Environment*, 3–31.

———. *The Ecological Indian: Myth and History*. New York: Norton, 1999.

Krupat, Arnold. *"That the People Might Live": Loss and Renewal in Native American Elegy*. Ithaca, NY: Cornell University Press, 2012.

LaCapra, Dominick. *History and Its Limits: Human, Animal, Violence*. Ithaca, NY: Cornell University Press, 2009.

LaDuke, Winona. *All Our Relations: Native Struggles for Land and Life*. Cambridge, MA: South End Press, 1999.

Latour, Bruno. "Agency at the Time of the Anthropocene." *New Literary History* 45 (2014): 1–18.

———. "An Attempt at a Compositionist Manifesto." *New Literary History* 41 (2010): 471–90.

———. *Facing Gaia: Eight Lectures on the New Climatic Regime*. Trans. Catherine Porter. Cambridge: Polity Press, 2017.

——. *The Politics of Nature: How to Bring the Sciences into Democracy.* Trans. Catherine Porter. Cambridge, MA: Harvard University Press, 2004.

——. *We Have Never Been Modern.* Trans. Catherine Porter. Cambridge, MA: Harvard University Press, 1993.

——. "Will Non-Humans Be Saved? An Argument in Ecotheology." *Journal of the Royal Anthropological Institute,* n.s., 15 (2009): 459–75.

Lawrence, D. H. *Studies in Classic American Literature.* 1923. Rpt. New York: Viking Press, 1964.

Leakey, Richard, and Robert Lewin. *The Sixth Extinction: Patterns of Life and the Future of Humankind.* New York: Doubleday, 1995.

Leland, Charles. *The Algonquin Legends of New England, or Myths and Folk Lore of the Micmac, Passamaquoddy, and Penobscot Tribes.* Boston: Houghton, Mifflin, 1884.

Leopold, Aldo. *A Sand County Almanac and Sketches Here and There.* 1949. Rpt. New York: Oxford University Press, 1987.

Lévi-Strauss, Claude. "We Are All Cannibals." 1993. Rpt. in *We Are All Cannibals: And Other Essays,* trans. Jane Marie Todd, 83–89. New York: Columbia University Press, 2016.

Levin, David. "Giants in the Earth: Science and the Occult in Cotton Mather's Letters to the Royal Society." *William and Mary Quarterly* 45 (1988): 751–70.

Levine, Robert S. *Race, Transnationalism, and Nineteenth-Century American Literary Study.* Cambridge: Cambridge University Press, 2018.

Lewis, M. W. *Green Delusions: An Environmentalist Critique of Radical Environmentalism.* Durham, NC: Duke University Press, 1992.

Lin, Maya. *Boundaries.* New York: Simon and Schuster, 2000.

——. "Share a Memory." In *What Is Missing?* Accessed November 24, 2020. http://www .whatismissing.net/#add-a-memory.

——. *What Is Missing? Creating a Global Memorial to the Planet.* Accessed November 24, 2020. http://www.whatismissing.net/#info/about-us.

Locke, John. *Two Treatises of Government.* Ed. Peter Laslett. 1960. 2nd ed. Cambridge: Cambridge University Press, 1970.

Long Now Foundation. Revive and Restore project website. Accessed December 2, 2020. http:// reviverestore.org/.

Lovelock, James. *The Revenge of Gaia: Earth's Climate Crisis and the Fate of Humanity.* New York: Basic Books, 2006.

Luisi, Pier Luigi. "Autopoiesis: A Review and Reappraisal." *Naturwissenschaften* 90 (2003): 49–59.

Lyell, Charles. *The Geological Evidences of the Antiquity of Man.* 4th ed. London: John Murray, 1873.

——. *Principles of Geology.* Vols. 1 and 2. London: John Murray, 1830, 1832.

Maddox, Lucy. *Removals: Nineteenth-Century American Literature and the Politics of Indian Affairs.* New York: Oxford University Press, 1991.

"Makah Whaling." Earth Island Institute. Accessed December 2, 2020. http://dev.earthisland.org /immp/archive_whale8.htm.

Malm, Andreas, and Alf Hornborg. "The Geology of Mankind? A Critique of the Anthropocene Narrative." *Anthropocene Review* 1 (2014): 62–69.

Marean, Curtis. "How *Homo sapiens* Became the Ultimate Invasive Species." *Scientific American* 313, no. 2 (August 2015): 32–39.

Martin, Calvin. *Keepers of the Game: Indian-Animal Relationships and the Fur Trade.* Berkeley: University of California Press, 1978.

Martin, Paul S. "Prehistoric Overkill: The Global Model." In *Quaternary Extinctions: A Prehistoric Revolution,* ed. Paul Martin and Richard Klein, 354–403. Tucson: University of Arizona Press, 1984.

———. *Twilight of the Mammoths: Ice Age Extinctions and the Rewilding of America.* Berkeley: University of California Press, 2005.

Martin, Paul S., and Christine Szuter. "War Zones and Game Sinks in Lewis and Clark's West." *Conservation Biology* 13 (1999): 36–45.

Martin, Ross. "Fossil Thoughts: Thoreau, Arrowheads, and Radical Paleontology." *ESQ* 65 (2019): 424–68.

Marx, Karl. *Economic and Philosophic Manuscripts of 1844.* Trans. Martin Milligan. Moscow: Foreign Languages Publishing House, 1961.

Mather, Cotton. *The Angel of Bethesda.* Ed. Gordon W. Jones. Barre, MA: American Antiquarian Society, 1972.

———. *Biblia Americana.* Vol. 1, *Genesis.* Ed. Reiner Smolinski. Grand Rapids, MI: Baker Academic, 2010.

———. *The Christian Philosopher: A Collection of the Best Discoveries in Nature, with Religious Improvements.* Ed. Josephine K. Piercy. 1721. Rpt. Gainesville, FL: Scholars Facsimiles and Reprints, 1968.

Mathews, Cornelius. *Behemoth: A Legend of the Mound-Builders.* 1839. Rpt. New York: Garrett Press, 1970.

Maturana, Humberto R., and Francisco J. Varela. "Autopoiesis: The Organization of the Living." 1973. In Maturana and Varela, *Autopoiesis and Cognition: The Realization of the Living,* 73–138. Dordrecht: D. Reidel, 1980.

Mayor, Adrienne. *The First Fossil Hunters: Dinosaurs, Mammoths, and Myth in Greek and Roman Times.* Princeton, NJ: Princeton University Press, 2011.

———. *Fossil Legends of the First Americans.* Princeton, NJ: Princeton University Press, 2005.

McBrien, Justin. "Accumulating Extinction: Planetary Catastrophism in the Necrocene." In *Anthropocene or Capitalocene? Nature, History, and the Crisis of Capitalism,* ed. Jason Moore, 116–37. Oakland, CA: PM Press, 2016.

McHugh, Susan. *Love in a Time of Slaughters: Human-Animal Stories Against Genocide and Extinction.* University Park: Pennsylvania State University Press, 2019.

Melville, Herman. "Benito Cereno." In *Herman Melville: Selected Tales and Poems,* ed. Richard Chase, 3–91. Fort Worth, TX: Harcourt Brace Jovanovich, 1950.

———. "Hawthorne and His Mosses." In *The Norton Anthology of American Literature,* Vol. B, *1820–1865,* ed. Robert S. Levine, Michael A. Elliott, Sandra M. Gustafson, Amy Hungerford, and Mary Loeffelholz, 1413–25. 9th ed. New York: Norton: 2017.

———. *Moby-Dick, or, The Whale.* New York: Penguin Books, 2003.

"Memorials of the Cherokee Indians, Signed by Their Representatives, and by 3,085 Individuals of the Nation." Rpt. in *Ethnocriticism: Ethnography, History, Literature,* by Arnold Krupat, 164–72. Berkeley: University of California Press, 1992.

Merrell, James. *The Indians' New World: Catawbas and Their Neighbors from European Contact Through the Era of Removal.* Chapel Hill: University of North Carolina Press, 1989.

Mignolo, Walter. *The Darker Side of the Renaissance: Literacy, Territoriality, and Colonization.* Ann Arbor: University of Michigan Press, 1995.

Miller, Perry. *The Raven and the Whale: The War of Words and Wits in the Era of Poe and Melville*. Westport, CT: Greenwood Press, 1977.

Miller, William. *Evidence from Scripture and History of the Second Coming of Christ, About the Year 1843*. Troy, NY: Kemble and Hooper, 1836.

Mithen, Steven. *After the Ice: A Global Human History 20,000–5000 BC*. London: Orion, 2004.

Molyneux, Thomas. "A Discourse Concerning the Large Horns Frequently Found Under Ground in Ireland." *Philosophical Transactions* 19 (1695–97): 489–512.

———. "An Essay Concerning Giants." *Philosophical Transactions* 22 (1700): 487–508.

Montgomery, James. "The Pelican Island." In *The Poetical Works of James Montgomery*, 2:3–114. Boston: Houghton Mifflin, 1880.

Mooney, James. *History, Myths, and Sacred Formulas of the Cherokees*. 1891, 1900. Rpt. Asheville, NC: Historical Images, 1992.

Moore, Jason. *Capitalism in the Web of Life: Ecology and the Accumulation of Capital*. New York: Verso, 2015.

Morris, Amy. "Geomythology on the Colonial Frontier: Edward Taylor, Cotton Mather, and the Claverack Giant." *William and Mary Quarterly* 70 (2013): 701–24.

Morton, Timothy. *Humankind: Solidarity with Nonhuman People*. London: Verso, 2017.

———. *Hyperobjects: Philosophy and Ecology After the End of the World*. Minneapolis: University of Minnesota Press, 2013.

Mulgan, Tim. *Ethics for a Broken World: Imagining Philosophy After Catastrophe*. Montreal: McGill-Queens University Press, 2011.

Nabokov, Peter. *A Forest of Time: American Indian Ways of History*. Cambridge: Cambridge University Press, 2002.

Nasady, Paul. "The Gift of the Animal: The Ontology of Hunting and Human-Animal Sociality." *American Ethnologist* 34 (2007): 25–43.

———. "Transcending the Debate over the Ecologically Noble Indian." *Ethnohistory* 52 (2005): 291–331.

National Oceanic and Atmospheric Administration. "Draft Environmental Impact Statement on the Makah Tribe Request to Hunt Gray Whales." February 2015. Accessed December 2, 2020. https://www.uscg.mil/Portals/0/Headquarters/Administrative%20Law%20Judges /NOAA%20files%202019/100.6%20ALJ_Ex_006_2015%20DEIS%20and%20Memo.pdf ?ver=2019-11-15-142017-673.

Newitz, Annalee. *Scatter, Adapt, and Remember: How Humans Will Survive a Mass Extinction*. New York: Anchor, 2014.

Nicolar, Joseph. *The Life and Traditions of the Red Man*. Ed. Annette Kolodny. 1893. Rpt. Durham, NC: Duke University Press, 2007.

Nixon, Rob. "Neoliberalism, Genre, and 'The Tragedy of the Commons.'" *PMLA* 127 (2012): 593–99.

———. *Slow Violence and the Environmentalism of the Poor*. Cambridge, MA: Harvard University Press, 2011.

Noble, Brian. "Treaty Ecologies: With Persons, Peoples, Animals, and the Land." In *Resurgence and Reconciliation: Indigenous-Settler Relations and Earth Teachings*, ed. Michael Asch, John Borrows, and James Tully, 315–42. Toronto: University of Toronto Press, 2018.

O'Brien, Jean. *Firsting and Lasting: Writing Indians out of Existence in New England*. Minneapolis: University of Minnesota Press, 2010.

O'Connor, M. R. *Resurrection Science: Conservation, De-Extinction, and the Precarious Future of Wild Things*. New York: St. Martin's Press, 2015.

Owen, Richard. *A History of British Fossil Mammals and Birds*. London: Van Voorst, 1846.

———. *Palaeontology, or a Systematic Summary of Extinct Animals and Their Geological Relations*. Edinburgh: A. and C. Black, 1860.

Parkinson, James. *Organic Remains of a Former World: An Examination of the Mineralized Remains of the Vegetables and Animals of the Antediluvian World: Generally Termed Extraneous Fossils*. Vol. 3. London: Sherwood, Neely, and Jones, 1811.

Parrish, Susan Scott. *American Curiosity: Cultures of Natural History in the Colonial British Atlantic World*. Chapel Hill: University of North Carolina Press, 2006.

Peale, Rembrandt. *An Historical Disquisition on the Mammoth, or, Great American Incognitum*. 1803. Rpt. in *The Selected Papers of Charles Willson Peale and His Family*, ed. Lillian B. Miller, vol. 2, pt. 1, 543–78. New Haven, CT: Yale University Press, 1983.

Pearce, Roy Harvey. *The Savages of America: A Study of the Indian and the Idea of Civilization*. Baltimore: Johns Hopkins University Press, 1953.

Pease, Donald. "Melville and Cultural Persuasion." In *Ideology and Classic American Literature*, ed. Sacvan Bercovitch and Myra Jehlen, 384–417. New York: Cambridge University Press, 1986.

Pennock, Caroline Dodds. *Bonds of Blood: Gender, Lifecycle and Sacrifice in Aztec Culture*. New York: Palgrave Macmillan, 2008.

Philbrick, Nathaniel. *In the Heart of the Sea: The Tragedy of the Whaleship "Essex."* New York: Penguin Books, 2001.

Philbrick, Nathaniel, and Thomas Philbrick, eds. *The Loss of the Ship "Essex," Sunk by a Whale*. New York: Penguin Books, 2000.

Pimentel, Juan. *The Rhinoceros and the Megatherium: An Essay in Natural History*. Trans. Peter Mason. Cambridge, MA: Harvard University Press, 2017.

Plumwood, Val. *Feminism and the Mastery of Nature*. London: Routledge, 1993.

Poe, Edgar Allan. *Poetry and Tales*. New York: Library of America, 1984.

Pontiac. *Journal of Pontiac's Conspiracy*. Ed. M. Agnes Burton. Trans. R. C. Ford. Detroit, MI: Clarence Monroe Burton, 1912.

Popper, Deborah E., and Frank J. Popper. "The Buffalo Commons: Metaphor as Method." *Geographical Review* 89 (1999): 491–510.

———. "The Great Plains: From Dust to Dust." *Planning* 53, no. 12 (December 1987): 12–18.

"Protect and Serve." Editorial. *Nature* 516 (December 10, 2014): 144. https://www.nature.com/news/protect-and-serve-1.16514.

Punke, Michael. *Last Stand: George Bird Grinnell, the Battle to Save the Buffalo, and the Birth of the New West*. New York: HarperCollins, 2007.

Radin, Paul. *The Trickster: A Study in American Indian Mythology*. London: Routledge and Kegan Paul, 1956.

Radus, Daniel M. "Printing Native History in *David Cusick's Sketches of Ancient History of the Six Nations*." *American Literature* 86 (2014): 217–43.

Rappaport, Rhoda. *When Geologists Were Historians, 1665–1750*. Ithaca, NY: Cornell University Press, 1997.

Raup, David M. *Extinction: Bad Genes or Bad Luck?* New York: Norton, 1991.

Regalado, Antonio. "A Stealthy De-Extinction Startup." *MIT Technology Review*, March 19, 2013. https://www.technologyreview.com/s/512671/a-stealthy-de-extinction-startup/.

Reid, Joshua L. *The Sea Is My Country: The Maritime World of the Makahs*. New Haven, CT: Yale University Press, 2015.

Richter, Daniel K. *Facing East from Indian Country: A Native History of Early America*. Cambridge, MA: Harvard University Press, 2001.

Rigal, Laura. *The American Manufactory: Art, Labor, and the World of Things in the Early Republic*. Princeton, NJ: Princeton University Press, 1998.

Robinson, Kim Stanley. *2312*. New York: Orbit, 2012.

———. *Green Mars*. New York: Bantam, 1995.

Rogin, Michael Paul. *Subversive Genealogy: The Politics and Art of Herman Melville*. New York: Knopf, 1983.

Rose, Deborah Bird. *Wild Dog Dreaming: Love and Extinction*. Charlottesville: University of Virginia Press, 2012.

Rose, Deborah Bird, Thom van Dooren, and Matthew Chrulew, eds. *Extinction Studies: Stories of Time, Death, and Generations*. New York: Columbia University Press, 2017.

Round, Phillip H. *Removable Type: Histories of the Book in Indian Country, 1663–1880*. Chapel Hill: University of North Carolina Press, 2010.

Rudwick, Martin J. S. *Bursting the Limits of Time: The Reconstruction of Geohistory in the Age of Revolution*. Chicago: University of Chicago Press, 2005.

Ruestow, Edward G. "Images and Ideas: Leeuwenhoek's Perception of the Spermatozoa." *Journal of the History of Biology* 16 (1983): 185–224.

Sahagún, Bernardino de. *Primeros Memoriales*. Trans. Thelma D. Sullivan. Norman: University of Oklahoma Press, 1997.

Sahlins, Marshall. "Culture as Protein and Profit." *New York Review of Books*, November 23, 1978, 45–53.

———. *Stone Age Economics*. 1972. Rpt. New York: Routledge, 2017.

———. *The Western Illusion of Human Nature*. Chicago: Prickly Paradigm Press, 2008.

Sale, Kirkpatrick. *After Eden: The Evolution of Human Domination*. Durham, NC: Duke University Press, 2006.

Sandom, Christopher, Søren Faurby, Brody Sandel, and Jens-Christian Svenning. "Global Late Quaternary Megafaunal Extinctions Linked to Humans, Not Climate Change." *Proceedings of the Royal Society B* (2014). https://doi.org/10.1098/rspb.2013.3254.

Saunders, Margaret Marshall. *Beautiful Joe*. 1894. Rpt. Peterborough, ON: Broadview, 2015.

Sayre, Gordon. "The Mammoth: Endangered Species or Vanishing Race?" *Journal for Early Modern Cultural Studies* 1 (2001): 63–87.

———. "The Mound Builders and the Imagination of American Antiquity in Jefferson, Bartram, and Chateaubriand." *Early American Literature* 33 (1998): 225–49.

Scammon, Charles M. *The Marine Mammals of the North-Western Coast of North America*. 1874. New York: Dover, 1968.

Scharnhorst, Gary. "Images of the Millerites in American Literature." *American Quarterly* 32 (1980): 19–36.

Schmalhausen, Ivan. *Factors of Evolution: The Theory of Stabilizing Selection*. Trans. Isadore Dordick. 1949. Rpt. Chicago: University of Chicago Press, 1986.

Schultz, Elizabeth. "Melville's Environmental Vision in *Moby-Dick*." *Interdisciplinary Studies in Literature and Environment* 7 (2000): 97–113.

Scott, James. *Against the Grain: A Deep History of the Earliest States*. New Haven, CT: Yale University Press, 2017.

Scranton, Roy. *Learning to Die in the Anthropocene: Reflections on the End of a Civilization*. San Francisco, CA: City Lights Books, 2015.

Semonin, Paul. *American Monster: How the Nation's First Prehistoric Creature Became a Symbol of National Identity*. New York: New York University Press, 2000.

Sewell, Anna. *Black Beauty*. 1877. Rpt. London: Puffin, 2008.

Shapiro, Beth. *How to Clone a Mammoth: The Science of De-Extinction*. Princeton, NJ: Princeton University Press, 2015.

Sheehan, Bernard. *Seeds of Extinction: Jeffersonian Philanthropy and the American Indian*. Chapel Hill: University of North Carolina Press, 2014.

Shell, Hanna Rose. "Introduction: Finding the Soul in the Skin." In Hornaday, *Extermination of the American Bison*, xiii–xxiii.

Silva, Cristobal. *Miraculous Plagues: An Epidemiology of Early New England Narrative*. New York: Oxford University Press, 2011.

Simmons, William S. *Spirit of the New England Tribes: Indian History and Folklore, 1620–1984*. Hanover, NH: University Press of New England, 1986.

Simpson, Leanne. "Looking After Gdoo-naaganinaa: Precolonial Nishnaabeg Diplomatic and Treaty Relationships." *Wicazo Sa Review* 23 (2008): 29–42.

Sluder, Lawrence L. "God in the Background: Edward Taylor as Naturalist." *Early American Literature* 7 (1973): 265–71.

Smith, Mick. "Environmental Anamnesis: Walter Benjamin and the Ethics of Extinction." *Environmental Ethics* 23 (2001): 359–76.

Smits, David D. "The Frontier Army and the Destruction of the Buffalo, 1865–1883." *Western Historical Quarterly* 25, no. 3 (1994): 312–38.

Spargo, R. Clifton. *The Ethics of Mourning: Grief and Responsibility in Elegiac Literature*. Baltimore: Johns Hopkins University Press, 2004.

Stanford, Donald E. "The Giant Bones of Claverack, New York, 1705." *New York History* 40 (1959): 47–61.

Steadman, David W. "Prehistoric Extinctions of Pacific Island Birds: Biodiversity Meets Zooarchaeology." *Science* 267 (1995): 1123–31.

Stengers, Isabelle. *In Catastrophic Times: Resisting the Coming Barbarism*. Trans. Andrew Goffey. London: Open Humanities Press, 2015. http://openhumanitiespress.org/books/download/Stengers_2015_In-Catastrophic-Times.pdf.

Stephens, Walter. *Giants in Those Days: Folklore, Ancient History, and Nationalism*. Lincoln: University of Nebraska Press, 1989.

Stiles, Ezra. *Extracts from the Itineraries and Other Miscellanies of Ezra Stiles, D.D., LL.D., 1755–1794*. Ed. Franklin Bowditch Dexter. New Haven, CT: Yale University Press, 1916.

Sullivan, Robert. *A Whale Hunt*. New York: Scribner, 2000.

Svenning, Jens-Christian. "Future Megafaunas: A Historical Perspective on the Potential for a Wilder Anthropocene." In *Arts of Living on a Damaged Planet*, ed. Anna Tsing, Heather Swanson, Elaine Gan, and Nils Bubandt, G67–G86. Minneapolis: University of Minnesota Press, 2017.

Sykes, Rebecca Wragg. *Kindred: Neanderthal Life, Love, Death, and Art*. London: Bloomsbury, 2020.

TallBear, Kimberly. "Shepard Krech's *The Ecological Indian*: One Indian's Perspective." *IIIRM Publications*, September 2000. http://www.iiirm.org/publications/Book%20Reviews/Reviews/Krech001.pdf.

Taylor, Edward. *Edward Taylor's Christographia*. Ed. Norman S. Grabo. New Haven, CT: Yale University Press, 1962.

———. *Edward Taylor's Minor Poetry*. Ed. Thomas M. Davis and Virginia L. Davis. Boston: Twayne, 1981.

———. *The Poems of Edward Taylor*. Ed. Donald E. Stanford. New Haven, CT: Yale University Press, 1960.

Taylor, Matthew. "Life's Return: Hylozoism, Again." *PMLA* 135 (2020): 474–91.

Thoreau, Henry David. *The Maine Woods*. In *"A Week on the Concord and Merrimack Rivers," "Walden," "The Maine Woods," "Cape Cod,"* ed. Robert F. Sayre, 589–845. New York: Library of America, 1985.

Tonino, Leath. "We Only Protect What We Love: Michael Soulé on the Vanishing Wilderness." *Sun*, April 2018. https://www.thesunmagazine.org/issues/508/we-only-protect-what-we-love.

Toulmin, Stephen. *Cosmopolis: The Hidden Agenda of Modernity*. New York: Free Press, 1990.

Treaty of Neah Bay, 1855. Governor's Office of Indian Affairs, State of Washington. Accessed December 2, 2020. https://goia.wa.gov/tribal-government/treaty-neah-bay-1855.

Turner, George. "Memoir on the Extraneous Fossils, denominated Mammoth Bones: principally designed to shew, that they are the remains of more than one species of non-descript Animal." *Transactions of the American Philosophical Society* 4 (1799): 510–18.

Tweedie, Ann M. *Drawing Back Culture: The Makah Struggle for Repatriation*. Seattle: University of Washington Press, 2002.

U.S. Department of Agriculture. *USDA Livestock Slaughter 2018 Summary*. April 2019. https://downloads.usda.library.cornell.edu/usda-esmis/files/r207tp32d/8336h934w/hq37vx004/lsslan19.pdf.

Ussher, James. *The Annals of the World Deduced from the Origin of Time*. London: F. Crook and G. Bedell, 1658. Early English Books Online.

van Dooren, Thom. "Care." *Environmental Humanities* 5 (2014): 291–94.

———. *Flight Ways: Life and Loss at the Edge of Extinction*. New York: Columbia University Press, 2014.

van Doren, Carl, ed. *Indian Treaties Printed by Benjamin Franklin, 1736–1762*. Philadelphia: Historical Society of Pennsylvania, 1938.

Vega, Garcilaso de la. *The Incas: The Royal Commentary of the Inca Garcilaso de la Vega, 1539–1616*. Trans. Maria Joals. New York: Orion, 1961.

Vincent, Howard. *The Trying-Out of Moby-Dick*. Kent, OH: Kent State University Press, 1980.

Viveiros de Castro, Eduardo. *Cannibal Metaphysics: For a Post-Structuralist Anthropology*. Trans. Peter Skafish. Minneapolis, MN: Univocal, 2014.

Vizenor, Gerald. *Harold of Orange*. Screenplay. Dir. Richard Weise. Vision Maker Video, 1984.

———. *Manifest Manners: Postindian Warriors and Survivance*. Hanover, NH: Wesleyan University Press, 1993.

Wallace, Alfred Russel. *The Geographical Distribution of Animals, with a Study of the Relations of Living and Extinct Faunas as Elucidating Past Changes in the Earth's Surface*. Vol. 1. New York: Harper and Brothers, 1876.

———. *The World of Life: A Manifestation of Creative Power, Directive Mind and Ultimate Purpose*. New York: Moffat, Yard, 1911.

Wallace, Anthony F. C. *Jefferson and the Indians: The Tragic Fate of the First Americans*. Cambridge, MA: Harvard University Press, 1999.

Waters, Michael, and Thomas W. Stafford Jr. "Redefining the Age of Clovis: Implications for the Peopling of America." *Science* 315 (2007): 1122–26.

Watters, Lawrence, and Connie Dugger. "The Hunt for Gray Whales: The Dilemma of Native American Treaty Rights and the International Moratorium on Whaling." *Columbia Journal of Environmental Law* 22 (1997): 319–52.

Watts, Edward. *Colonizing the Past: Mythmaking and Pre-Columbian Whites in Nineteenth-Century American Writing*. Charlottesville: University of Virginia Press, 2020.

Webb, Robert Lloyd. *On the Northwest: Commercial Whaling in the Pacific Northwest, 1790–1967*. Vancouver: University of British Columbia Press, 1988.

Webb, Walter Prescott. *The Great Plains*. 1931. Rpt. Lincoln: University of Nebraska Press, 1981.

Weisman, Alan. *The World Without Us*. New York: Thomas Dunne, 2007.

Wells, H. G. "The Grisly Folk." In *The Short Stories of H. G. Wells*, 607–21. 1927. Rpt. London: Ernest Benn, 1952.

"The Whale Fishery." *North American Review* 82 (1834): 84–115.

Wheeler, Richard S. *The Buffalo Commons*. New York: Forge-Tom Doherty, 1998.

White, Hayden. *Metahistory: The Historical Imagination in Nineteenth-Century Europe*. Baltimore: Johns Hopkins University Press, 1973.

"Why Efforts to Bring Extinct Species Back from the Dead Miss the Point." Editorial. *Scientific American* 308, no. 6 (June 1, 2013): 12. https://www.scientificamerican.com/article/why-efforts-bring-extinct-species-back-from-dead-miss-point/.

Williams, John. *Butcher's Crossing*. 1960. Rpt. Boston: Gregg Press, 1978.

Wilson, Clint. "Sacrificial Structures: Waste, Animals, and the Monumental Impulse." *Resilience* 6 (2019): 86–101.

Wilson, Edward O. *The Future of Life*. New York: Knopf, 2002.

Wilson, Eric. "Melville, Darwin, and the Great Chain of Being." *Studies in American Fiction* 28 (2000): 131–50.

Winterbotham, William. *An Historical, Geographical, Commercial, and Philosophical View of the American United States*. Vol. 3. London: J. Ridgeway, 1795.

Wisecup, Kelly. "'Meteors, Ships, Etc.': Native American Histories of Colonialism and Early American Archives." *American Literary History* 30 (2018): 29–54.

Wittgenstein, Ludwig. *Philosophical Investigations*. Trans. G. E. M. Anscombe. New York: Macmillan, 1958.

Wolfe, Cary. *Animal Rites: American Culture, the Discourses of Species, and Posthumanist Theory*. Chicago: University of Chicago Press, 2003.

———. "Condors at the End of the World." In *After Extinction*, ed. Richard Grusin, 107–22. Minneapolis: University of Minnesota Press, 2018.

Womack, Craig. "There Is No Respectful Way to Kill an Animal." *Studies in American Indian Literatures* 25 (2013): 11–27.

Woodward, Walter W. *Prospero's America: John Winthrop, Jr., and the Creation of New England Culture, 1606–1676*. Chapel Hill: University of North Carolina Press, 2010.

Wray, Britt. *Rise of the Necrofauna: Science, Ethics, and the Risks of De-Extinction*. Vancouver: Greystone Books, 2017.

Wright, Ronald. *A Short History of Progress*. New York: Carroll and Graf, 2005.

Youatt, Rafi. *Counting Species: Biodioversity in Global Environmental Politics*. Minneapolis: University of Minnesota Press, 2015.

Young, Elizabeth. *Pet Projects: Animal Fiction and Taxidermy in the Nineteenth-Century Archive.* University Park: Pennsylvania State University Press, 2019.

Zalasiewicz, Jan. *The Earth After Us: What Legacy Will Humans Leave in the Rocks?* Oxford: Oxford University Press, 2008.

Zalasiewicz, Jan, Mark Williams, Richard Fortey, Alan Smith et al. "Stratigraphy of the Anthropocene." *Philosophical Transactions of the Royal Society A* 369 (2011): 1036–55.

Zárate, Agustín de. *The Discouerie and Conquest of the Prouinces of Peru, and the Nauigation in the South Sea, along that Coast, and also the Ritche Mines of Potosi.* Trans. Thomas Nicholas. London: Richard Jones, 1581. Early English Books Online.

Žižek, Slavoj. *Less Than Nothing: Hegel and the Shadow of Dialectical Materialism.* Brooklyn, NY: Verso, 2012.

Zontek, Ken. *Buffalo Nation: American Indian Efforts to Restore the Bison.* Lincoln: University of Nebraska Press, 2007.

Zubrin, Robert. *Entering Space: Creating a Spacefaring Civilization.* New York: Tarcher/Putnam, 1999.

INDEX

ACKNOWLEDGMENTS

My first, best reader has been Dennis Allen: thank you for your advice and encouragement on this as on so many projects. Other colleagues from West Virginia University (some elsewhere now) have been helpful as well, including Brian Ballentine, Cari Carpenter, Ryan Claycomb, Julia Daniel, Lowell Duckert, Lara Farina, Stephanie Foote, Lea Herron, Jason Phillips, the participants in the English Department's faculty colloquium and environmental humanities reading group, and students in my ecocriticism and American literature courses, especially Mariah Crilley, Sam Horrocks, Frank Izaguirre, and Clint Wilson. Thanks are due to my research assistants Aaron Rovan and especially Frank Izaguirre and Beth Staley for their thoughtful, critical reading as well as meticulous attention to the manuscript. To all WVU librarians, thank you for your help with access to materials during the pandemic shutdown. Thanks to Marilyn Van Winkle at the Autry Museum for extra effort in providing an image file. Thanks also to Reiner Smolinski for sending me pages from his edition of Mather's *Biblia Americana*.

Beyond WVU, I've benefited from conversations with John Barnard, Stephanie Bernhard, Colleen Boggs, Kris Bross, Larry Buell, Hal Bush, Joe Campana, Jeffery Cohen, Matt Cohen, Kim Evans, Randall Fuller, Amy Green, Jim Greene, Tom Hallock, Ursula Heise, Tom Kinnahan, Dana Luciano, Tony McGowan, Dennis Moore, Dana Nelson, Tom Nurmi, Scotti Parrish, Peter Remien, Judith Roof, Gordon Sayre, Scott Slovic, Brian Yothers, Elizabeth Young, Laura Walls, Ned Watts, Mike Ziser, audiences at ASLE, MLA, and SEA conferences, and students at Duquesne University, Rice University, and West Point. I've been working on this project for so long that two people who had significant input in its early stages are no longer with us: Frank Shuffelton and Jeff Richards, you are dearly missed.

I can't begin to thank Laura Brady enough, not only for her love and support all these years, but also for asking critical questions about the project and for playing Max Perkins on occasion (I hope I have not been as difficult as Tom Wolfe).

I'm grateful for Jerry Singerman's patient encouragement and productive skepticism throughout the process. I'm grateful to Randall Fuller and Scotti Parrish, who read the manuscript anonymously for the University of Pennsylvania Press and offered very helpful recommendations. All faults, of course, remain mine. I'm grateful to the staff at the Press for shepherding the work through production. It has been a pleasure to work with them.

Part of this work was supported by a summer research grant from the WVU Humanities Center and other parts by a sabbatical leave. Research funds from the Eberly Foundation supported reproductions and permissions for the images. I would also like to thank the Eberly family for endowing the professorship in American literature that I hold.

Parts of two chapters have been published elsewhere in a different form: "The Eighteenth-Century *Archives du Monde*: The Question of Agency in Extinction Stories," in *The Year's Work in the Oddball Archive*, edited by Jonathan Eburne and Judith Roof (Indiana University Press, 2016), 219–45, and "'Will He Perish?' *Moby-Dick* and Nineteenth-Century Extinction Discourse," in *Above the American Renaissance: David S. Reynolds and the Spiritual Imagination in American Literary Studies*, edited by Hal Bush and Brian Yothers (University of Massachusetts Press, 2018), 87–103, used with permission.